BELIEFS IN GOVERNMENT

Volumes of a Research Programme of the European Science Foundation

Series Editors: Max Kaase, Kenneth Newton, and Elinor Scarbrough

BELIEFS IN GOVERNMENT

This set of five volumes is an exhaustive study of beliefs in government in post-war Europe. Based upon an extensive collection of survey evidence, the results challenge widely argued theories of mass opinion, and much scholarly writing about citizen attitudes towards government and politics.

The **European Science Foundation** is an association of its fifty-six member research councils, academies, and institutions devoted to basic scientific research in twenty countries. The ESF assists its Member Organizations in two main ways: by bringing scientists together in its Scientific Programmes, Networks, and European Research Conferences to work on topics of common concern, and through the joint study of issues of strategic importance in European science policy.

The scientific work sponsored by ESF includes basic research in the natural and technical sciences, the medical and biosciences, the humanities, and the social sciences.

The ESF maintains close relations with other scientific institutions within and outside Europe. By its activities, ESF adds value by co-operation and co-ordination across national frontiers, offers expert scientific advice on strategic issues, and provides the European forum for fundamental science.

This volume arises from the work of the ESF Scientific Programme on Beliefs in Government (BiG).

Further information on ESF activities can be obtained from:

European Science Foundation
1, quai Lezay-Marnésia
F-67080 Strasbourg Cedex
France

Tel. (+33) 88 76 71 00
Fax (+33) 88 37 05 32

BELIEFS IN GOVERNMENT VOLUME FIVE

BELIEFS IN GOVERNMENT

MAX KAASE

and

KENNETH NEWTON

OXFORD UNIVERSITY PRESS

1995

Oxford University Press, Walton Street, Oxford OX2 6DP

Oxford New York
Athens Auckland Bangkok Bombay
Calcutta Cape Town Dar es Salaam Delhi
Florence Hong Kong Istanbul Karachi
Kuala Lumpur Madras Madrid Melbourne
Mexico City Nairobi Paris Singapore
Taipei Tokyo Toronto
and associated companies in
Berlin Ibadan

Oxford is a trade mark of Oxford University Press

Published in the United States
by Oxford University Press Inc., New York

British Library Cataloguing in Publication Data
Data available

Library of Congress Cataloging in Publication Data
Kaase, Max.
Beliefs in government / Max Kaase and Kenneth Newton.
—(Beliefs in government; v. 5)
Includes bibliographical references.
1. Europe—Politics and government—1945– . 2. Political participation—Europe. 3. Public
opinion—Europe. I. Newton, Kenneth, 1940– . II. Title. III. Series.
JN94.A91K33 1995 320.94'09'049—dc20 95–16268

ISBN 0–19–827956–6

1 3 5 7 9 10 8 6 4 2

Typeset by J&L Composition Ltd, Filey, North Yorkshire
Printed in Great Britain
on acid-free paper by
Biddles Ltd, Guildford and King's Lynn

FOREWORD

This is one of five volumes in a series produced by the Beliefs in Government research programme of the European Science Foundation. The volumes, all published by Oxford University Press in 1995, are as follows:

i *Citizens and the State*, edited by Hans-Dieter Klingemann and Dieter Fuchs

ii *Public Opinion and Internationalized Governance*, edited by Oskar Niedermayer and Richard Sinnott

iii *The Scope of Government*, edited by Ole Borre and Elinor Scarbrough

iv *The Impact of Values*, edited by Jan van Deth and Elinor Scarbrough

v *Beliefs in Government*, authored by Max Kaase and Kenneth Newton

The first chapter of *Beliefs in Government* presents a brief history of the research project, its general concerns, approach and methods, and an outline of the relationship of each volume to the project as a whole.

All five books share a debt of gratitude which we would like to acknowledge on their behalf. The European Science Foundation (ESF) supported and funded the research programme throughout its five long and arduous years. Eleven of the research councils and academies which are members of the ESF have made a financial contribution to the overall costs of the project—Belgium, Denmark, Finland, France, the Federal Republic of Germany, Ireland, Italy, the Netherlands, Norway, Sweden, and the United Kingdom. We would like to thank the ESF and these member organizations five times over—once for each book.

All five volumes were copy-edited by Heather Bliss, whose eagle eye and endless patience are unrivalled in the Western world. At Oxford University Press we were lucky indeed to have two understanding editors in Tim Barton and Dominic Byatt.

In particular, John Smith, the Secretary of the ESF's Standing Committee for the Social Sciences, and his staff put in huge efforts and gave us encouragement at every stage of the project. Having gone through the process with other ESF research programmes a few times before, they knew when we started what an immense task lay in wait for us all, but were not daunted. We cannot lay claim to any such bravery, and have only our innocence as an excuse.

Max Kaase
Kenneth Newton
Elinor Scarbrough

December 1994

PREFACE

Academic research invariably accumulates debts of gratitude to many people. This book has accumulated far more than most. Apart from anything else, it is based upon a collective research project which stretches across West Europe from Portugal to Finland and from Ireland to Greece, and it has absorbed the energies and talents of some sixty scholars. Our thanks go to these people whose work can be read in the four companion volumes of the Beliefs in Government series. A list of chapters and authors appears on pp. xiv–xv.

Eleven member organizations (research councils and academies) of the European Science Foundation agreed to make a financial contribution to the programme—that is, Belgium, Denmark, Finland, France, the Federal Republic of Germany, Ireland, Italy, the Netherlands, Norway, Sweden, and the United Kingdom. Their help is gratefully acknowledged.

At the outset we had the support of Jean Blondel. His role in the project is described in the introduction which follows. It is sufficient to say here that his energy and huge enthusiasm were crucial in getting the project going in the first place.

In Strasbourg we had the unfailing help of the European Science Foundation at every stage of the work. Helga Nowotny was Chair of the ESF's Standing Committee for the Social Sciences, and then Guido Martinotti took over. Both facilitated our work with care and concern. Stein Kuhnle kept a kindly watching brief over us for the ESF Standing Committee, offering good and timely advice and a steadying presence. In the office of the ESF we had the unfailing help of the staff, especially Liz Altham who was always ready and willing to assist.

At the Essex office we were fortunate enough to have had the help of three wonderfully cheerful and efficient staff. Chris Wilkinson got the show on the road with skill and panache, Helen Sibley took over and drove it like hell (she may yet pass her driving test), and Sharon Duthie finished it off with the calm assurance it needed. All of them coped with recalcitrant photocopiers, wilful software, illegible faxes, e-mail messages from outer space, phones that never stopped ringing, and the incessant and exacting demands of researchers from all over Western Europe. John Simister and Steven Studd collected data, compiled tables, ran computer programs, checked bibliographies, searched the literature, and mastered the finest details of SPSS and Word for Windows. Last but not least, we also profited greatly from the quiet but highly skilful secretarial support of Jutta Hoehne of the Wissenschaftszentrum Berlin für Sozialforschung.

Our first plenary sessions were held at the Wissenschaftszentrum Berlin für Sozialforschung where Konstanza Prinzessin zu Löwenstein, with her inimitable charm and unrivalled efficiency, went to great trouble to provide us with excellent working conditions and memorable hospitality. The second plenary meetings were held in Essex, were Elinor Scarbrough and Chris Wilkinson laboured long and hard to make things run smoothly and successfully.

Our final meeting at Le Bischenbourg in the Alsace was beautifully organized by Liz Altham—in addition to all her other work. It was an important meeting for us because we benefited from the invaluable advice of Richard Eichenberg, Ronald Inglehart, Helmut Klages, Beate Kohler-Koch, William Lafferty, William Miller, Ekkehard Mochmann, Gunnar Sjöblom, and Albert Weale. Their comments have greatly improved the quality of the final product.

The project had an insatiable appetite for quality data, more quality data, and still more quality data. The appetite was (almost) satisfied by the prompt services of national archives—especially the ESRC Archive at Essex, the Steinmetz Archive in Amsterdam, the NSD in Bergen, the DDA in Odense, and the SSD in Göteborg. Above all, Ekkehard Mochmann, the Director of the Zentralarchiv in Cologne, and the ZA staff showed great understanding and consideration of the special needs of a cross-national comparative project of this kind.

To all these people we offer our grateful thanks, but two names stand out from all the rest—John Smith and Elinor Scarbrough. John Smith has been tremendous—patient, understanding, humorous, diplomatic, and enormously encouraging at all times. It is a simple fact that we could not have begun, never mind finished, this project without him.

Last and most important, Elinor Scarbrough has been Research Co-ordinator for the BiG project since it started. She has worked exceedingly hard and taken the most meticulous care over it. On behalf of the whole of the Beliefs in Government research team, we express our affection, our admiration, and our thanks to her.

Max Kaase
Kenneth Newton

December 1994

CONTENTS

List of Figures   x
List of Tables   xi
Abbreviations   xii
List of Chapters and Authors in Volumes i–iv   xiv

1.   The Tale of a Comparative Political Science Project   1

2.   Theories of Crisis and Catastrophe, Change and
          Transformation   17

3.   Political Attitudes and Political Behaviour   40

4.   The Growth and Decline of the State?   65

5.   International Government   97

6.   Citizens and the State   126

7.   A Crisis of Democracy?   150

Appendix Project Proposal for Decision by the General
          Assembly of the European Science Foundation
          on 2 November 1988.   173

References   185
Author Index   201
Subject Index   204

LIST OF FIGURES

3.1. Proportion of people who frequently discuss politics with
      friends, EC countries, 1973–89   46
3.2. Trends in satisfaction with democracy in Western Europe,
      1976–91   61
5.1. Support for the European Union, 1973–94   101
5.2. Military and non-military co-operation in the EU, 1991   105

LIST OF TABLES

3.1. Relevance of birth cohorts, education, and occupation to
materialism–postmaterialism in EC-12 countries, 1973–91   45
3.2. Total effects of the three voting types in Western Europe   49
3.3. Political participation in Western Europe, 1959–90   50
3.4. Political participation in Western Europe, by country,
1959–90   51
3.5. Modes of political involvement, 1974–90   52
3.6. Evolution of partisanship across time in fourteen West
European countries and the United States: linear regression
analysis using national election studies and Eurobarometer
data   54
3.7. Party membership in ten West European countries,
1960–89: party records   56
3.8. Support for new social movements in five West European
countries, 1982–9   59
3.9. Trends in satisfaction with democracy in thirteen West
European countries, 1976–91   62
4.1. Attitudes towards government responsibility, 1974   69
4.2. Attitudes towards government responsibility, 1985 and 1990   70
4.3. Attitudes towards spending in eight policy fields: Germany,
Britain, and Italy, 1985   74
4.4. Attitudes towards government spending, 1985 and 1990   83
4.5. Support for different socio-economic equality policies, 1987   84
4.6. Attitudes towards issues of tax fairness   87
4.7. Policy distance and satisfaction with democracy in eight
West European countries, 1979–83   93
5.1. Structure of attitudes towards the EC, NATO, and UN, 1989   99
5.2. Indicators of support by length of EC membership, 1970–89   110
5.3. National pride and support for EC membership, 1985   116
5.4. Community-wide levels of trust in other EC nationals,
1976–90   120
5.5. Levels of trust among nine member states of the EU,
1976–90   120

ABBREVIATIONS

BASS	Belgian Academic Survey Data Archive
CESSDA	Council of European Social Science Data Archives
COMECON	Council for Mutual Economic Aid
EB	Eurobarometer
EC	European Community
ECPR	European Consortium for European Research
EEC	European Economic Community
EFTA	European Free Trade Association
ERM	Exchange Rate Mechanism
ESF	European Science Foundation
ESRC	Economic and Social Research Council (UK)
EU	European Union
GATT	General Agreement on Tariffs and Trade
G7	Group of Seven
ICPSR	Inter-university Consortium for Political and Social Research (University of Michigan)
IMF	International Monetary Fund
ISSP	International Social Survey Programme
NATO	North Atlantic Treaty Organization
OECD	Organization for Economic Co-operation and Development
OPEC	Oil Producing and Exporting Countries
SCSS	Standing Committee for the Social Sciences (of the ESF)
UN	United Nations
UNESCO	United Nations Educational, Scientific and Cultural Organization
UNICEF	United Nations Children's Fund
USIA	United States Information Agency

Standard country abbreviations used in the tables and figures

AU	Austria
BE	Belgium
DK	Denmark

FI	Finland
FR	France
GB	Britain
GE	Germany
GR	Greece
IC	Iceland
IR	Ireland
IT	Italy
LU	Luxembourg
NI	Northern Ireland
NL	Netherlands
NO	Norway
PO	Portugal
SP	Spain
SV	Sweden
SW	Switzerland

LIST OF CHAPTERS AND
AUTHORS IN VOLUMES I–IV

Volume i. Citizens and the State

1. Citizens and the State: A Changing Relationship?
   Dieter Fuchs and Hans-Dieter Klingemann
2. Electoral Participation
   Richard Topf
3. Beyond Electoral Participation
   Richard Topf
4. Political Parties in Decline?
   Hermann Schmitt and Sören Holmberg
5. Party Membership and Party Representativeness
   Anders Widfeldt
6. Party Positions and Voter Orientations
   Hans-Dieter Klingemann
7. Relationships between Citizens and Political Parties
   Roberto Biorcio and Renato Mannheimer
8. Intermediate Organizations and Interest Representation
   Kees Aarts
9. The Dynamics of Trust in Politicians
   Ola Listhaug
10. Confidence in Political and Private Institutions
    Ola Listhaug and Matti Wiberg
11. Support for the Democratic System
    Dieter Fuchs, Giovanna Guidorossi, and Palle Svensson
12. Political Support in East–Central Europe
    Gábor Tóka
13. Support for Democratic Values
    Jacques Thomassen
14. Citizens and the State: A Relationship Transformed
    Dieter Fuchs and Hans-Dieter Klingemann

Volume ii. Public Opinion and Internationalized Governance

1. Introduction
   Oskar Niedermayer and Richard Sinnott
2. Bringing Public Opinion Back In
   Richard Sinnott
3. A Typology of Orientations
   Oskar Niedermayer and Bettina Westle
4. Trends and Contrasts
   Oskar Niedermayer
5. Economics Calculus or Familiarity Breeds Content
   Agusti Bosch and Kenneth Newton
6. Development of Support: Diffusion or Demographic
   Replacement?
   Bernhard Wessels
7. Evaluations of the EC: Élite or Mass Driven?
   Bernhard Wessels
8. Europeans and the Nation State
   Guido Martinotti and Sonia Stefanizzi
9. Is There a European Identity?
   Sophie Duchesne and André-Paul Frognier
10. Trust and Sense of Community
    Oskar Niedermayer
11. Policy, Subsidiarity, and Legitimacy
    Richard Sinnott
12. Democratic Legitimacy and the European Parliament
    Oskar Niedermayer and Richard Sinnott
13. The View from Within
    Bettina Westle
14. The View from EFTA
    Frank Aarebrot, Sten Berglund, and Thomas Weninger
15. The View from Central and Eastern Europe
    Sten Berglund and Frank Aarebrot with
    Jadwiga Koralewicz
16. NATO, the European Community, and the United Nations
    Philip Everts
17. Conclusion: European Publics and the Legitimacy of
    International Governance
    Philip Everts and Richard Sinnott

Volume iii. The Scope of Government

1. The Scope of Government
   Ole Borre and Michael Goldsmith
2. The Growth of Government
   Michael Goldsmith
3. Political Agendas and Beliefs about the Scope
   of Government
   Edeltraud Roller
4. Attitudes towards the Size of Government
   Beate M. Huseby
5. Taxing and Spending: Tax Revolt or Tax Protest?
   Maria A. Confalonieri and Kenneth Newton
6. Politics, Economics, Class, and Taxation
   Kenneth Newton and Maria A. Confalonieri
7. The Welfare State: The Equality Dimension
   Edeltraud Roller
8. The Welfare State: The Security Dimension
   Per Arnt Pettersen
9. Government Intervention in the Economy
   Ole Borre and José Manuel Viegas
10. Government, Communications, and the Media
    Peter Golding and Leo van Snippenburg
11. Protecting the Environment
    Olof Johansson
12. Scope-of-Government Beliefs and Political Support
    Ole Borre
13. Beliefs and the Scope of Government
    Ole Borre
14. Public Attitudes and Changes in Health Care Systems:
    A Confrontation and a Puzzle
    Achille Ardigó

Volume iv. The Impact of Values

1. Introduction: The Impact of Values
   Jan W. van Deth
2. The Concept of Values
   Jan W. van Deth and Elinor Scarbrough

 3. A Macro Setting for Micro Politics
    Jan W. van Deth
 4. Secularization and Church Religiosity
    Wolfgang Jagodzinski and Karel Dobbelaere
 5. Materialist–Postmaterialist Value Orientations
    Elinor Scarbrough
 6. Left–Right Materialist Value Orientations
    Oddbjørn Knutsen
 7. Religious Cognitions and Beliefs
    Karel Dobbelaere and Wolfgang Jagodzinski
 8. Religious and Ethical Pluralism
    Wolfgang Jagodzinski and Karel Dobbelaere
 9. Feminist Political Orientations
    Carina Lundmark
10. Green, Greener, Greenest
    Masja Nas
11. Postmodernism
    John Gibbins and Bo Reimer
12. Status Tensions
    Etienne Schweisguth
13. Political Efficacy and Trust
    Oscar W. Gabriel
14. Political Interest
    Oscar W. Gabriel and Jan W. van Deth
15. Grass-Roots Activity
    Peter Gundelach
16. Electoral Participation
    Sami Borg
17. Party Choice
    Oddbjørn Knutsen
18. Cleavage Politics
    Oddbjørn Knutsen and Elinor Scarbrough
19. Perspectives on Value Change
    Jan W. van Deth and Elinor Scarbrough

1

The Tale of a Comparative Political Science Project

How It All Came About

In 1986 Jean Blondel, then chairman of the Government and Law Committee of the Economic and Social Research Council of the UK (ESRC), proposed that the Standing Committee for the Social Sciences (SCSS) of the European Science Foundation (ESF) hold a conference to discuss comparative research in Western Europe. The intention was to strengthen links between the national research councils, the ESF, and individual researchers, and to discuss ways of promoting comparative research. The SCSS agreed, and a meeting was jointly organized by Jean Blondel, John Smith, the Secretary of the SCSS, and Ken Newton, then chair of the Research Board of the European Consortium for Political Research (ECPR). Some twenty representatives from ESF member organizations in sixteen countries, most of them social scientists, discussed research modes and priorities and considered substantive projects which would particularly benefit from a comparative approach.

One of the many ideas that came up during the meeting was 'Beliefs in Government', a study of changing mass attitudes towards government in Western Europe in the post-war period. It was felt that a great deal on this topic had already been done, mainly from a national perspective, and that there was a strong case for bringing leading scholars together to re-examine the data with a fresh eye, a comparative approach, and an interest in long-term stability and change. The meeting recommended that an intensive, specialist workshop should be organized in order to explore the potential for the project.

This suggestion was enthusiastically accepted by the SCSS as the first activity of its third (1988–92) mandate. Max Kaase, of the University of Mannheim, and Ken Newton, of the University of Essex, were asked to prepare a working paper for the workshop, which was held in September 1988 in Strasbourg. It was attended by eighteen specialists in mass survey research from twelve nations. They considered the rationale of the research and the difficult problem of suitable and available data. There was a great deal of enthusiasm for the project and a belief that the data situation, while very far from ideal, was at least satisfactory. As a result, the workshop was able to agree an outline research programme. It also made a most important decision that the project should be divided into four sub-topics, namely: attitudes towards democratic politics; the internationalization of government; the scope of government; and the impact of values.

Kaase and Newton put some finishing touches to the research programme agreed by the workshop, and Kaase presented it to the November 1988 meeting of the ESF General Assembly. It was unanimously accepted. Work started on the project in 1989. A steering committee was set up which first met at the University of Mannheim in May 1989.

Six long years later, the end product of the Beliefs in Government research programme is a series of five books published by Oxford University Press, as follows:

   i *Citizens and the State*, edited by Hans-Dieter Klingemann and Dieter Fuchs
   ii *Public Opinion and Internationalized Governance*, edited by Oskar Niedermayer and Richard Sinnott
   iii *The Scope of Government*, edited by Ole Borre and Elinor Scarbrough
   iv *The Impact of Values*, edited by Jan van Deth and Elinor Scarbrough
   v *Beliefs in Government*, by Max Kaase and Kenneth Newton

The rest of this chapter outlines the logic of the research, its approach and methods, and the relationship of each volume to the project as a whole.

Of Time and Space

If there is one sub-discipline of the social science where the famous Merton (after Isaac Newton) dictum 'On the shoulders of giants' applies, it is empirical and cross-national comparative research (for an account of the major developments, see Scheuch 1990). Such work is built on the four corner-stones of theory, methodology, empirical studies, and an appropriate infrastructure. In all these respects the pioneers of comparative politics of the 1950s and 1960s created the basics of modern political science. They taught us the need for systematic comparative research, for broad-based comparisons, and for historical perspectives. In addition they laid down the foundations of university and private research centres, and of data archives such as the Inter-university Consortium for Political and Social Research (ICPSR) at Michigan, the national data archives of Western Europe, and the Roper Center in the United States. There is no question that a project like Beliefs in Government could never have started without the intellectual and institutional basis created by the pioneers of comparative government since the 1960s.

From the very outset the whole purpose of the project was to reconsider and re-analyse secondary data. To commission a European survey of our own covering all aspects of beliefs in government would have been impossibly expensive. In any case it would not have met the central aim of considering trends and developments over as long a (post-war) time period as possible. Given the logic of time-series research, we were bound to use published data sources. Besides its theoretical and financial logic, the project would also add an extra dimension to published material by setting it in a comparative and time-series framework—in the modern jargon, the research would have considerable value-added potential.

When the project was conceptualized, the organizers had, of course, a good knowledge of the relevant comparative work—Almond and Verba's *The Civic Culture*, Verba, Nie, and Kim's *Participation and Political Equality*, Barnes, Kaase, *et al.*'s *Political Action*, the Inglehart-driven European Values Survey (now the World Values Survey), and the surveys of the International Social Science Programme (ISSP). However, national work was less widely known, and, unfortunately, national data archives, like those in Denmark, Sweden, Norway, Germany, Britain, and the Netherlands, are not so well developed in other countries. What was worse, the documentation and dissemination of machine-readable national data files had not at that time reached a point where compatible studies could be identified without enormous initial effort. It was hoped that such data could be used for comparative purposes, but, if that proved impossible, it was believed that its lack would not ruin the project.

Perhaps the most important source of information, which tipped the balance in favour of the study, was the bi-annual Eurobarometer surveys of the populations (aged 17 years and over) of the member states of the European Union. In addition, the data problem was subsequently eased by an agreement of the Council of European Social Science Data Archives (CESSDA) that the Cologne Zentralarchiv für Empirische Sozialforschung would take on the vital role of supplying secondary data to the project. The agreement with the Cologne Zentralarchiv even allowed resources to be pooled so as to prepare questionnaire data from the United States Information Agency (USIA) covering attitudes towards politics, especially foreign affairs, in Europe. As a result of the Beliefs in Government project the data are now available from the Cologne archive.

In an ideal world, the complete information needs of the project could be represented in a three-dimensional matrix of time, countries, and variables. Measured against this ideal, the real situation is poor indeed. First, few surveys cover as long a time span as the Eurobarometers. Indeed, most are recent and cover only two or three time points. With the exception of *The Civic Culture* and the USIA surveys, there is little material before 1970. This hampered us enormously. Secondly, it is frequently the case that countries covered in comparative studies are chosen not on theoretical grounds but because survey teams happen to be available, or for some chance reason. For example, the regular country coverage of the Eurobarometers depends on which countries join the European Union (EU) and when. Thirdly, and most importantly, the areas of substantive research interests vary across time and space. Some questions are intensively investigated in some countries and at some periods, but not others.

Consequently, our high hopes at the outset of the project mellowed quickly. Nevertheless, we have managed to retain as a minimum criterion for inclusion in the project the requirement of studying at least two countries over at least two time points. Most chapters in the books cover many more countries and time points. This has demanded not just close and time-consuming collaboration between scholars in different countries, but also a huge effort to collect and collate the relevant data. Although the effort was huge, we believe that the pay-off is worth it in terms of more systematically comparative research which tracks changes over time.

When this project was conceived, no one anticipated the breathtaking political events of 1989–90 which resulted in the collapse of the Soviet empire. As fascinated observers of these momentous events, we discussed whether the whole scope and nature of the project should be transformed by them. The result was a clear-cut decision: neither the theoretical focus of the project on mass attitudes towards democracy, nor the lack of comparative longitudinal survey evidence, allowed us to extend the research into Central and Eastern Europe. In the special case of Germany, this meant that we could cover the Federal Republic only until 3 October 1990. However, the intellectual challenge is such that parts of *Citizens and the State*, Volume i, and *Public Opinion and Internationalized Governance*, Volume ii, consider the implications of the politics of the new Europe.

The Analysis of Socio-Political Change

Millions of deaths, the atrocities of the holocaust, and the expulsion of countless people from their homes and communities have sharpened the desire of scholars, politicians, and the public to search for conditions that would prevent the repetition of such things. Though challenged by the Cold War, the West has held firmly to its liberal belief that pluralist democracy, in the form of a *Rechtsstaat* (legal state), is the best guarantee. This view was widely though not universally accepted, while a reversion to authoritarian or totalitarian rule in the West was not entirely discounted either (Huntington 1991). Democracy is not to be taken for granted. As a consequence, it is important to study why democracy may fail (Linz and Stepan 1978) and, no less important, why most nations of Western Europe have stabilized themselves institutionally and maintained at least an acceptable level of public support. The Beliefs in Government project is firmly located in this tradition.

Methodologically, understanding the conditions that make for political stability and change requires one to examine various levels of the political system simultaneously. It has become customary to think of three such levels: the micro level of the individual, the meso level of intermediary organizations, and the macro level of the whole system. Given the survey data base of most of our project, it is the individual citizen who is the core of our analysis. This concern is also grounded in democratic theory which centres on the rights and duties of the individual, and on the principle of formal political equality between individuals, including, of course, the central idea of one person, one vote.

Voting, like other types of political participation and political action, is thought to be based upon individual cognitions, feelings, and evaluations, which in turn are moderated and influenced by situational circumstances such as group membership, institutional settings, and the mass media. The model that most closely corresponds to this way of conceptualizing and explaining micro-political behaviour is the attitude→situation→behaviour model which is the basis for much research. It is also a model that can be applied to the study of attitude change.

Unfortunately, this approach is best suited to the analysis of *short-term phenomena* which, though they are interesting in their own right, have contributed precious little to the understanding of long-term change. For example, monthly or even weekly measurement of party preferences may be important for politicians, the public, and scholars to follow, even if these changes are not translated into actual votes on election day. But one of the potential pitfalls of research is that short-term fluctuations in mass attitudes may be misinterpreted as harbingers of great transformations to come, although in fact they simply represent the ebb and flow of the public mood without lasting political significance.

In sum, the attitude→situation→behaviour model is not well suited to the analysis of those *long-term changes* with which the Beliefs in Government project is most concerned. Any judgement of how Western democracy has fared must consider stability and change in the long term—that is, from one generation to the next over a period of thirty to forty years.

We need to identify generational changes and separate them from short-term fluctuations and life-cycle changes, as Inglehart does by using cohort analysis in his study of value change. This approach is important, not least because it permits the researcher to study the effects of population replacement and the ability of society to reproduce itself, democratic values included. After all, OECD nations replace some 30 to 40 per cent of their populations over a thirty-year period.

By using cohort analysis, researchers can come closer to understanding the *meaning* of observed changes, although not necessarily their *causes*. Theories of change usually assume one or both of two things. First, structural and institutional shifts at the macro level somehow trickle down through the mass media and different organizations and social groups to individual citizens. Secondly, changes at the mass level bubble up through group and institutional channels of communication to the élite level. Such a multi-level process of reciprocal cause-and-effect can be used as a heuristic device to try to understand the process by which micro and macro factors interact.

Thinking abstractly about micro–macro interactions and studying them with an appropriate multi-level research design are quite different matters. For a start, it cannot be assumed that relevant empirical data are available. For example, post-industrial society, which epitomizes the core of modern society for many, emphasizes the importance of secularization, but this itself is difficult to study. The chapter by Jagodzinski and Dobbelaere in *The Impact of Values*, Volume iv, amply demonstrates that it is a major scholarly achievement in its own right just to document differences between countries in such things as church attendance. To go further than this and relate macro and micro variables with respect to such things as secularization requires the logic of what Przeworski and Teune (1970) term 'most similar systems design'. This singles out units of analysis, particularly nation states, which differ only on a limited number of theoretically meaningful macro variables in order to test their causal importance. Of course, this is difficult enough, but to trace changes over time in order to test a dynamic model is an even greater challenge.

Since Western Europe consists of a set of nations which are quite similar in terms of economic development and democratic government, it was initially thought to be an ideal setting for the most similar systems design. Our initial scan of the data sources showed that some longitudinal information for both macro and micro variables was available, but that cross-national comparative data were relatively scarce. In the process of coming to grips with data difficulties, however, we became aware of another problem that we had not realized quite so clearly before.

Most of the standard macro variables of comparative research are of rather limited explanatory value for our purposes; country size, unitary and federal government, presidential and parliamentary systems, centre and periphery, corporatist and non-corporatist, Christian democratic and social democratic. One exception is the work of Lijphart (1984) on majoritarian and consensus democracies, which deserves the highest praise. Another is the book by Klingemann, Hofferbert, and Budge (1994), which compares the relationship between party programmes, government programmes, and government outputs. Beyond this there is comparatively little information about core variables, or their indicators, which dig deep into the internal structures and processes of pluralist democracies. It may be that many Western political scientists have been so mesmerized by the ideological confrontation of East and West that they have not felt it necessary to examine or compare the internal functioning of Western democracies, how they have changed over time, or how they vary in operation and performance.

This leaves us with something of a puzzle. On the one hand, we suspect that the 'most similar' systems of the Western European family of democracies turn out to differ in some crucial respects in terms of government structures and processes. On the other, we also know that most have managed to sustain rather high levels of public satisfaction with democracy over the past three or four decades. In short, different systems seem to be associated with generally rather similar public opinion profiles. Perhaps this is because democracies, whatever their type, maintain citizen satisfaction through the operation of functional equivalents. But this still leaves us with the puzzle (discussed in a later chapter) of what explains the levels of citizen satisfaction: is it due to a close and constant process of mutual adaptation between democratic states and their citizens, or, on the contrary, to the distance between the two, and to the political indifference or resilience of citizens?

'Beliefs in Government'

Two themes implicit in the title of the project deserve brief elaboration: what is meant by government, and why beliefs 'in' and not 'about' government? By 'government' we do not mean only that group of people or political parties who are put into power by popular election. The term has a much broader meaning and covers all the political institutions of the executive, the legislative, and the judiciary and their associated activities, decisions, and outputs. In this vein, the project deals with the attitudes of individual citizens which directly and indirectly relate to their role in the political process, their views of individual and corporate political actors, and their assessment of the institutions of government and its democratic rules of the game.

Given this necessarily wide focus it would have been enormously attractive and desirable to organize the analysis around a tightly knit and broadly conceived framework, but this turned out to be impossible for theoretical and empirical reasons. It would have required an entirely fresh look at the whole subject while, at the same time, being constrained by empirical material which had already been collected with different theoretical concerns in mind. It would require, for example, marrying Easton's theoretical distinction between authorities, regime, and community (Easton 1965, 1975) with Almond and Verba's empirical analysis built around the distinctions between system, input, output, and self (Almond and Verba 1963). Extensive use is made of both sets of concepts in Beliefs in Government research, but of necessity they are used in a pragmatic and eclectic fashion for different theoretical purposes.

A major example of the piecemeal development of research concerns *The Civic Culture,* which, while it was a theoretical breakthrough, did not stimulate a concerted effort to develop the theoretical underpinnings of the concept of political culture or a systematic account of how it changes over time. As a result, there are research voids. The same may be said of the early promising work on the authoritarian personality (Adorno *et al.* 1950), on political dogmatism (Rokeach 1960), democratic attitudes (Prothro and Grigg 1960; McClosky 1964), and political ideology (Lane 1962). In short, research has proceeded in an understandably piecemeal and *ad hoc* fashion in which the 'self' dimension, identified by Almond and Verba, has been largely underdeveloped in national and cross-national research. Instead, clusters of intensive research efforts have concentrated on various research objects according to the influence of major research figures (Rokkan, for example), or idiosyncratic factors, or on the fads and fashions from which social science suffers no less than other disciplines.

As a result, the particular concerns of this and the other four volumes in the series are inevitably shaped to some extent by the past concerns of research communities and the work they have left us. For theoretical and descriptive reasons it would have been desirable to combine information about élite and mass attitudes in order to understand how the two interact. Unfortunately, élites are rarely sampled systematically over time in single countries, let alone comparatively.

The second question concerns the use of 'in' rather than 'about' government. While we do not want to make too much of the point, to believe *in* something implies a sense of involvement, a moral or emotional commitment. Beliefs *about* something imply detachment, the position of the outside observer. In this sense, 'Beliefs in Government' is concerned with sense of citizen identification with, and emotional attachment to, democratic government. At the outset, the hypothesis was that democratic stability depends upon mass beliefs in the legitimacy of the democratic order. Constitutions are like fortresses: they must be well designed and well manned if they are to withstand their enemies.

This does not mean commitment, come what may, as Sniderman (1981) points out. On the contrary, a lively democracy depends upon active, attentive, and critical citizens. Nevertheless, the criticism and the inevitable disappointments of a competitive political process must be combined with a basic identification with, and commitment to, norms and institutions if democracy is to thrive.

The idea that democracy involves a balanced tension between identification and criticism, commitment and detachment, extends the study of political attitudes beyond the cognitive realm. This was recognized in the theoretical scheme of *The Civic Culture,* which argued that political orientations entail cognitive, affective, and evaluative dimensions. Unfortunately, the three dimensions have not figured equally in empirical research; the cognitive has been studied most frequently, the affective less so, and the evaluative least. For example, a great deal of information has been produced by commercial polling agencies about how citizens evaluate governments, opposition parties, and their programmes, but comparatively little on how citizens evaluate their political regimes, in the Eastonian sense of the term. In short, there is less information than we would like about regime evaluation of the kind necessary for a study of beliefs in government.

A good example is the case of political parties where the affective dimension has traditionally been studied in terms of party identification. Holmberg and Schmitt's chapter in *Citizens and the State* shows how rich the returns can be for this type of work, but, unfortunately, there is rather little comparative material of this kind. As a result, it is difficult to assess the claim that there is rising dissatisfaction with all political parties in the West. The same difficulty applies to the regime level of the political system, and hence it is also difficult to assess claims about the legitimacy crisis or overloaded governments. Beliefs *in* government seems to be a topic which merits more scholarly attention in the future.

The Scope of 'Beliefs in Government'

It is generally acknowledged that the two and a half decades following 1950 were unusual for economic growth and democratic consolidation in OECD countries. This was also a time when continued economic expansion seemed guaranteed and when many OECD countries moved through a period of transition from the social state, which protected individuals in times of emergency, to the all-encompassing welfare state. This seems to have been a crucial period in the development of Western European society which had a major impact on political attitudes and beliefs.

Although good comparative data are lacking, there is German evidence of a generational shift of outlook between 1965 to 1970 among the young, well-educated post-war cohorts. They became the leaders of what was later termed postmaterialism, the élite challenge, and the participatory revolution (Allerbeck 1976; Meulemann 1985). In retrospect, we can see it was probably growing political engagement outside established party channels which generated the crisis theories of democracy of the 1970s. We consider these theories later in the book, but meanwhile point out that both the Marxist theories (Offe 1972; Lieberam 1977) and the liberal and conservatives ones (King 1975; Birch 1984) were based on the assumption that the upward spiral of expectations would inevitably drive democracy beyond its limits.

Two decades later, we can see that this assumption was unwarranted and try to understand why, but the main point is that speculation about the legitimacy crisis and government overload encouraged scholars to look more closely at how state and citizens relate. The main thrust of the Beliefs in Government project is also to examine the relationship from the citizen perspective, but to do it both comparatively and over time. The members of the project felt this was a useful enterprise because the literature is full of rogue evidence, deviant cases, contradictions, and counter-intuitive findings.

Election studies have long been an important source of information, although they are strong in depth but weak in comparative breadth—they are usually national studies. As such they form an immensely rich but diverse body of data, which opens up possibilities for the study of changing public opinion. They allow us to track changing attitudes towards parties and interest groups; to study the unfreezing of parties; together with studies of political participation, they provide insights into the processes of politicization and de-politicization; at the micro level they help to clarify the circumstances of institutional and non-institutional political action; and at the meso level, they link the study of established parties and interest groups with the study of new social movements (see Kriesi 1993). In sum, for both theoretical and practical reasons the first volume in the Beliefs in Government series concentrates on the topic of *Citizens and the State* and makes extensive use of national voting studies as well as comparative social surveys.

The crisis of the welfare state, caused by slow economic growth and tax strain in the late 1970s, generated the literature which forms the core of the second volume. In its title, 'scope of government' refers both to the range of state activities and to the depth of its penetration into everyday life. After the long boom it was increasingly argued that big government undermined economic growth, wasted taxpayers' money, eroded incentives, and slowed innovation. Attention was increasingly turned to the free-rider and over-consumption problems of public goods, the need to optimize scarce resources, and the claim that the state had outgrown itself. In short, the assumptions and the philosophy of the 1950–70 period were challenged and the welfare state came under scrutiny. Continuing tension between state expansion and contraction, and mass attitudes towards the proper role of government as a service supplier, are the main themes of *The Scope of Government*, Volume iii. It is ironic, however, that the very assumption of the 1960s and 1970s, that the state would continue to expand, means that data about public opinion on some aspects of the matter are sparse before the 1980s.

The argument that mass attitudes towards government and its services were beginning to change in the 1970s is closely tied up with the discussion of materialism and postmaterialism. Only feint traces of the silent, postmaterialist revolution could be detected in 1971 when Inglehart first formulated his theme, but since then an enormous amount of evidence has been assembled. As a result, his theory of postmaterialism is likely to remain one of the most influential and stimulating so far as socio-political change is concerned. This achievement is the more laudable because Inglehart has also ensured that Eurobarometer surveys of the European Commission regularly contain a (not uncontroversial) battery of four questions. A rank-ordering of responses to these allows the identification of four value types: the pure types of materialist and postmaterialist, and two mixed types. However, it may be that rank-ordering distorts the real nature of value change if this involves a symbiotic merger of the old and the new, rather than replacement of one by the other. Rank-ordering is more likely to pick up replacement; valence scoring is more likely to pick up a merging of agendas. The Beliefs in Government research finds good evidence to show that the new political agenda has not replaced the old one, but has merged with it in a symbiotic fashion. However, even if this is true, there remains overwhelming empirical evidence of a broad range of implications stemming from the sorts of value change observed by Inglehart.

The Beliefs in Government Volume iv, entitled *The Impact of Values*, deals with this sort of issue, although the book is not only or even mainly concerned with the materialism–postmaterialism debate. Its scope is much wider than this, including, among other things, religion and secularization, gender, age, class, postmodernism, and 'green' political culture. It also considers the impact of values on such things as political participation, new social movements, political interest, and life styles.

The remaining volume in the series deals with one of the most conspicuous, important, and far-reaching trends of government in the late twentieth century—the trend towards the internationalization of government. The prescience of Deutsch and his colleagues who wrote on this topic almost forty years ago (Deutsch *et al.* 1957) is revealed in the fact that the EU currently has fifteen members. Expansion into Central and Eastern Europe is also in prospect. This situation alone makes the study of popular attitudes towards the EU mandatory for the project. Yet the EU is only one part, though a very significant part for Western Europeans, of the broader trend involving the creation of a supranational or international level of government. Public opinion about the EU, European integration and international government in general is the concern of *Public Opinion and Internationalized Govern-ance*, Volume ii. Two aspects of this topic merit attention here.

The first concerns the democratic deficit of the EU. While the Maastricht Treaty enhanced the role of the European Parliament, the EU is still dominated by the Commission, the Council of Ministers, and, in a more basic sense, the European Court. The tensions between democratic member nations and the EU are likely to surface more and more in the future. So also is tension between the EU and individual citizens as the EU makes decisions with a direct and every-day impact on citizens. So far, policy effects have been rather remote and abstract, or have impacted on particular and specific interests and groups. But as the EU develops it is increasingly likely to make decisions which have a real and immediate effect upon the general public. The symbolic issue of a European banknote is a case in point. Even the German public, normally highly supportive of the EU, reacted against the suggestion that it should lose its Deutschmark. As recent referendums in Denmark and France suggest, and as subsequent referendums in Austria, Finland, Sweden, and Norway also indicate, public opinion is likely to become more important. Public controversy is likely to grow over the issues of deepening and broadening, especially since there is not yet consensus about the constitutional structure of the EU.

The second point deals with international government beyond the EU. This particularly concerns the UN and NATO, so far as Western Europe is concerned. As international regimes spread in scope and power as a response to the globalization of politics, international communications, and economic integration, their relationship with national governments will increasingly become a controversial matter. This will raise in an acute form the issues of internationalism and centralization, on the one hand, and decentralization and subsidiarity, on the other. Once again, these issues are likely to be hammered out in the context of an increasingly vocal and active public opinion. Therefore the issues of nationalism and internationalism, public opinion and European integration, democracy in international organizations, and mass attitudes towards the EU, UN, and NATO, are also examined.

In concluding this section, a few words should be said about this fifth and final volume of the series. We are aware of steering a difficult course between the dangers of Scylla and Charybdis. On the one hand, this volume is not concerned with mere summary and repetition of the other volumes; readers are directed to them for full and detailed discussion of research. It includes some statistics to illustrate the arguments, but the four companion volumes provide detailed supporting argument and evidence. On the other hand, this volume does set the results of the other four into a wider reference frame of social science, though without departing too much from the central core of the project. In other words, this book is grounded in the detailed research of the other volumes, but tries to go beyond them and to relate their conclusions in a more speculative fashion to over-arching theories of public opinion, political institutions, and political change in the democracies of Western Europe. Consequently, the book starts off with more specific chapters, and moves on to more general and abstract matters.

The End of an Era?

In their underrated book discussing the critical disposition of modern intellectuals, Hamilton and Wright (1986: 417) say:

For many people within the intellectual ranks, the critical outlook is not data based. Their conclusions . . . do not stem from systematic review and analysis of evidence. The tendency, for many, exists prior to analysis and . . . is frequently accompanied by an indifference to evidence, especially to findings that challenge or bring into question key elements of their *Weltanschauung* . . . We have seen numerous examples of this data indifference—or worse, data denigration—in previous chapters. Many intellectuals, in short, are depending on a consensus as opposed to an evidential truth. Expressed in other words, they are responding to processes of group dynamics rather than to processes of data collection and assessment.

The authors come to this judgement having confronted widely held theories about American society in the 1960s and 1970s with survey evidence. Although they are mainly concerned with the cultural and media intelligentsia of America, a reading of the book shows that they regard many social scientists as part of the intelligentsia. Their conclusion might be extended to cover the data-blindness and data-prejudice of social scientists in Europe. In contrast, the goal of this project is both demanding and modest: it seeks to confront major theories of government and politics in modern democratic societies with a body of appropriate evidence; and in doing so it seeks to compile reliable empirical information about the state of, and changes in, public attitudes towards government in Western Europe for as much of the postwar period as possible and for as many nations as possible. The aim is to accumulate evidence in the best traditions of 'On the shoulders of giants'. In doing so, we hope to identify black spots in the research landscape and even, perhaps, stimulate research on them.

At the start of this project the collapse of the Soviet bloc was inconceivable. The project was set up because it seemed a propitious time to review the fate of European democracy against the survey evidence which had accumulated with increasing weight since the 1970s. With the virtually overnight changes of the velvet revolution, however, we began to wonder whether the changes in Central and Eastern Europe did not mark the end of an era in the democracies of the West. Two thoughts triggered this speculation. The first concerns the extent to which the revolution of 1917 and the continuing threat of communism until 1989 has encouraged nations of the West to soften their hard-nosed capitalism and engage in some redistribution of wealth and power.

The second thought involves turning this idea around and asking what the loss of the ideological alternative would mean to contemporary democracies. One outcome might be that co-operation in the face of the Soviet threat is replaced by peaceful competition which strengthens the liberal democracies. Another might be depoliticization and estrangement from democracy now that we are released from our quasi-religious struggle with communism. Democratic faith may be further undermined by political apathy, hedonism, individualism, and by the antisocial calculation of personal interests, as some of the theorists of postmodernism argue.

In contrast to this line of argument, Huntington, in his *Clash of Civilizations* (1993), says that the void created by the collapse of communism will be replaced by new conflicts which thrive on cultural rather than political differences. As one would expect, this idea has drawn critical fire which need not concern us here. It is significant, though, that both sides of the debate agree that Westerners universally, and as if by instinct, place an enormous priority on individualism. If this is the hallmark of the West which brings it into conflict with other cultures, then it may turn out that the 'open society' (to use Karl Popper's famous term) still has its enemies.

The lesson of the Beliefs in Government research is that democracies can stand considerable internal and external pressure while at the same time adjusting to changing environments. Our speculation is that after an initial period of irritation and disorientation, liberal democracies will measure themselves against fresh challenges—religious, cultural, environmental, for example—and survive by adapting.

2

Theories of Crisis and Catastrophe, Change and Transformation

From Post-War to Post-Wall Europe

Western Europe has only twenty or thirty years of democracy left
in it; after that it will slide, engineless and rudderless, under the
surrounding seas of dictatorship, and whether the dictation comes
from a politburo or a junta will not make that much difference.

Willy Brandt; quoted in Crozier, Huntington, and Watanuki
(1975: 2)

Western Europe has passed through an unprecedented era of relative
peace, affluence, and democratic stability in the latter half of the
twentieth century. During this period almost all nations on the sub-
continent have had political difficulties and disturbances, and in some
instances these have been acute and serious. But by comparison with
almost any other period in its history, the last forty-five years have been
a truly golden era.

Nevertheless, many political scientists and political commentators
have expressed a ceaseless flow of serious worries and anxieties about
the present state and future prospects of democracy. Each period has
had its favourite theory or theories about democracy. In the 1960s it was
mass theory. In the 1970s it was various forms of 'legitimacy crisis' and
theories of 'overload' and 'ungovernability'. These were followed in
the late 1970s and early 1980s by a concern for the challenge new social
movements posed to the orthodox political order of Western democracies. Class and partisan political dealignment, it was said, destabilized
traditional mass parties and pressure groups, causing dangerous
unpredictability and political instability. Most recently, the theory of

postmodern politics or the 'new politics' has analysed the ways in which modern liberal democracy is being undermined by the emergence of a new type of citizen and new types of political interests.

In their different ways these five theories of crisis, contradiction, and catastrophe, which predict a gloomy and difficult future for Western democracies, argue that they will either come under extreme strain or else collapse altogether. As such they present us with a paradox: on the one hand, Western Europe has passed through a period of relative peace, affluence and democratic stability; on the other hand, political scientists have offered us theories of crisis and catastrophe.

There is also another general stream of thought in the social sciences which does not predict crisis or collapse, but rather fundamental change and transformation. In the 1960s the 'end of ideology' writers foresaw a new style and content for the democratic politics of the West. In the 1990s, the 'end of history' predicted something similar. The theory of postmaterialism also argues that culture shift and a 'silent revolution' is currently transforming Western government and politics. These three theories argue that democracies will change, sometimes in fundamental ways, but will not crumble or collapse.

Perhaps by laying out the theories and their evidence side by side we can learn, first, something about both the current state and the future prospects of the liberal democracies of Western Europe. We may also learn, secondly, something about the way in which political scientists have gone about their job of analysing government and politics in the post-war period. And, thirdly, it may be that studying the experience of the established democracies of Western Europe will show something of value for the newly emerging democracies of the globe.

The rest of this chapter will review the theories of democratic crisis and of democratic transformation. The review will be brief since the main thrust of the different theories is well known and widely understood. This chapter will then draw out the implications of the theories for modern democratic politics in a way which helps to put them to an empirical test. In the next chapter we will consider evidence relevant to the theories.

Theories of Contradiction, Crisis, and Catastrophe

Mass Society Theory

Social science writing of the 1940s and 1950s about extremist and anti-democratic politics culminated in Kornhauser's influential book *The*

Politics of Mass Society (1960). He deals with the social and economic bases of Fascist, Communist, and Nazi governments in Europe in the inter-war period, and with the conditions in which extremist political movements emerged in the post-war period in Europe and the United States. The book draws together a great mass of theory and data to produce a subtle and complex theory which seems to fit a great deal of empirical evidence. As such it should be as useful in understanding contemporary movements, such as Le Pen's National Front in France or the extreme-right Republicans in Germany, as it was for Poujadism or McCarthyism in earlier times.

Kornhauser argues that modern societies are integrated by a large number and wide diversity of formal and informal social groups and organizations. At the informal level, the ties of family and community locate people in their society and give them a rooted sense of belonging, identity, and personal security. At the formal level, a great variety of secondary associations (also known as voluntary associations, citizens' associations, and intermediary organizations), act as channels of communication between citizens, and between citizens and political élites. These associations—churches, professional organizations, trade unions, community associations, and sports, charity, education, and leisure clubs of all kinds—bind together individuals with the same interests. They also create an overlapping and interlocking network of different and competing interests which, in Simmel's (1955) words, 'bind society together by its own internal divisions'. Such groups are also a means of mobilizing public opinion against unpopular governments and policies, on the one hand, and of creating a complex set of cross-cutting cleavages which help stabilize and moderate political conflict, on the other.

Societies that are built upon stable and cohesive informal groups and communities, and which sustain a whole range of formal organizations and associations, are called pluralist societies. In contrast, mass societies are made up of an amorphous mass of unrelated, undifferentiated, isolated and atomized individuals. Such individuals lack social roots, are poorly integrated into society, and tend to be alienated politically. They are prepared to support extremist and anti-democratic political movements.

Anything which produces a sharp tear in the social fabric—defeat in war, widespread unemployment, sudden urbanization and industrialization—tends to create the conditions of mass society and hence extremist politics. But modern liberal democracies also contain the seeds of mass society, and therefore of social and political alienation. Kornhauser lists those aspects of modern urban-industrial societies which present a danger: the breakdown of the old, autonomous, self-employed middle class and the rise of the modern organization man who lives and works in the large-scale corporation; the devaluation of churches and communities; the expanding bureaucracy and centralization of modern life; the rise of mass communications; the increasing complexity of modern social and political issues which heighten the citizen's sense of ineffectiveness and powerlessness; the decay of old class and community ties which tends to increase the nihilistic attitude of the masses; and the increasing sensitivity and responsiveness of political élites to mass demands, which leaves them exposed to populist and anti-democratic movements.

Kornhauser (1960: 237–8) is careful to point out that modern society contains within itself the capacity to create both pluralist democracy and mass society extremism.

these conditions of modern life carry with them both the heightened possibility of social alienation *and* enhanced opportunities for the creation of new forms of association. Modern industry destroys the conditions for a society of small enterprises, but it also provides the condition of abundance which frees people to seek new ways of life. Modern urban life atomizes traditional social groups, but it also provides a variety of contacts and experiences that broaden social horizons and the range of social participation. Modern democracy diminishes the legitimacy of elites, but it also encourages a multiplicity of competing elites.

Therefore Kornhauser does not equate modern society with mass society, but claims that modern Western society can generate some of the features of mass society which threaten democratic politics. His theories lead us to look for particular signs of democratic pathology. As far as social conditions are concerned, the decay of community and the erosion of secondary associations (including the established parties) are warning signs. In terms of political attitudes, growing alienation and a mass sense of inefficacy and low competence are important. So also is a loss of élite legitimacy. And so far as political behaviour is concerned, the indicators of a democratic breakdown are a decline in membership of voluntary organizations, and the increasing use of direct, anti-democratic, and sometimes violent forms of political participation.

The Legitimacy Crisis

Mass society theory was largely but not wholly driven by a desire to understand the politics of authoritarianism and totalitarianism between the 1930s and 1950s. It tried to explain the rise of Communism under Stalin, of Nazism under Hitler, and Fascism under Franco and Mussolini as well as the extremist and anti-democratic movements in other countries in the 1950s. In the late 1960s, however, the radicalism of student and worker movements, especially the events of 1968, resulted in the replacement of mass theory with a concern for legitimacy. Theories of the legitimacy crisis are generally complex, involving many different conceptual refinements and analytical variations which, fortunately, are not particularly relevant to present concerns. There are two main versions of the general theme: the first focuses on the economic contradictions of the modern state; the second concentrates rather more heavily on its political contradictions.

The purest form of the first is found in O'Connor's *The Fiscal Crisis of the State* (1973), which argues that the state must fulfil two contradictory functions. First, it must create the conditions favourable to capital accumulation, which calls for greater and greater investment not just in physical capital—roads, airports, communications—but also in social capital—a healthy, well-educated, and productive workforce. Secondly, the state must legitimate itself by creating conditions promoting social and political order, and this calls for increasingly expensive welfare state provisions for health, housing, unemployment, income maintenance, and so on.

In meeting these demands the state faces a fundamental contradiction: too little expenditure on legitimation runs the risk of serious social and political unrest, even revolution; too much expenditure on social welfare eats into capitalist profits and deprives the accumulation process of resources and profit. On the one hand, governments cannot reduce social expenditure without serious risk of electoral defeat or social disturbance; on the other hand, they must reduce social expenditure and increase investment expenditure in order to support capital. Unable to resolve the incompatible demands of workers, who want better and more expensive welfare provisions, and capitalists, who want tax cuts but infrastructural investments, the modern democratic state runs into increasing fiscal crisis.

This, in turn, provokes political crisis. Different sections of society withdraw their support from the state: monopoly capital because the necessary conditions for capital accumulation have been undermined; the middle class expresses its resentment through tax revolts, which simply make the situation worse; state workers become militant because their occupational and professional base is eroded by cuts in state spending; and the clients of the welfare state are left with nothing to do but revolt. The result is a steep increase in political involvement of a radical kind. With this goes a sharp loss of trust in state agencies and officials, and increasing conflict between different interests—class, race, region, workers in monopoly and competitive capitalist sectors.

A similar theory of crisis was proposed in the early 1970s by Claus Offe. In his view, the modern state is increasingly forced to intervene in the contradictions of the capitalist economy. It must preserve the conditions of capital accumulation and an expanding economy, and it must also protect the interests of the capitalists themselves, particularly property rights, private enterprise, and economic freedom. On the other hand, the state must also look to its own legitimation among the mass of the population. This requires the provision of public services and facilities, and at least the minimum requirements of a welfare state. In other words, the state must protect the interests of both capital and workers, but at the same time it must appear to be a neutral and impartial arbiter of conflicting interests within the state. It must not undermine belief in the private sector, but at the same time it must maintain the appearance of social fairness for the population as a whole.

As a result, so this theory goes, mass loyalty to 'welfare capitalism' will start to be eroded as the fundamental contradictions of the system surface. The state becomes ungovernable and overloaded. Demands for expenditure outrun the state's capacity to pay. The more it tries to solve these problems by promising to fulfil citizen demands, the more it encourages those demands. And the more it is unable to meet the contradictory demands of increased public spending and tax cuts, the more its policy failures will provoke widespread frustration. The state will be unable to resolve basic conflicts, and so citizens will turn to other, more direct ways of expressing their demands. Citizen action groups and new social movements will begin to replace the old interest organizations and parties.

Faced with declining membership and support the established political parties try to adapt by converting themselves into 'catch-all' parties by broadening their appeal and trying to win votes from a wide range of social groups and interests. This simply results in loss of party identification and membership which accelerates the decline.

With their non-conventional aims and methods, new action groups and social movements come to rival, then replace, the orthodox parties and interest groups, and to challenge traditional forms of government and politics. Offe's (1984: 175) view of the new action groups and social movements is that 'although they are not in any traditional sense "political", [they] still release astonishing amounts of collective energy mixed with elements of anger and protest'. The level of direct political action rises sharply—protest behaviour, strikes, demonstrations, occupations, petitions, marches, sit-ins, and political violence.

Habermas's version of the legitimation crises focuses rather more directly on the political aspects of the process (Habermas 1973). He argues that the advanced capitalist state must maintain a critical level of support and loyalty. Laws must be obeyed, bureaucratic procedures and practices followed, the rules of the game must be observed. The problem here is that the capitalist state must protect the interests of capitalism, and at the same time it must appear to be fair, impartial, and just to all citizens. Its dilemma increases as the scope of state activity expands in advanced capitalism. In doing so the visible hand of the state replaced the invisible hand of the market, with the consequence that the real ambiguities and contradictions of the state are laid bare to citizens.

The state is forced to intervene more energetically to try to solve the contradictions of capitalist economics, so the argument goes, but the truth of the matter is that it cannot. The result is that problems are shifted into the political sphere when it becomes only too clear that the basic difficulty is that the state is trying to accomplish two incompatible objectives (see Beetham 1991: 166). Wider and wider areas of social and economic life are politicized, rationalized, and demystified. Greater demands are made for political participation and consultation. Meanwhile, the very success of capitalism destroys the values that helped both create it and regulate it—the work ethic, religion, the moral order which defined fairness and justice (Habermas 1975: 75–8) Unrestrained self-interest on the part of individuals replaces the old order of religion, community, and hierarchy. The more the advanced capitalist state tries to legitimate itself in this climate of opinion the more it undermines the basis of its legitimacy. The result is a growing cynicism and alienation among citizens, and the withdrawal of support for the state and its institutions. The first signs of a legitimation crisis will be seen in the changing values and behaviour of the young (Birch 1984: 147). Habermas claims that the breakdown of bourgeois individualism means an erosion of a sense of autonomy and individuality: he talks of 'the end of the individual' (1976: 124–5). At this point he comes close to Korn-hauser's picture of the atomized, isolated, amorphous, and alienated individuals of mass society.

Overload and Ungovernability

Theories of the legitimacy crisis argued that economic interests made increasingly heavy and contradictory demands upon the state. The claim that modern democratic states are overloaded or ungovernable was also made by a different school of thought, though one which came, for the most part, from different political and disciplinary traditions (King 1975; Brittan 1975; Rose and Peters 1978; Birch 1984).

Overload theory argues that the modern democratic state is faced with an increased level of popular political participation and an increasing range and variety of political demands. The state responds by increasing its level of activity and expanding into new policy areas. King (1975: 288) put it memorably: 'Once upon a time man looked to God to order the world. Then he looked to the market. Now he looks to government.' In response to growing popular expectations, governments are under pressure to increase spending and taxation, produce more and better services, allow more public participation, and to consult more widely. Many of the new areas of public activity are inherently complex social and political problems where the chances of success are relatively slight, or where even success is slow and qualified and serves only to create losers as well as winners.

Moreover, the greater complexity of modern government means that the state is increasingly dependent upon a wide variety of interests, groups, and organizations. This makes it difficult to pick a safe political pathway through different interests and problems, and exceedingly difficult to define the national interest, as opposed to the particular interests of special groups. The demands of the immediate present overwhelm the social interests of the future (Maier 1992: 146), and the authority of the state as the supreme allocator of values and resources for the immediate present is diminished.

As a result, the authority of government is impaired, and its ability to resolve political problems reduced. At precisely the time when service demands escalate and proliferate, government's capacity to deliver is reduced. Even its capacity to make decisions, never mind its capacity to carry them out satisfactorily, is increasingly undermined by the cacophony of competing, conflicting, and incompatible demands.

Consequently, said Crozier, Huntington, and Watanuki (1975: 159), 'Dissatisfaction with and lack of confidence in the functioning of the institutions of democratic government have thus become widespread.' Non-compliance with government decisions and dissatisfaction with government policies increases. This feeds the vicious circle whereby governments try to save themselves by making promises which they cannot deliver. As a result there is a delegitimation of authority and a loss of trust in leadership, as well as an undermining of trust and co-operation among citizens. At the same time, political conflict increases while the old political parties decline, fragment, or decompose into many special interests. A parochial and nationalist style of politics is forced upon political leaders (Crozier, Huntington, and Watanuki 1975: 161–8).

Although the present book is concerned with Western Europe and not the United States, it is interesting to take a side-long glance at some American writing of the 1970s on the future of democracy. Discussing what he called 'the democratic distemper', Huntington (1976: 11) argued that an excess of democracy in the United States caused governments to promise more than they could deliver. 'The apparent vitality of democracy in the 1960s', he wrote, 'raises questions about the governability of democracy in the 1970s.' Associated with this was a growing public disillusionment with political representatives and distrust of government. The participation of marginal groups, which were previously politically apathetic, risked 'the danger of "over-loading" the political system with demands which extended its functions and undermined its authority' (Huntington 1976: 37).

Similarly, Daniel Bell (1975, 1976*a*, 1976*b*) discussed the decline of party identification and of the party system, the loss of confidence in government and institutions, generalized and widespread discontent, and a growing sense of alienation in America. Tied up with these trends was the rise of issue politics which resisted compromise, tended to be all-or-nothing (rather than more-or-less) and symbolic in a way which excited intensely partisan feelings. 'And when such issues multiply, the level of distrust of the system rises, and individuals support extremist leaders . . .' (Bell 1976*a*: 220). The result was a crisis of the regime. Elsewhere, Bell (1975) discussed the problem of overload and ungovernability in America. (For a review of American writing on overload and ungovernability see McKay 1979.)

In contrast to the theory of the legitimacy crisis, some of those who wrote about government overload used the concept of 'contradiction', but not in the sense of a problem which is unresolvable. In his essay on 'The Economic Contradictions of Democracy', Samuel Brittan (1975: 129) wrote: 'liberal representative democracy suffers from internal contradictions, which are likely to increase over time . . . on present indications, the system is likely to pass away within the lifetime of people now adult'. He went on to argue, however, that this conjecture did not have the inevitability of a historicist prediction. Rather, the point of shouting 'Fire' is not to sit back and contemplate the blaze, but to summon the fire brigade to put it out (Brittan 1989: 191).

Though they often talk of 'crisis' and sometimes of 'contradiction', overload theorists are inclined to see the problem as reversible if the revolution of rising expectations can be replaced by a revolution of declining expectations, if the state can re-establish its authority among the welter of competing special interests, and if a clear boundary between the private and the public, the political and the non-political can be redrawn. A legitimation crisis is born of contradictions which can only result in the destruction of the system. Overload theory diagnoses problems—sometimes severe problems or crisis—which can be solved, albeit only after great efforts and with considerable difficulties and political will.

New Social Movements

It has already become clear that writing on government overload and ungovernability spread into a discussion of new social movements which challenged the established political order. Writing on new social movements also drew upon and overlapped a little with mass theory (see e.g. Parkin 1968: 15), and with some writings on the legitimacy crisis (see e.g. Offe 1984: 168–9).

At the heart of the literature is the idea that post-industrial society not only creates a new set of social cleavages but also a new and varied set of social values which form the basis of a new set of political demands. These are articulated by the new social movements. Touraine (1981), for example, suggested that the transition from industrial to post-industrial society entailed shifting from relatively clear-cut bases of political organization—workers, factories, communities—to more amorphous groupings, such as consumers or the public. The institutions of the established political order were incapable of responding adequately to these new demands, which therefore found their expression in extra-institutional or uninstitutional ways. Hence the movements were described as anti-political, anti-party, or anti-state, for they challenged both conventional political goals and means, and they stood outside the sphere of conventional politics. The movements included those of the feminists, the environmentalists, peace, and anti-nuclear movements, and a variety of social and cultural minorities, including sexual, racial, religious, and ethnic groups. They often used the means of direct political action and protest—strikes, boycotts, sit-ins, occupations, petitions, street blockades, direct protest, or civil disobedience. Some new social movements used violent means, most did not, but many used direct and disruptive forms of action (Tarrow 1994: 103–17).

New social movements are not typically located on the conventional left–right spectrum of traditional mass parties, and nor do they fit comfortably into the world of the established pressure groups. They are often single-issue groups created around a particular interest of post-industrial society, that is to say fragmented, decentralized, and rapidly changing society (Huntington 1974). They are often involved in zero-sum politics, which are the antithesis of compromise and moderation (Melucci 1980: 207; Bell 1976*a*: 220). Ironically, the politics of the class struggle, which according to Marxists leads inevitably to the final revolution, is frequently the politics of bargaining and compromise (Alford 1964: 339). Class and industrial conflict can often be solved by incremental change—alterations to wages, working hours, or working conditions. In contrast, the new social movements are about black-and-white issues such as abortion, the environment, or nuclear energy, and they not unusually entail non-negotiable demands. New social movements, therefore, tend to undermine the old (class, region, religion) basis of politics, and introduce an unpredictable and unstable element into the political system. The fact that they are often loose-knit and anti-bureaucratic organizations, usually with supporters rather than members, and sometimes with populist tendencies, enhances their potential for unpredictability and volatility.

New social movements undermine the social basis of the old and established parties and pressure groups, and are therefore a cause of the decomposition, fragmentation, shrinking, or even failure of the party system (Merkl 1988: 562). They also contribute directly to the political pressures which are said to create a legitimacy crisis and overloaded government. Consequently, they not only challenge the conventional forms of politics in modern democracies, but they challenge the very basis of the modern democratic state itself.

Postmodern Politics

New social movements are an integral part of postmodern politics because both have a common origin in post-industrial society. Nevertheless, it is difficult to encapsulate the theory of postmodern politics. Writing on the subject tends to be loose, ambivalent, fragmentary, fluid, and illusive—like postmodern society and politics, in fact. As Harvey says, there is little agreement about the meaning of postmodernism, except that it is a reaction to modernism, but since modernism is a vague term, postmodernism is doubly so (Harvey 1989: 7). Rather than an integrated theory built on a structure of logically related concepts and propositions, postmodernism consists of a kaleidoscopic array of notions which can be arranged in different ways to reach different conclusions.

The origin of postmodern politics is said to be in the transformation of modern capitalism. The old-style capitalism is described as 'Fordist'—after Henry Ford's use of the mass production line—and characterized by the rational, centralized, and hierarchically organized large-scale industrial plant and mass production factories located in large-scale cities with large-scale bureaucracies and a massed labour force, all co-ordinated and regulated by a large-scale and centralized state. The postmodern economy, in stark contrast, is built around small-scale and flexible production units which are spatially dispersed and organizationally decentralized, even disorganized (Lash and Urry 1987). Instead of mass production, the emphasis is on flexible specialization and niche marketing based upon information technology which links the cash register directly to the factory to tell it what is selling today. The model is not the Ford factory turning out millions of identical cars, but the Italian clothing firm Bennetton, which employs only 1,500 people, but contracts work out to another 10,000 who work in small factories employing 30–50 people each, and switches its designs and production according to computerized daily sales returns to the main office (Murray 1989: 57). Fordist production is based on highly centralized, high-energy, heavy industry, and mass production engineering. The postmodern economy is based on decentralized, high technology, fast-changing, and highly skilled production of customized products. In the wider economy there is a shift from industry to services. In the labour market there is a shift towards flexi-hours, part-time, job-shares, and the new cottage industry of people working at home. In all areas of the economy the practice of contracting out means small-scale flexibility and greater uncertainty as consumption patterns change, production methods switch, and new, small-scale but hi-tech producers and suppliers enter the market.

The result is the breakdown of the old capitalist class structure and the emergence of an increasingly fragmented, diverse, differentiated, and changing social structure. New work patterns break up the 9 a.m.–5 p.m. routines and small work teams break down the imperatively co-ordinated hierarchies of bureaucracies and factories. The old occupational and class communities which created solidaristic and collectivist political forms are replaced by a skilled but rapidly changing, atomized, and mobile workforce. A 'new politics' emerges which expresses hostility towards the modern state, especially its centralized and large-scale bureaucracies, including its orthodox political parties and interest groups. The new politics is clearly opposed to the centralized state, but it is not necessarily in favour of the liberal market either. It is based upon localism, small-scale co-operation, and individualism, and it prefers to work through loose-knit grass-roots coalitions. A new political culture emerges built around self-expression, diversity, post-materialism, and direct democracy. The old civic culture is replaced by forms of new populism, distrust of the state and its institutions, and (according to Beer 1982) a romantic revolt against orthodox politics. Community, stability, and collectivism are replaced by individualism, consumerism, and self-interested calculation—people become the sum of their shopping.

The old class and party alignments start to dissolve, and with them trade unions and the mass party system starts to change. New parties and fragmentary alliances emerge. Political and electoral volatility increases. Traditional loyalties decay, trust and confidence in the state, its political élites, and major social institutions declines (Crook, Pakulski, and Waters 1992: 133–49).

For some theorists, postmodern politics means individualism, self-expression, participation, and freedom. The 'black postmodernists' take a gloomier view. Streek (1987—as recounted in Fuchs, Guidorossi, and Svensson, Volume i) believes that postmodern citizens calculate the costs and benefits of political involvement and support. Political loyalty is replaced by an instrumental assessment of political performance, and its costs and benefits for the individual. Citizens are more critical, more demanding, and less reliable supporters of the state and political institutions. On the one hand, this has the effect of defusing the moral basis of political commitment, and therefore reducing the chances of fundamental political conflict. On the other hand, it means that the basis of politics is shifting, changing, unreliable, and unpredictable. Citizens are no longer bound by tradition, trust, loyalty, or a sense of solidarity, but by calculation of individual interest. They sell their souls to the highest bidder—until a better offer comes along. Moreover, in the postmodern and fragmented world with postmodern and fragmented life-styles, they no longer buy into a party, a movement, or the community, but rather take bits and pieces from here and there, as rapidly changing moods and conditions dictate.

The mass media play a crucial role in postmodern society, partly because the influence of the mass media is growing rapidly, and partly because postmodern individuals make great use of the media for entertainment and political information (Volume iv, Chapter 11). The contemporary mass media have a penchant for catastrophes, disasters, crime and murder, corruption, terrorism, and political failure of all kinds. Bad news is good news because it helps to sell newspapers and increase audience ratings. Fed with a constant diet of bad news the mood of the postmodern world is one of cynicism, distrust, alienation, and withdrawal into an apolitical world of consumer individualism.

In sum, postmodern politics and its media erode old political ties and loyalties, creating a new breed of self-centred and calculating citizens. The 'new politics' or 'life-style politics' which they favour will not focus on community or public or national interest, but on 'me and mine'. The result, it is said, will be a volatile, unpredictable, and instrumental form of mass politics, without much attachment to places, organizations, or political principles.

Theories of Political Change and Transformation

Not all theories of change, however, predict such alarming outcomes as the five theories briefly summarized above. There is a second major stream of thought in post-war social science which predicts not crisis, contradiction, and catastrophe, but political change and transformation. These theories see change taking place in a more gradual, moderate, and peaceful way. Liberal democracies might be transformed, but in a way which preserves and changes them rather than threatening or destroying them. In addition to the most general theories of liberal, pluralist, or polyarchical democracy, there are three more specific theories of this kind. They are concerned with the end of ideology, the end of history, and with postmaterialism. We now turn to these theories of the peaceful and gradual transformation of democracy.

The End of Ideology

At the end of the 1950s Daniel Bell wrote of the exhaustion of political ideas in the West (Bell 1960: 393–402). The old ideological passions, he said, were spent. On the one hand, the 'truth' of the old political ideologies and their utopian appeals had been battered by events such as the Moscow trials, the Nazi–Soviet pact, concentration camps, and the suppression of Hungarian workers in 1956. On the other hand, the humanization of capitalism and the rise of the welfare state had under-mined the appeals of extremist political ideas. In their place had emerged a rough consensus among intellectuals on political issues such as the welfare state, decentralized power, the mixed economy, and political pluralism.

Though concerned particularly with the loss of ideological convic-tions on the part of the intellectuals, Bell also stated (1960: 399) that the same had happened to the workers.

The irony, further, for those who seek 'causes' is that the workers, whose grievances were once the driving energy for social change, are more satisfied with the society than the intellectuals. The workers have not achieved utopia, but their expectations were less than those of the intellectuals, and the gains correspondingly large.

As a result, the West had turned to the politics of moderation, compro-mise, and social reform. Politics naturally lost its excitement as a consequence, but it also left behind its extremism, turbulence, and violence.

Lipset developed much the same theme (Lipset 1960: 403–17) at the same time. He argued that serious intellectual conflict between different political values had declined in the democratic West. The political problems of the industrial revolution had been solved and the workers had achieved industrial and political citizenship. The political right had come to accept the welfare state, just as the left accepted that an increase in state powers carried with it more dangers to freedom than solutions to economic problems. It was not that class politics had come to an end, but that the very triumph of the democratic social revolution in the West had rendered serious conflict between ideologists and utopians all but defunct. 'The democratic class struggle will continue, but it will be a fight without ideologies, without red flags, without May Day parades' (Lipset 1960: 408).

Like Bell, Lipset was mainly concerned with the decline of ideological politics among the intellectuals, and like Bell he also suggested that much the same thing had occurred among ordinary citizens as well. He argued that the politics of affluence, bureaucracy, and democracy in America resulted in mass over-conformism and caution. The rise of the 'organization man' was linked to the decline in the intensity of political conflict because politics was changing into administration, as the manager and the expert took over in government as in business (Lipset 1960: 414).

For Bell and Lipset the politics of the intellectuals and the masses in the second half of the twentieth century had become a contest between moderates who accepted the rules of the democratic game and who competed for the centre ground. With the exception of a small minority of the permanently disaffected, the politics of alienation and extremism had been replaced by a liberal democratic consensus and a general satisfaction with social and political life. This could not be in starker contrast to the five theories of crisis and catastrophe discussed earlier. Bell and Lipset's end of ideology conclusions also stand in contrast to their writing on American government overload and ungovernability only a few years later—as we have already seen in the summary of overload theory above.

The End of History

Thirty years after Bell and Lipset had written about the end of ideology, a very similar theme was developed by Fukuyama, although he refers to 'the end of history' rather than the end of ideology (Fukuyama 1989, 1992). In a passage strikingly reminiscent of Bell and Lipset he writes, 'On both the communist Left and the authoritarian Right there has been a bankruptcy of serious ideas capable of sustaining the internal political cohesion of strong governments' (Fukuyama 1992: 39). He argues that by 1990 an almost world-wide consensus has emerged concerning liberal democracy as the only legitimate form of government. It had conquered all its rival ideologies like hereditary monarchy, fascism, and communism, leaving it unchallenged as the only acceptable form of government in the largest part of the globe. Indeed, in the modern world, only Islam and nationalism offered any resistance to the ideological hegemony of liberal democracy. The former, however, lacks world-wide ideological appeal, and the latter lacks ideological breadth. Fukuyama (1992: xi) writes that 'liberal democracy may constitute the "end point of mankind's ideological evolution" and the "final form of human government", and as such constituted the end of history"'.

According to Fukuyama, there will be no further progress in the development of its underlying principles and institutions, because all the really big questions have been settled. While the principles of liberal democracy might well be imperfectly applied in particular places and at particular times, the principles themselves, founded on the twin values of liberty and equality, cannot be improved upon. Consequently, liberal democracy has triumphed as the only viable form of government for the modern world.

In spite of this, Fukuyama is pessimistic about the present and future spiritual and political well-being of citizens. The end of history means the last man, in the sense that the last man is essentially the victorious slave who has successfully struggled for freedom and self-esteem. After that there are no big issues to fight for—only possessive individualism, consumerism, materialism, self-absorption, and a life without passion or struggle, without blood or sweat or tears, and without real achievement or triumph. After the last man, people will stick out their chests, only to find that they are hollow. Life will become so meaningless and so empty that there may even be a reversion to the bloody and pointless political struggles and chaos of earlier epochs (Fukuyama 1992: 328).

According to Fukuyama, the citizens of ordinary democracies will initially loose their attachment to political passions and ideologies, but in doing so may also come to demonstrate some of the pathologies of postmodern politics—meaningless materialism, isolated individualism, and social rootlessness with little sense of collective identity born of struggle, or of communal purpose created by common goals. In the end, history may turn back on itself as people are driven by alienation, disillusionment, and anomie to the atavistic struggles and wars of historical times. Thus, Fukuyama starts from Bell and Lipset's 'end of ideology' position, but ends up with the possibility that people will return to the bad old days of political extremism and violence in an attempt to recapture the meaning, excitement, and value of life.

It is difficult to draw out concrete hypotheses from Fukuyama's very general and rather abstract treatment of liberal democratic politics in the West, but he seems to be suggesting three historical stages of political development. First, he argues that liberal democracy is based upon consensus politics and a rejection of extremism. Liberal democracy is synonymous with the loss of ideology and passionless, low-temperature politics. Mass politics will be marked by possessive individualism, consumerism, and materialism. This account of modern politics is an almost exact replica of Bell and Lipset's end of ideology thesis. In the second historical stage, and developing out of the dull and drab world of the first, there is, or may be, a growing sense of mass alienation, futility, disillusionment, anomie, and rootlessness, together with a loss of identity and individual pride. This is a similar picture in many respects to that painted by the gloomier theorists of postmodernism, or 'black' postmodernists. In the third historical stage, and as a result of the developments of the second, people may turn increasingly to old-style ideologies, conflicts, and battles. This is most like the apocalyptic theories of mass society and some of the earlier literature on social movements.

Postmaterialism

Inglehart's accumulation of research on postmaterialism is fundamentally at odds with theories about the end of ideology and the end of history, although like them he argues that modern democracy is in the process of transforming itself gradually and peacefully (Inglehart 1977b; 1990). Rather than eliminating the need for ideology, the peace and prosperity of Western liberal democracies is fashioning a new set of political aspirations. What people want out of life is changing, but this does not mean that ideology is disappearing. Rather it is being reshaped by a new set of concerns. It is true, as the end of ideology school argues, that the old left–right dichotomies based upon class cleavages are beginning to dissolve, but the new circumstances of the postmaterialist world are gradually and imperceptibly generating new concerns and a new set of ideological goals. Inglehart and Abramson (1994) produce evidence to show an increase in postmaterialism in eighteen out of twenty countries spread across five continents, but especially in the advanced democracies of the Western world.

The old materialist order focused on material well-being, and particularly economic matters. These include: fighting inflation; maintaining a high rate of economic growth; economic stability; defence of the nation; and the fight against crime. The newly emerging postmaterial era, however, is associated with a new set of ideological goals. These focus not on material things and money, but on individual freedom and self-expression; not on salary or status, but on the quality of life and personal relations; not on law, order, and hierarchy, but on participation and self-determination; not on the traditional issues of left and right politics, but on the new ideas involving internationalism, freedom and equality, and environmental protection. As indicators of postmaterial-ism in his mass surveys Inglehart uses questions about giving people more say in the decisions of government, protecting freedom of speech, giving people more say in how things are decided at work and in their community, making cities and the countryside more beautiful, moving towards a friendlier, less impersonal society, and moving towards a society where ideas count more than money (Inglehart 1990: 74–5).

Changes in the political culture and ideas of western societies are so slow as to be virtually unnoticeable, but they are none the less massive in their consequences. Originally held by the young, the most affluent, and the best educated, they will gradually percolate through the system, until the postmaterialist generation rises to positions of political power and influence. By this time the silent revolution will be well on its way to transforming Western society and politics. There will be no end of ideology or end of history, but a new postmaterial ideology and a new historical period.

The consequences of the silent revolution are far-reaching for Wes-tern democracies. First, there will be rising levels of mass political interest and participation. At the same time postmaterial politics cre-ates new forms of political participation, new political organizations, and new channels of political communications. As a result, certain types of political participation may decline, especially those which do not require high levels of cognitive mobilization and which tend to be élite directed, such as voting. Postmaterial participation is more likely to occur outside the traditional and established political parties and inter-est groups, and in the workplace, the community, and new parties and social movements.

Postmaterial politics is also unconventional politics. It increasingly expresses itself in forms of direct participation and action—petitions, demonstrations, boycotts, unofficial strikes, occupations, and civil disobedience (Inglehart 1990: 360). Because postmaterialist participa-tion takes this form, attachment to and involvement in the orthodox political parties and interest groups will decline. There will be a concomitant increase in involvement and participation in new parties and new social movements—the Social Democrats in Britain, the West German Greens, the French and Belgian Ecologists, the Dutch Demo-crats '66, the Proletarian Democrats in Italy, the National Front in

France, and the peace movement in Europe in the 1980s (Inglehart 1990: 367–8, 373).

The Theories Compared

Each of the eight major schools of thought about the conditions of modern democracy have their own local variations. Some of these seem to be of major importance to the participants in the debate, but much less worthy of note to outside observers. The theories also originate in different political perspectives, different academic disciplines, and different intellectual traditions: Marxist, liberal and conservative thought; sociology, philosophy, economics, and political science; the grand theory of European thought and the empirical approach of the Anglo-Saxon tradition. Not surprisingly, the theories arrive at different conclusions. Given their diverse origins and nature, however, it is remarkable that the theories also have some important features in common, three of which are particularly significant.

First, in writing about the conditions of modern democracy, all theories agree that mass behaviour and attitudes are of central importance. The theories are not always explicit, but some seem to hold that mass behaviour is a cause of crisis or change, while others seem more inclined to the view that mass attitudes and behaviour are a symptom. All theories converge, however, on a discussion of mass, popular, or public opinion and behaviour, and all agree that this plays a pivotal role in the problems modern democracies face and the ways they deal with them.

Secondly, they focus on the impact of fundamental and rapid social and economic change, and extrapolate from these to government and politics. That is, the theories assume that economic, social, and technological developments are the driving forces which have a more or less automatic and direct impact on government and politics. Some concentrate on the effects of economic changes—legitimacy crisis, postmodernism, and postmaterialism. Some concentrate rather more heavily on social causes such as education, occupational and class changes, or rapid social change—postmodernism and postmaterialism, mass theory. Others mix economic and social change. All assume the causal primacy of economic and social change, and argue in different ways that these will inevitably and directly create difficulties for democratic politics which will cause it to change fundamentally, or to crumble or collapse altogether.

In this respect, overload theory stands apart from the others in that it locates the origin of democratic problems primarily in political, rather than social or economic factors. The causes of overload and ungovernability are the growing range and strength of political demands upon government. Since democracy encourages popular participation, and is supposed to be responsive to it, these demands are increasingly strident and powerful in pluralist or hyper-pluralist systems. In short, overload theory sees politics, not economic or social change, as the source of the problem.

The third common feature of many, but not all, the theories is that that they are agreed on the indicators or symptoms of democratic *malaise*. The theories are not always explicit about what is cause, what is effect, and what is sympton, but they all see the same sort of features of modern society as cause or effect or sympton. The five theories of crisis and catastrophe talk in terms of growing mass alienation and anomie, increasing political distrust, political disillusion-ment, dissatisfaction with democracy, declining political participation, falling membership of established parties, pressure groups, and com-munity groups, an increase in electoral volatility, support for extremist and anti-democratic politics and movements, and a rise of direct political participation, including illegal and violent action. In the case of the end of history, Fukuyama suggests that many of these will start to become features of society when the last man realizes the futility and pointlessness of life without passion or struggle.

The indicators of democratic pathology of the six theories can be stated formally and systematically. For the empirical purposes, it is useful to group them under four general headings, namely; conven-tional politics, unconventional politics, linkage politics, and legitimacy, as follows:

Conventional Politics

(1) Decreasing sense of political competence or efficacy
(2) Decreasing levels of voting behaviour based upon old and established social and economic differences such as class or religion (cleavage voting)
(3) Decreasing levels of political interest and rising levels of apathy
(4) Either a decline in voting turnout or a sharp increase which mobilizes the apathetic
(5) Sudden increases in the level of electoral volatility and change which tend to destabilize the party system

Unconventional Politics

(6) Increasing level of political distrust, cynicism, alienation, and disillusionment
(7) Increasing beliefs in direct political action, including illegal and violent action

Linkages

(8) Decreasing levels of identification with established political parties (party identification)
(9) Declining membership of voluntary organizations of many kinds
(10) Increasing support for and participation in new social movements, including anti-party, anti-politics, and anti-state movements which challenge orthodox government and politics

Legitimacy

(11) Decreasing levels of confidence and trust in public institutions
(12) Declining beliefs in democracy, both as a principle of government in general, and as practised in particular countries

The convergence of the six schools of thought on a common set of attitudinal and behavioural indicators is not just of theoretical interest. They allow us to put the theories to an empirical test. As we shall see, this is much easier said than done, but nevertheless it remains a possibility on paper.

Of the eight theories of modern democracy, two remain—the end of ideology and postmaterialism. It is difficult to draw out concrete hypotheses from the end of ideology thesis, other than the general conclusion that the main features of democracy will henceforth be moderation, compromise, social reform, a liberal democratic consensus, and a general satisfaction with social and political life. In other words, the theory argues that we will find few of the attitudinal and behavioural indicators of democratic pathology just listed, and where they are present at all it will be in a comparatively weak form. The end of ideology thesis therefore serves as a counterpoint to the theories of crisis and catastrophe.

Lastly, the consequences of postmaterialism for mass politics are easy to draw out of Inglehart's work. They are:

(1) Rising levels of mass political interest and participation (cognitive mobilization)

(2) An increase in unconventional and direct forms of political participation (petitions, demonstrations, boycotts, unofficial strikes, occupations, and civil disobedience)

(3) A decrease in conventional forms of political participation which are amenable to élite manipulation

(4) A growth of international attitudes (foreign aid, forms of international government which promote international co-operation and peace)

(5) Support for racial, ethnic, gender, and minority group equality and freedom

(6) Support for new parties, social movements, and community organizations—green politics, the women's movement, anti-nuclear groups, animal rights, grass-roots organizations, and 'rainbow coalitions'

In the following three chapters we look at the empirical evidence relevant to the eight theories we have outlined, and the hypotheses we draw from them.

3

Political Attitudes and Political Behaviour

Guided by the hypotheses laid out at the end of the last chapter, we now turn to some of the empirical evidence collected by Beliefs in Government. We will not dwell again on the difficulties of finding good empirical data that are comparable across nations and over time. Nor will we go into details of research. These are readily available in other Beliefs in Government volumes, together with a full account of theory, methods, and empirical findings. Rather we will summarize the most important results of the books. But before starting a few preliminary observations are in order.

Given the long-term perspectives of this research, empirical findings have to be scrutinized for what they can tell us about change and stability over a lengthy period of time. Most theories of change assume that basic shifts in socio-economic structure will lead, eventually, to changes in social and political attitudes of citizens, especially over the long haul as one generation replaces another. The gradual nature of such change makes the application of a parsimonious model of linear trends plausible, and, therefore, the testing of the model by means of time-series regression analysis. By these methods, it is possible to obtain a composite, though not necessarily refined, measure of long-term change. Chapter 11 by Fuchs, Guidorossi, and Svensson ('Support for the Democratic System') in Volume i provides a good example of this research strategy.

Though simple, this approach seems warranted because the hypotheses in the concluding section of the previous chapter anticipate certain long-term trends across OECD nations, notwithstanding short-term oscillations around the trend lines which are mainly national or event-specific. For the most part, we will be examining the long-term comparisons of multivariate summary statistics such as betas,

R-squares, or marginal distributions of individual responses to items, indices, or scales measuring political attitudes and behaviour. Usually, the population of voting age is surveyed and in many cases the data are broken down according to conventional social, economic, and political variables such as age, income, class, education, gender, postmaterialism, party identification, and so on.

Cross-national comparisons are, of course, at the heart of a project like Beliefs in Government. Two types of comparison are useful. The first refers to the nature of relationships within a given country at the individual level, and whether the same relationship is generally found in other countries. For example, one might ask whether supporters of new social movements are generally of a left-wing persuasion—a question Kees Aarts takes up in his chapter on 'Intermediate Organizations and Interest Representation' in Volume i. In regression analysis such comparison involves examining the regression slope between two variables within a given country, and comparing it with the slope in other countries. If the slopes are not comparable, then the question arises whether the institutional properties of different political systems help explain the observed differences.

There is a second type of comparison which concerns differences between nations, rather than between individuals within nations. The first Political Action study found evidence of similar relationships at the individual level in different nations, but of disparities between countries at the absolute level. In the terminology of regression analysis the focus of attention here is not the slope of the regression line but its intercept. For example, the countries covered in Political Action varied considerably in their repression potential (Barnes, Kaase, *et al.* 1979: 557) with the Netherlands at the lowest end, and Austria and Germany at the highest. This suggests different cultural and political traditions which are difficult to explain. For example, in their 'Support for the Democratic System' in Volume i, Fuchs *et al.* find that Italy and France show very low levels of 'satisfaction with democracy', and speculate that this is partly a reflection of the high polarization of the party system in both countries.

In this and the following two chapters we will be especially concerned with both individual level and national comparisons, and with trend analysis of the ways in which these change over time. In this way we can relate empirical data to the main theoretical concerns laid out in the previous chapter, and, at the same time, hope to say something about long-term political change and its causes in Western Europe.

Social Structure and Values

Although the notion of values has been a core idea in sociological theory since Weber and Parsons, the empirical study of mass values is relatively underdeveloped, no doubt in part because there is rather little agreement about how to conceptualize values in the first place. Perhaps this is why a major stock-taking survey of values commissioned by the newly elected West German government of 1969 resulted in a set of rather ambiguous and inconclusive findings (Klages and Kmieciak 1979). Nevertheless, the topic of values had been in the air, and of more than purely academic interest, as a result of the student revolts of 1968, public reaction to the Vietnam war, and the entrance of the baby-boomer generation into the adult population—a generation that had no direct memory or experience of the Second World War. It was left to Inglehart (1971) finally to put the empirical study of values successfully on to the political science agenda with his seminal work on the silent revolution.

Lack of systematic comparative study makes it difficult to trace value change much before the 1970s. German research by Allerbeck (1976) and Meulemann (1985) hinted at the possibility of the first sweep of change occurring in the late 1960s as a result of the expansion of higher education coinciding with a growing awareness of issues such as the environment and political participation. Concern with such issues was later integrated into the broader and more coherent framework of 'the new politics' (Miller and Levitin 1976; Hildebrandt and Dalton 1978; Baker, Dalton, and Hildebrandt 1981).

In his chapter on 'A Macro Setting for Micro Politics' in Volume iv, Van Deth, documents major trends and changes in the social structure of post-war Western Europe which may be assumed to have contributed greatly to changing political beliefs—growth in per capita GNP, the industrialization and the subsequent tertiarization of the economy, along with growth of the mass media, especially television. Most importantly, it seems to be no coincidence that the dramatic expansion of higher education in the early 1960s and its continued growth thereafter happened at much the same time as the rise in non-material concerns.

A beneficial side-effect of the Inglehart-generated interest in values was the explicit recognition that values have always played an important role in citizen politics. Knutsen and Scarbrough, in their chapter 'Cleavage Politics' in Volume iv, rightly point out that in order to achieve its full analytic potential the concept of cleavage must be understood in terms of a combination of social and value differences which, together, are translated into institutionalized conflict between collective social actors such as parties and interest groups.

Knutsen and Scarbrough convincingly argue against extending the notion of the social cleavage model to the notion of value cleavage as a way of understanding voting behaviour. They prefer the concept of value conflict. They develop a framework which distinguishes 'structure voting' from 'cleavage voting', and from 'value voting'. In structure voting divisions in the social structure are what count. In value voting it is values, not social-structural differences, that matter. And in cleavage voting a combination of both is at work. The materialist–postmaterialist division involves value voting, whereas cleavage voting in Western Europe has often embraced both the conflicts of class and the corresponding values of the left–right dimension, and religious and secular values.

It is possible to use this broad framework to explore changes in voting and political behaviour in Western Europe over the past two decades, and to discover whether one or more of the three types has grown in importance in this period. We discuss the empirical findings in the following section on conventional political behaviour.

Political Interest, Cognitive Mobilization, and the Vote

Since involvement in democratic politics is a complex matter which can take many forms, it is necessary to be clear at the outset about different dimensions and subdimensions of politics. In this section we will deal with what Barnes, Kaase, *et al.* (1979) refer to as conventional political participation, which is to say, those forms of political involvement that are institutionalized. Political discussion, election campaigning, and voting are prime examples.

Political interest is not easily measured. After all, it costs respondents nothing to say that they are interested. On the contrary, to express lack of interest may carry the social stigma attached to apathy. Therefore, questionnaire responses may produce inflated figures for political interest. However, since there is little reason to believe that the problem changes much over time, its importance is reduced for longitudinal analysis. Moreover, Klingemann (1979) has convincingly shown that political interest has an impact on the way people think about politics which is independent of education, making political interest worthy of study in its own right.

According to data put together by Dalton (1988: 22–3) there is no question that the electorates of France, Great Britain, West Germany, and the United States became substantially more politicized during the period from 1950 to 1970. It is an open question, however, whether this is related to the rise of education or to the spread of television, as both Dalton (1988) and Noelle-Neumann (1988) suspect. Since education is almost universally associated with higher levels of political interest, it may be assumed that the huge expansion of further and higher education has had the biggest impact.

On closer examination it turns out that most of the increase in political interest occurred before 1975, even though higher education continued to expand after that date. Using the indicator of frequency of political discussion in their chapter on 'Political Interest' in Volume iv, Gabriel and Van Deth are unable to detect a systematic trend towards further politicization after 1975 (see Figure 3.1). It would, of course, require panel data to find out whether the overall stability they discover after the mid-1970s hides individual cycles of shifting involvements (Hirschman 1982), or whether aggregate stability is based upon individual stability.

The relationship between education and postmaterialism which Inglehart (1977b: 82) discovered among younger people in the 1970s seems to have persisted in later years. The point is made effectively in Scarbrough's chapter on 'Materialist–Postmaterialist Value Orientations' in Volume iv (see also Table 3.1 in this chapter). It is no surprise, therefore, that Gabriel and Van Deth find that their composite measure of political interest has an association with postmaterialism, although not to four other value dimensions, i.e. secularization, left–right materialism, political libertarianism, and new egalitarianism. This, they say, indicates that the processes of cognitive mobilization encourage the growth of postmaterialism and, thereby, an interest in the issues of 'new politics' among particular parts of the population.

We pointed out in Chapter 2 that some theories of the 1960s and 1970s speculated that increased politization of mass publics was a prelude of coming political crisis. Fears were reinforced by evidence of growing electoral volatility and a tendency to favour more direct forms of political participation than the vote. (For early empirical tests, see Pedersen 1983; Maguire 1983.) However, the Bartolini and Mair study of volatility (1990) and Topf's broadly based approach to trends

TABLE 3.1. *Relevance of birth cohorts, education, and occupation to materialism–postmaterialism in EC-12 countries, 1973–91*

	Birth cohorts	Education	Occupation	R^2	N
Belgium					
Eta	0.19	0.25	0.22	0.076	38,246
Beta	0.11	0.17	0.09		
Denmark					
Eta	0.23	0.32	0.21	0.118	37,642
Beta	0.16	0.26	0.08		
France					
Eta	0.23	0.27	0.25	0.103	40,055
Beta	0.18	0.17	0.12		
Germany					
Eta	0.24	0.23	0.18	0.091	39,306
Beta	0.24	0.16	0.12		
Britain					
Eta	0.19	0.15	0.12	0.048	39,607
Beta	0.20	0.09	0.07		
Greece					
Eta	0.23	0.25	0.24	0.090	24,226
Beta	0.16	0.15	0.11		
Ireland					
Eta	0.23	0.15	0.15	0.059	37,448
Beta	0.23	0.06	0.07		
Italy					
Eta	0.25	0.25	0.23	0.092	40,464
Beta	0.21	0.16	0.11		
Luxembourg					
Eta	0.24	0.22	0.20	0.082	11,713
Beta	0.22	0.12	0.10		
Netherlands					
Eta	0.22	0.24	0.22	0.087	38,710
Beta	0.17	0.15	0.11		
Portugal					
Eta	0.19	0.21	0.23	0.071	14,000
Beta	0.14	0.09	0.13		
Spain					
Eta	0.32	0.27	0.29	0.128	14,067
Beta	0.26	0.10	0.10		

Notes: Entries are coefficients from multiple classification analysis. All coefficients are significant at the 0.01 level at least.

Source: Eurobarometer cumulated data (1973–91), as presented in Vol. iv, *The Impact of Values*, Table 5.6.

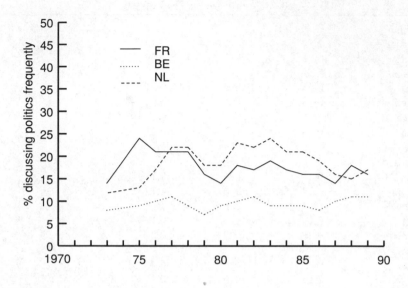

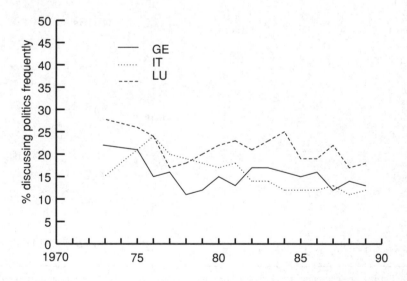

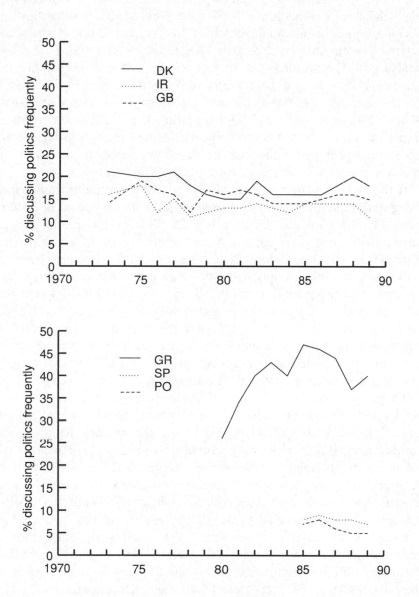

FIGURE 3.1. *Proportion of people who frequently discuss politics with friends,*
EC countries, 1973–89

Sources: European Community Study (1973); Eurobarometer, Nos. 3–22, as presented
in Vol. iv, *The Impact of Values*, Fig. 14.1.

in voting turnout across Western Europe in his chapter in Volume i show that speculations about an impending crisis have to be taken with a pinch of salt. In addition, Topf refines his analysis by taking into account those demographic changes in Western Europe which are related to voting turnout (see also Miegel and Wahl 1993). In the final analysis, his conclusion is that there has been neither major decline nor increase in turnout, and that there is unlikely to be either in the future if present demographic trends persist. This conclusion is consistent with Verba, Nie, and Kim's (1978) suggestion that various intermediary organizations in Europe (especially parties and interest groups) manage to compensate for the lack of individual resources in the lower social strata, at least as far as voting turnout is concerned.

If the turnout pattern is one of stability and continuity rather than change, the question naturally arises whether the same can be said of party identification and party voting. In Western Europe the biggest change to the party system has been the emergence of green parties, although, as Masja Nas shows in her chapter 'Green, Greener, Greenest' in Volume iv, the description 'green' may mean different things. In a recent comparative analysis Müller-Rommel (1993: 170–1) found that both postmaterialism and macro-structural variables, such as type of party system, have strongly affected the rise of green parties. If postmaterialist values are important in this respect we would expect (to return to the Knutson–Scarbrough analysis of party choice) a rise in pure value voting, compared with structure or cleavage voting.

They do, indeed, find such a tendency for pure value voting, particularly among the post-war age cohorts and in the wealthiest countries in Western Europe. However, the picture Knutsen and Scarbrough paint is also more complex than this. In general, their figures point to stability rather than change so far as the impact of religion, class, and values on voting are concerned (see Table 3.2). As a result, the 'old' parties have survived remarkably well on the voter market and have managed to do so by reinforcing old values while simultaneously adapting to new ones. Nevertheless, the emergence of 'new politics' has placed a particular strain upon the social democratic parties by obliging them to accommodate to the policy preferences of the 'old' left and the 'new' left (Kaase and Klingemann 1982). Not least, it is their inability to cope with this challenge which has allowed new, green parties into the system. In general, however, so far as parties and voters are concerned the saying 'plus ça change, plus c'est la même chose' seems to apply.

TABLE 3.2. *Total effects of the three voting types in Western Europe*

% of total discrimination power	Structural voting	Value voting	Cleavage voting
60–65		Iceland, Sweden, Britain	
50–59		Norway	Netherlands
40–49	Ireland	Denmark, Germany, Ireland, France, Italy, Spain	
35–39		Belgium, Portugal	Belgium, Italy, France
30–34	Portugal		Denmark, Germany, Spain, Portugal
20–29	Denmark, Norway, Belgium, Britain, Germany, France, Italy, Spain	Netherlands	Sweden, Norway
10–19	Iceland, Sweden, Netherlands		Iceland, Britain, Ireland

Notes: The total effects are decomposed into the portions of the total discriminating power of the conflict model accounted for by the three voting types. The average for 1981 (Eurobarometer, No. 16) and 1990 (European Values Survey) is shown for eight countries. For five countries, only results for the 1990 European Values Survey are shown.

Source: Vol. iv, *The Impact of Values*, Table 18.5.

Unconventional Participation

After the first Political Action study paved the way for the study of direct legal and illegal political behaviour, latter work refined the approach. In place of a single type of direct action, different types were distinguished, including illegal, non-violent (civil disobedience), and violent behaviour (Uehlinger 1988; Kaase and Neidhardt 1990). However, in the 1970s the most interesting theoretical question was how conventional and unconventional political behaviour were related. A growing divergence between the two, in which people increasingly opted for one rather than the other, would signal a challenge to conventional politics. A merger of the two, in which people opted for both types depending upon circumstances and issues, would suggest a change from élite-directed modes of participation (voting) to élite-challenging participation which could express individual preferences more directly and precisely (Inglehart and Klingemann 1979: 207). The empirical data suggested a fusion of conventional and unconventional forms of political behaviour which resulted in an extension of the repertory of political action. If sustained, this trend would mean a wider range of participation while not necessarily threatening democracy.

The chapters by Topf in Volume i and Gundelach in Volume iv corroborate the early speculations of Political Action. It is now safe to conclude that legal forms of direct action, such as boycotts, citizen initiatives, and demonstrations, have become a standard part of the citizen repertory of political behaviour in modern pluralist democracies (see Tables 3.3 and 3.4). While these two chapters look at participation itself, Kaase (1992) emphasizes the gap between expressing favourable attitudes towards unconventional behaviour and the behaviour itself, which is still quite sporadic and infrequent. The gap suggests a need for research on the circumstances in which favourable attitudes are converted into actual behaviour. This, in turn, suggests the need for further study of the corporate actors and political entrepreneurs who mobilize individuals. We will return to the matter of mobilization in the next section when we examine the linkages between individuals and the polity.

Before that, however, we would like to consider two problems related to the extension of the political repertory of modern democratic mass publics. The first concerns the implications of the growth of the political repertory for democratic political processes, a theme picked up in the concluding chapter of *Political Action*. It was assumed that rational, goal-directed behaviour would make for better politics than purely

TABLE 3.3. *Political participation in Western Europe, 1959–90*

	1959	1974	1981	1990
None	85	69	55	44
Some	11	27	38	46
Active	4	4	7	10
N	2,734	6,148	13,315	15,107

Note: Entries are aggregate percentages. All the original data have been re-analysed.

Sources: Civic Culture (1959); Political Action (1973–6); European Values Survey (1981); World Values Survey (1990), as presented in Vol. i, *Citizens and the State*, Table 3.2.

TABLE 3.4. *Political participation in Western Europe, by country, 1959–90*

	1959	1974	1981	1990
Denmark	—	—	48	59
Finland	—	26	40	38
Iceland	—	—	40	55
Norway	—	—	58	68
Sweden	—	—	58	74
Belgium	—	—	27	51
Britain	18	31	66	77
Ireland	—	—	32	46
Netherlands	—	28	37	54
West Germany	16	34	48	57
France	—	—	52	57
Italy	10	34	50	56
Spain	—	—	32	32

Note: Entries are percentage of adult population who engage in some form of political participation beyond voting.

Sources: Civic Culture (1959); Political Action (1973–6); European Values Survey (1981); World Values Survey (1990), as presented in Vol. i, *Citizens and the State*, Table 3.3.

hedonistic or expressive participation, which is an end in itself. The latter was found to be a minority phenomenon (Kaase and Barnes 1979: 528)

In passing, it is worth noting that hedonistic or expressive participation comes rather close to what is now called postmodern politics, although the term was not used at the time. It is interesting, therefore, that Topf's replication of the Political Action study, using recalculated measures of reported action, discovers a remarkable stability in the use of different types of action over time. He finds this stability in the four countries included in the initial Political Action study (Austria, Britain, the Netherlands, and West Germany) and in other nations as well. He also finds that expressive action—as well as political apathy—appears more frequently in the less economically developed countries of Western Europe (Belgium, Ireland, and southern Europe), while the 'postmodern' nations of Central and northern Europe are dominated by instrumental behaviour (Table 3.5). Of course, a linear development from the former to the latter should not be assumed. In addition, it is important to note that the shift towards hedonistic politics, which Gibbins and Reimer discuss in their chapter on 'Postmodernism' in Volume iv, finds little empirical support in the data which Topf presents.

Political Attitudes and Behaviour

TABLE 3.5. *Modes of political involvement, 1974–90*

Mode of involvement	1974	1981	1990
Four Political Action countries			
Apathetic	27	32	23
Detached	13	12	12
Expressive	19	28	25
Instrumental	42	29	41
N	5,118	5,105	6,620
Western Europe			
Apathetic	27	36	29
Detached	11	14	11
Expressive	21	23	24
Instrumental	41	27	35
N	7,713	16,282	20,054

Notes: Entries are average percentages. The entries in the upper part of the table are for West Germany, Netherlands, Italy, and Britain. The entries in the lower part are for up to fourteen countries.

Sources: Civic Culture (1959); Political Action (1973–6); European Values Survey (1981); World Values Survey (1990), as presented in Vol. i, *Citizens and the State*, Table 3.5.

Topf does not deal with political violence. The findings of both Uehlinger (1988) and Kaase and Neidhardt (1990) point to the problem that there is a fine line between legal and illegal participation, and between illegal participation and political violence. One may well flow into the other, depending upon the situation. The results confirm the need to study political mobilization and the relationship between citizens and the state, particularly between political activists and the police. Unfortunately, lack of empirical evidence has made this impossible for the Beliefs in Government project.

The second point deals with the consequence of political action on political outcomes. We have already noted that the policy preferences of political activists differ from the public at large. As various studies point out (Verba and Nie 1972; Parry, Moser, and Day 1992; Verba *et al.* 1993), the result is that the use of direct means of political action on the part of activists is likely to give them undue weight in politics; this raises the problem of political equality. The fact that the Beliefs in Government study presents clear evidence of the growth of the political repertory to include direct political action, particularly on the part of citizens with more political resources, underlines this problem.

It is a truism that most people do not participate in politics as part of daily life. Therefore, the way that citizens are linked to the polity, and the means of doing so, has been a constant theme of political science since the earliest days. It was pointed out in the previous chapter, for example, that Kornhauser (1960) was concerned that a loss of the integrative power of intermediary organizations would lead to the atomization and alienation of individuals and thus to a separation of élites and the mass public. The theme is taken up again by Beck (1986).

Many theories of political crisis and collapse since Kornhauser have been based on the assumption that major social change will lead to major political change without careful scrutiny of the available evidence. For example, it has been suggested that the widespread decline of established parties has undermined their mediating and linkage functions. Yet the evidence of Beliefs in Government suggests otherwise. For example, Schmitt and Holmberg's chapter in Volume i, 'Political Parties in Decline?', finds such variation across fourteen West European party systems and the United States that no general conclusion is possible. Although there is some evidence of a decline in the intensity of partisanship, there is overall stability in aggregate party identification. This seems to be the result of an interplay of macro variables including the degree of ideological polarization of parties and the intensity of issue conflicts. As a result, parties seem not to be in general decline (see Table 3.6).

Party identification is an intangible and one-directional link of citizens to parties, while party membership is a harder and better indicator of the connection. In the chapter on 'Party Membership and Party Representativeness' in Volume i, Anders Widfeldt looks at empirical evidence about the level of party membership and its development over a period of almost thirty years. The figures show, first, that party penetration in society varies across political systems according to distinct political and cultural traditions. Penetration is deepest in Scandinavia and Great Britain. Secondly, it is precisely in these countries that a decline in membership occurs—with the slight exception of Norway. In Central and southern Europe party membership figures are more stable (see Table 3.7). Overall, however, there are clear indications that political parties have lost some of their grip on the electorates of Western Europe (see also Poguntke 1994).

Kees Aarts raises similar questions about trade unions in his chapter

TABLE 3.6. *Evolution of partisanship across time in fourteen West European countries and the United States: linear regression analysis using national election studies and Eurobarometer data*

	Data source	Time span cover	No. of observations	Strong identifiers		All identifiers	
				Intercept	b-values	Intercept	b-values
USA	NES	1952–92	11	36.7	−0.25*	78.4	−0.44**
Ireland	EB	1978–92	15	35.6	−0.96**	61.8	−1.83**
Italy	EB	1978–92	15	45.8	−1.00**	78.6	−1.50**
France	EB	1975–92	18	26.9	−0.60*	66.9	−0.86**
Britain	NES	1964–92	9	46.0	−1.21**	92.0	−0.78**
	EB	1978–92	15	33.4	0.02	60.5	−0.81*
Sweden	NES	1956–91	12	48.6	−0.65**	n.a.	n.a.
	NES	1968–91	9	38.0	−0.49*	66.1	−0.70**
Luxembourg	EB	1975–92	18	28.5	−0.56**	61.9	−0.74*
Germany	NES	1961–90	9	n.a.	n.a.	38.6	0.26
	NES	1972–90	6	16.1	−0.38	52.8	−0.66
	EB	1975–92	18	33.2	−0.26	69.8	−0.52
Netherlands	NES	1971–89	6	22.4	−0.01	38.9	−0.11
	EB	1975–92	18	36.3	−0.42*	75.7	0.09

Norway	NES	1965–89	7	36.9	−0.08	66.9	−0.04
Denmark	NES	1971–89	7	28.9	−0.07	50.3	0.07
Belgium	EB	1976–92	17	36.7	−0.37*	67.4	0.01
	EB	1975–92	18	25.7	−0.37	50.8	−0.10
Portugal	EB	1985–92	8	14.8	−0.62	60.3	0.18
Greece	EB	1981–92	12	35.6	−0.17	63.0	0.52
Spain	EB	1985–92	8	10.5	0.37*	35.9	0.81
EC-9	EB	1978–92	15	35.6	−0.47*	71.2	−0.89**

*p < 0.05 **p < 0.005. Two-tailed t-tests applied.

Notes: Country-specific OLS regressions were performed with proportion of party identifiers as the dependent variable and year as the independent variable. 'Number of observations' means number of elections in the case of national election studies (NES), and number of years covered in Eurobarometers. For NES, the number of elections is not equivalent to the number of surveys; in some cases more than one survey contained the party identification measure, and the findings are averaged; in other instances (e.g. in Denmark) some election studies did not include the party identification measure. Some data for Sweden 1956–91 and for Germany 1961–90 cannot be estimated because of changes in question wording. EC-9 is the 'old' European Community of nine member-countries (Belgium, Denmark, France, Germany, Ireland, Italy, Luxembourg, Netherlands, and Britain). For these countries, equivalent Eurobarometer data are available from 1978 onwards; pooled analyses are run on the basis of weighted data with national sample sizes adjusted to the relative population weight within the Community. We used the Irish 'closely attached' to exemplify how to read these figures. Strong party identifiers comprised, in 1978, an estimated 35.6 per cent of the adult population. This level has been declining by approximately 1 per cent per year since (precisely −0.96 per cent) and approaches the 20 per cent mark in 1992 (35.6 +(15*−0.96)).

Source: Vol. i, *Citizens and the State*, Table 4.1.

Political Attitudes and Behaviour

TABLE 3.7. *Party membership in ten West European countries, 1960–89: party records*

	BE	DK	FI	GE	IR	IT	NL	NO	SV	GB
1960		21							10	
1961	8			3				16		
1962			19							
1963						13	9			
1964		19							10	9
1965	7			3				16		
1966		17	19							9
1967							6			
1968	8	16				12			8	
1969				3				15		
1970			17						8	8
1971	8	14					4			
1972			17	4		13	4			
1973		11						13	8	
1974	9									6
1975		10	15							
1976				5		10			8	
1977	9	8			1		4	14		
1978	9									
1979		8	15			10			8	5
1980				5						
1981	9	8			2		4	15		
1982					2		4		8	
1983			14	4		9				4
1984		7								
1985	9							16	8	
1986							3			
1987	9	7	13	4	5	10				3
1988		7							8	
1989					5		3	13		

Notes: Entries are party members as a percentage of the total electorate, based on membership figures supplied by the parties. The Swedish figures have been adjusted to exclude collectively enrolled members of the Social Democratic Party, assuming an individual membership of 20 per cent of the reported total membership.

Sources: Katz, Mair, *et al.* (1992); Katz and Mair (1992*b*), as presented in Vol. i, *Citizens and the State*, Table 5.1.

in Volume i, and in many ways his conclusions are like those of Widfeldt. First, there are substantial national differences in unionization rates in Western Europe. Secondly, like political parties, union membership seems to be declining, excepting the Netherlands. It is important to keep in mind, however, that the time series ends in 1985, thereby excluding recent and possibly important developments from study. However, if we take membership of all organizations, rather than trade unions alone, as an indicator of social integration, then, once again, the overall picture is one of stability over time, even of increasing membership. Finally, Aarts confirms previous findings that membership of intermediate organizations seems to be conducive to political involvement and to developing a party preference. In sum, he finds no evidence either of mass society or of an end of ideology.

Of course, it can be argued that membership is too coarse an indicator to get at the most interesting changes in the linkage between intermediary organizations and the electorate. These concern the nature of the exchange between organizations and their members, and the ideological and emotional strength of the relationship. It has been suggested that the linkage between people and organizations is losing its strong and affective basis and becoming more instrumental, thereby forcing the organizations to rely upon selective rewards and incentives for membership (Streeck 1987: 474–82). There is some evidence to support this speculation but it is usually of an impressionistic kind, leaving the field wide open for future research.

New social movements are one of the most significant innovations in the world of intermediary organizations. Rucht (1994: 76–7) conceives of them as groups and organizations with collective identities which are mobilized to generate action aimed at producing, preventing, or reversing social change through political protest. Their newness is believed to surface in their unique leftist, egalitarian, and emancipatory concept of politics (Rucht 1994: 154). A detailed look at the theoretical debate, however, shows no coherent analytical framework or explanatory theory to help the study of them as a whole. Therefore, research tends to deal with particular movements, such as the women's movement or the peace movement, but not movements in general.

Likewise, Aarts ('Intermediate Organizations and Interest Representation', Volume i) also deals empirically with support for the new social movements in terms of two questions; approval and disapproval, and psychological membership—that is, considering oneself a member or a potential member in the sense of expressing an emotional adherence to the cause. He uses four Eurobarometer surveys which cover five nations (France, Britain, Italy, the Netherlands, and West Germany) during the period from 1982 to 1989 (for an excellent analysis of the same data see Fuchs and Rucht 1994). Aarts uses a 'support' indicator to identify people who both support the movements and who are, or might become, members. His research covers the ecology, anti-nuclear, and anti-war movements.

Setting aside the question of what his results tell us about social movement membership, given its rather intangible nature, we will concentrate on levels and trends in support for the three movements in the five nations. First, like party, trade union, and intermediary organization membership, support varies in different countries. It is consistently low in France and high in West Germany. Secondly, support fluctuates in different countries and in different ways: it increases for all three social movements in the Netherlands and West Germany and declines in Italy and France, while support for the ecology movement increases in Britain but declines for the other two (see Table 3.8).

The most important conclusion suggested by the data is that a majority in four of the five countries support the ecology and peace movements. Britain is the exception (see also Fuchs and Rucht 1994: 109–11). The anti-nuclear movement is more controversial, although less so after the Chernobyl disaster. However, because membership of the new social movements is very loose, they cannot be regarded as full functional equivalents of traditional organizations such as parties, trade unions, or social clubs. Nevertheless, there is no question that the organizational logic of new social movements, as *ad hoc* networks of networks (Neidhardt 1985) which can be activated for political purposes, has added a new element to the intermediary level of modern democracies. From this Neidhardt and Rucht (1993; see also Tarrow 1994: 187–98) derive the concept of 'movement society' (*Bewegungsgesellschaft*), although they are quick to add that this term does *not* involve the disappearance of traditional organizations from society.

The fluid 'membership' of the new social movements may even point to their weakness compared with established collective actors, such as parties, although, if true, this applies mainly to the level of mass support rather than to integration into the broader political system. So far as this is concerned, Aarts shows that for all five countries, all three movements types, and all time points there is a distinct leaning of movement supporters towards left and green parties. This suggests that political parties may well act as a stabilizing element for the new social movements—a kind of political anchor. This suggestion is reinforced by the finding that organizationally parties and movement élites increasingly

TABLE 3.8. *Support for new social movements in five West European countries, 1982–9*

	GE	NL	GB	FR	IT
Ecology movement					
1982	33	32	22	15	31
N	1,170	1,200	989	1,169	1,217
1984	31	31	18	11	21
N	849	973	984	983	1,003
1986	29	32	20	11	19
N	865	977	941	964	1,042
1989	41	44	30	13	20
N	1,079	936	854	1,027	983
Anti-nuclear movement					
1982	31	17	24	8	17
N	1,178	1,193	1,061	1,163	1,156
1984	23	16	10	4	11
N	829	992	993	971	984
1986	26	15	15	4	11
N	849	985	1,000	947	1,013
1989	40	20	15	7	11
N	1,075	941	896	1,005	966
Anti-war movement					
1982	47	23	26	14	34
N	1,219	1,203	1,065	1,164	1,241
1984	43	24	14	9	19
N	868	996	1,006	975	1,003
1986	44	19	16	10	19
N	889	984	1,007	961	1,042
1989	49	24	17	10	16
N	1,088	948	905	1,012	979

Notes: Entries are percentages of respondents classified as activists or potential activists for each of three new social movements. The percentage base is all respondents in the sample with valid scores on the 'support' indicator.

Sources: Eurobarometer, Nos. 17, 21, 25, and 31a, as presented in Vol. i, *Citizens and the State*, Table 8.9.

interpenetrate and overlap in the sense that they occupy leader positions in both (Kriesi 1993).

The concept of a movement society assumes that the new social movements are here to stay in modern democracies. It is an open question whether they are. Indeed, Rucht (1994: 166–78) shows that new social movement supporters in Europe form a well-established group of people who are marked by individual resources, left-wing ideology, postmaterialist values, and an inclination to use direct action. It is this combination which make the new social movements and their supporters the epitome of the political changes which we have mapped out in the Beliefs in Government research.

Legitimacy

This topic has been discussed in the previous chapter and we do not wish to reiterate the ideological and theoretical background of the legitimacy crisis writings of the 1970s. Rather, we will look at the evidence which is available and which may throw light on the theory.

At the outset it must be recalled that beliefs about legitimacy are not all of a piece. As *Citizens and the State*, Volume i, shows, trust, support, confidence, and legitimacy are all closely related terms, but are used in the literature in different ways in different theoretical contexts (see also Westle 1989; Fuchs 1993: 235–40). While there is virtue in trying to refine the concept, the crux of the matter is that that there is no agreement in the literature on how this should be done. Nor, unsurprisingly, do the available empirical data fit nicely into one single frame of reference. An unfortunate consequence is that the data are not easily interpreted in a coherent fashion.

But to give the analysis some shape here, we will use the core logic of democratic politics—the competition for power within a set of impartial rules—as a starting point. Since the struggle for political office (the authority level) is bound to create winners and losers, this necessarily generates ambivalent attitudes towards authorities on the part of the losers. Therefore, the legitimacy of the democratic order must depend on a sense of allegiance to the regime—the rules of the game. This must be so notwithstanding the fact that under certain circumstances opposition to authorities may carry over to opposition to the regime, particularly if the same groups are on the losing side for a long period of time. Consequently, it makes sense for studies of legitimacy to concentrate on the authority and regime levels of the political system. Two studies in Volume i of the Beliefs in Government project do this. First Fuchs *et al.* (Chapter 11) focus on a level of the political system which is both between authority and regime, and which combines both—that is 'the way democracy works in a given country'. Secondly, in their chapter on 'Confidence in Political and Private

Institutions', Listhaug and Wiberg analyse attitudes towards aspects of the regime, namely the legal system, parliament, the police, civil service, and the educational system.

So far as satisfaction with the way democracy works, Fuchs *et al.* discover three national trends; increasing dissatisfaction in Germany, stability in Belgium, Denmark, Britain, Ireland, and Spain, and increasing satisfaction in France, Italy, Luxembourg, Northern Ireland, and the Netherlands (see Figure 3.2 and Table 3.9). Much more might be said about how different countries compare, but the most important point is a simple one: there is no pervasive or general trend towards decreasing satisfaction with the way democracy works in the member states of the European Union between 1976 and 1991. This, in fact, is also the main conclusion of Listhaug and Wiberg's study of confidence in institutions. In sum, the empirical evidence does not support legitimacy crisis theory.

However, it is also necessary to point out some interesting recent

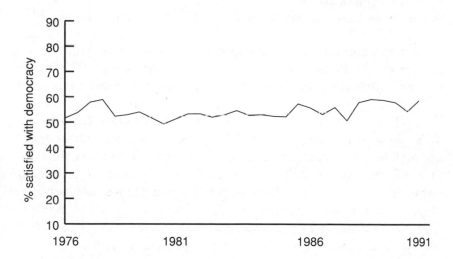

FIGURE 3.2. *Trends in satisfaction with democracy in Western Europe, 1976–91*

Notes: The data base is the total population. The data are pooled and weighted by population size. EC-12 consists of Belgium, Britain, Denmark, France, Germany, Greece, Ireland, Italy, Luxembourg, Netherlands, Portugal, and Spain. Northern Ireland is entered as a separate case.

Source: Eurobarometer, Nos. 6–35, as presented in Vol. i, *Citizens and the State*, Fig. 11.1.

TABLE 3.9. *Trends in satisfaction with democracy in thirteen West European countries, 1976–91*

	B	Beta	R^2	Sig.	t-statistic
DK	0.03	0.28	0.08	0.12	1.58
BE	0.04	0.26	0.07	0.15	1.47
GB	−0.02	−0.20	0.04	0.29	−1.07
GE	−0.03	−0.29	0.09	0.11	−1.64
IR	−0.02	−0.14	0.02	0.45	−0.76
NI*	0.10	0.65	0.43	0.00	4.64
LU	0.06	0.52	0.27	0.00	3.31
NL	0.06	0.39	0.15	0.03	2.30
FR	0.04	0.33	0.11	0.07	1.87
IT	0.08	0.76	0.58	0.00	6.39
GR	−0.14	−0.63	0.39	0.00	−3.68
SP	0.06	0.24	0.06	0.44	0.81
PO	0.30	0.58	0.33	0.04	2.34

* Northern Ireland.

Note: Linear regression on time.

Sources: Eurobarometer, Nos. 6–35, as presented in Vol. i, *Citizens and the State*, Table 11.3.

developments in the European Union where satisfaction with the way democracy works has fallen quite precipitously since 1992. In the autumn of that year, and for the first time since the question was asked in 1976, the percentage dissatisfied exceeded the percentage satisfied. This is likely to be the result of a combination of causes. Listhaug and Wiberg find that government instability, poor economic performance, and high levels of unemployment are related to a decline of confidence in public institutions, and all may play a role in post-1992 developments. Beyond this, the collapse of the Communist bloc may also have played a significant part, since as an external enemy it had been the focus of critical attention. Now European citizens are free to look inwards at the internal state of their own political systems.

As before, the European average masks large and important differences between nations. In France, Greece, and Italy satisfaction improved after changes of government in 1993, a fact which emphasizes the legitimizing effect of 'throwing the rascals out'. Nevertheless, the recent and sharp downturn in satisfaction with democracy is significant and in need of further study and explanation.

In concluding this section of the chapter, it must be mentioned that there is an almost total absence of comparative and longitudinal data on internal and external efficacy. Internal efficacy refers to the belief of individuals that they can exercise political influence, whereas external efficacy refers to a belief in the responsiveness of the government and the political system as a whole. Comparing *The Civic Culture* and *Political Action*, it seems that between 1959 and 1974 external efficacy rose in Britain and especially in West Germany. Given this, an improvement in individual resources available for mobilization, and an expansion of the political repertory, a similar increase in subjective efficacy might also be predicted for Europe in the last decade or so. But since there is no data we cannot say more about these two aspects of efficacy.

Conclusions

We find substantial support for the model which traces social changes to value changes, and value change into changes in political attitudes and behaviour, especially through the process of generational replacement. It does not follow that social change always has an impact on political orientations, even less on political organizations and institutions. Nor does it follow that social (and economic) change is the only cause of political change. However, it is clear that the decline of religious values and the rise of postmaterialist values have transformed the cultural composition of Western democracies in recent decades. In the political arena, the most noteworthy developments are the growth of participation and the broadening of the political repertory to cover a wider range of political behaviour and action. This is evident in the tactics used by local citizen groups as well as in the broader range of activities of the new social movements.

It would be useful to have comparative studies which trace the impact of these shifts in mass attitudes and behaviour on political institutions and processes, but the relevant evidence is simply not available. Nevertheless, when we take, among others, the evidence presented by Klingemann in his chapter in Volume i on 'Party Positions and Voter Orientations', or the study by Klingemann, Hofferbert and Budge (1994), then it seems that democratic procedures and institutions are more flexible, adaptable, and responsive than the theories of crisis and catastrophe would have us believe. The extent to which the issue of the environment has emerged on the West European agenda is evidence of the capacity of established political organizations to adjust to new demands from the electorate. In turn, the electorate has not become apathetic, antagonistic, or hostile; there is no question, though, that it responds more quickly and more directly than it did, and that it may not be more impatient and more selective than it once was. Before we draw a conclusion on this matter, however, two other major aspects of modern mass politics should be considered.

In the next chapter we examine mass attitudes towards the welfare state because this has undoubtedly been the backbone of Western democratization in the post-war period. In the following chapter we look at mass attitudes towards international or supranational government not only because this represents a level of government which is increasing in power, but also because it may well be the most important innovation in contemporary West European politics.

4

The Growth and Decline of the State?

The growth of the state is one of the most notable features of twentieth-century politics. Whatever the measure—taxes exacted, money spent, people employed, services delivered, laws passed, regulations implemented, people affected—the amount and the range of state activity has grown out of all recognition in the twentieth century, especially in the latter half. It is not just the scope of government which has expanded, but also the depth of its influence on the everyday lives of citizens. This combination of scope and pervasiveness gives the state its paramount significance in Western Europe.

Three major twentieth-century events helped create big government. The Great Depression of the 1930s prepared the political ground for a Keynesian approach to economic management and social policy. The war efforts of 1939–45 then accustomed people to higher levels of government intervention and helped create a sense of community and national solidarity which was conducive to the development of public services (Peacock and Wiseman 1967; Goodin 1988). And third, post-war reconstruction, with its goals of creating a land fit for heroes and destroying forever the social and economic bases of political extremism, consolidated the public mood in favour of government services.

However, it was the peace and economic growth of the 1950s and 1960s which resulted in the most rapid expansion of the state. As Goldsmith shows in his chapter on 'The Growth of Government' in Volume iii (see also Gould 1983), this period saw an unprecedented escalation of government activity, especially public expenditure. On the income side, average government receipts almost doubled as a percentage of GDP from 27 per cent in 1950 to 45 per cent in 1990. Tax revenues increased 40 per cent. On the spending side, the cost of social and health services almost doubled as a proportion of GDP, while education spending rose by nearly two-thirds. Social security contributions and social security transfers almost trebled in the same period. Defence expenditure alone declined.

In other words, the post-war growth of the state in Western Europe was, in large part, a growth of the welfare state. Indeed, among the wealthiest nations in the world, the welfare state is particularly associated with those of Western Europe. Other OECD nations, such as the United States, Canada, New Zealand, and Japan, are not particularly outstanding in this respect, although they too have expanded the scope of the public sector.

The European experience seems to confirm Wagner's law which states that the public sector share of the economy will grow faster than the economy as a whole. By the mid-1970s, however, Wagner's prediction was beginning to lose its law-like quality. The first oil shock of 1971–2 brought the long boom of the 1950s and 1960s towards its close. Lower economic growth and rising unemployment created social problems and greater need for public expenditure. At the same time inflation and higher taxes started to cut into take-home pay so that citizens began to feel the economic squeeze acutely. Consequently, the post-war mood of active support for public services, and perhaps a passive acceptance of the tax levels they incurred, seems to have been replaced by a tax revolt and welfare state backlash.

The new public mood was taken up quickly by parties and political movements. In Denmark, the Glistrup 'anti-tax party' took 16 per cent of the poll in 1973 to become, almost overnight, the second largest party in the Danish Parliament. In Britain, local tax increases provoked civil disturbances—the ratepayer revolts of the 1970s. In Sweden in 1976 the Social Democrats were voted from office for the first time since the 1930s and high taxes were a major election issue. A German anti-tax party was formed in 1978, though it was unsuccessful and short-lived. Anti-tax parties were also formed in Norway and Finland, though with little more success.

The new climate of public opinion in the 1980s encouraged many governments in Western Europe to rethink their welfare state, restructure their public sectors, and cut public spending. Kohl in Germany, Thatcher in Britain, and Schluter in Denmark best exemplify the new politics, but equivalents were to be found all over Western Europe. Most notably the majority of Western states remodelled their tax regimes. In fact, the scale, speed, and radical nature of the changes in many Western countries in the 1980s were quite remarkable (see e.g.

Peters 1991*a*: 271–99; Pechman 1988). In a relatively short time many of the OECD countries had restructured their tax regimes, and in rather similar ways.

The forty-five years from 1945 to 1990 in Europe seem to divide into two periods. From 1945 to about 1975 the public sector expanded rapidly, and public opinion appears to have favoured state activity as a solution to social and economic problems. By the end of the 1970s the scope and pervasiveness of state activity were at their maximum in many countries. From about 1975 the expansion seems to have been halted, if not reversed. As Claus Offe (1984: 157) put it, perhaps with some exaggeration, 'nowhere is the welfare state believed any longer to be the promising and permanently valid answer to the problems of the socio-political order of advanced capitalist economies'. Doubts were raised about the efficiency and effectiveness of public solutions to social and economic problems, politicians favoured rolling back the state, privatization became the watchword, and individualism and the market began to replace collectivism and the state. It was not just the welfare state's taxing and spending that was called into question, but the entire role of the state in modern society (Peters 1991*b*: 116–17). Government action was increasingly presented not as a solution to public problems, but as a cause of them (Douglas 1989; Hadenius 1986).

In the first part of this chapter we look at public opinion evidence about the scope of government in West European nations. In particular we examine evidence of declining support for government services. Is there a growing belief that the scope of government should contract? If so, what sort of people are leading the trend? Has the welfare state backlash and tax revolt been led by the middle mass, or by the young, well-educated, and affluent postmaterialists? Or perhaps slow economic growth and disillusionment with overloaded government and high taxes is so widespread that the new mood pervades the whole of society?

Underneath these questions there lies a matter of basic significance for the development of West European society and government. Are we at the start of a new era of restricted or minimal government? Are we moving back towards a caretaker state which regulates private activities rather than providing public services?

The central focus of this chapter is on mass beliefs about the proper scope of government. These beliefs cover both cognitive—knowledge of government activities—and evaluative judgements about what should happen. In other words, the chapter is concerned with mass beliefs, opinions, and judgements about the proper role and the scope of the public sector in West European states. In many ways this comes close to what political scientists refer to as policy demands or the policy inputs of public opinion.

The empirical evidence on which this chapter is based is drawn mainly from Volume iii of the Beliefs in Government volumes, *The Scope of Government*. As in the previous chapter, we do not go into research details, which are presented in full in Volume iii. Rather, we provide a few statistical tables to illustrate the argument.

The Scope of Government and the Welfare State

A Tax Revolt and Welfare State Backlash of the Middle Mass?

Many of the theories of the 1960s and 1970s which explain the contraction of the state assume that public opinion was a driving force behind the trend. The first, and in many ways the most prescient, theory on the scene, was Wilensky's theory of 'the middle mass' (Wilensky 1975: 116–19). Wilensky argues that fundamental social change in modern society generates a complex division of labour, high rates of social and geographical mobility, a diffuse 'success ideology', and economic individualism. These changes will produce a growing middle mass of lower middle class and skilled workers who are detached from the old social class groupings and the values of industrial society. Looking upwards in the social hierarchy the middle mass sees the upper middle class—libertarian, privileged, educated, living well but apparently paying little in taxes, and allowing its children to run wild at university, often at public expense. Looking down, the middle mass sees the lazy, amoral, often criminal and undeserving poor living off welfare.

The middle mass's reaction to this 'unholy alliance' of immoral poor and educated libertarians is to reaffirm the virtues of hard work, law, order, and self-discipline. Taxes and the welfare state serve as symbols for its grievances. Consequently, it expresses an anti-state feeling covering not just welfare and taxes, but also the issues of public morality, law and order, liberalism, and a 'sick society'. According to Wilensky, the movement will be led by the middle mass initially, but as public service costs rise and the tax burden grows, it will be joined by the upper middle class. Together they will form a political alliance against the working class to turn the welfare backlash into a powerful political force.

Looking back, we can see that Wilensky's book foreshadowed some recent writing on postmodern individualism and life-styles. We can also see that he exaggerated some local events and over-interpreted a short-lived though quite widespread shift of mood. The evidence about public opinion towards taxes, public services, and public policy painstakingly collected and analysed in *The Scope of Government*, Volume iii, shows that there was no fundamental or sustained shift of public opinion in the 1970s or 1980s. On the contrary, support for the state and its services has remained surprisingly and consistently strong, as a comparison of figures for 1974, 1985, and 1990 show (see Tables 4.1 and 4.2). By 1990, no less than in 1985, very large majorities (usually over 70 per cent) in seven West European nations continued to believe that it was

TABLE 4.1. *Attitudes towards government responsibility, 1974*

	GE	GB	NL	AU	IT	SW	FI	Mean
Elderly	93	88	93	89	92	90	96	92
Medical care	94	95	93	94	96	86	95	94
Education	93	92	98	90	93	89	88	92
Housing	88	85	94	81	92	71	77	84
Equalization of wealth	71	52	82	68	72	75	58	68
Job security	94	85	90	94	94	89	94	91
Low prices	96	—	94	92	95	—	94	94
Minority rights	66	59	73	53	—	68	61	63
Equal rights for sexes	76	49	75	63	64	72	63	66
Pollution control	93	85	92	85	89	92	87	89
Crime prevention	97	87	90	94	95	82	96	92
Energy supply	96	—	95	94	91	—	96	94
Mean	88	78	89	83	88	81	84	85
N	1,483	1,483	1,201	1,585	1,779	1,290	1,224	

Note: Entries are percentages who think it is essential or important that government take responsibility in the policy field stated. Question: 'Now we would like to know how you feel about some of the particular issues and problems that people often talk about these days. We would like to know (*a*) How important these issues and problems are in your view, and (*b*) How far you feel [the] government has responsibility for them.' Codes: Is it something that you feel (1) is essential for government to do; (2) something that government has an important responsibility to do; (3) some responsibility to do; (4) no responsibility at all to do? Entries in the table are category (1) and (2) from question (*b*).

Source: Political Action (1973–6), as presented in Vol. iii, *The Scope of Government*, Table 4.1.

TABLE 4.2. *Attitudes towards government responsibility, 1985 and 1990*

	GE	GB	IT	AU	IR	SV	NO	Mean
Provide health care								
1985	98	99	100	98				99
1990	95	100	99		99	97	99	98
Provide for elderly								
1985	97	98	100	99				99
1990	95	99	99		98	97	99	98
Provide for the unemployed								
1985	85	86	85	68				81
1990	78	80	78		91	90	91	85
Provide jobs								
1985	82	72	89	84				82
1990	74	63	85		71	75	84	75
Control prices								
1985	76	93	98	93				90
1990	70	89	96		92	86	92	88
Assist growth of industry								
1985	54	95	84	75				77
1990	52	94	82		90		67	77
Reduce income differences								
1985	67	75	84	78				76
1990	64	74	78		82	74	72	74
Mean								
1985	80	88	91	85				86
1990	75	85	88		89	87	86	85
N								
1985	1,048	1,530	1,580	987	—	—	—	
1990	2,812	1,197	983	—	1,005	1,320	1,517	

Notes: Entries are percentages who think it is probably or definitely the government's responsibility. Question: 'On the whole, do you think it should be or should not be the government's responsibility to . . . ?' Response codes: definitely should be = 1; probably should be = 2; probably should not be = 3; definitely should not be = 4.

Sources: Data for Germany, Britain, Austria, Italy, Ireland, and Norway are from ISSP 1985 and 1990. Data for Sweden are from the Research Programme on Comparative Political Culture, G. Gustafsson and O. Johansson, Umeå University. The table appears in Vol. iii, *The Scope of Government,* Table 4.2.

government's responsibility to provide health care, services for the elderly and the unemployed, to provide jobs, control prices, assist industry, and reduce income differences (see Table 4.2).

Nor is there much evidence to indicate a backlash of the middle mass or the liberal, educated, upper class. On the contrary, social variables such as class and education are not generally or strongly associated with attitudes towards tax, the welfare state, or the scope of government (see the chapters by Huseby, Confalonieri and Newton, Pettersen, and Roller in *The Scope of Government*). The figures do not confirm the middle mass hypothesis. Rather they suggest a simple, linear relationship in which support for the public sector tends to decline, though only marginally, as one goes up the education, income, and socio-economic ladder.

The flaw in the middle mass, backlash theory seems to be the assumption that post-industrial changes in the division of labour will result in individualism and a new success ideology which would automatically translate into opposition to taxes and the welfare state. The survey evidence of the 1980s and 1990s makes it clear that there has been no conspicuous shift towards a success ideology based upon economic individualism. On the contrary, traditional attitudes towards social and economic equality and towards the core services of the welfare state seem to have held quite firm. Perhaps it will take another generation or two before social-structural change percolates through to mass opinion, but meanwhile there is little evidence to suggest a tax revolt or welfare state backlash among the middle mass—or sustained revolt or backlash on the part of any other social group in Western Europe, for that matter.

Government Overload?

Like the theory of the middle mass, the theory of ungovernability or government overload also emphasizes the importance of public opinion as a political force undermining the expansion of the modern state. Unlike middle mass theory, however, it claims that opposition to the state and its activities will come not from particular groups or social strata, but from all quarters of public opinion.

According to overload theory, modern society generates an ever expanding range of special groups and interests each of which urgently presses its case for benefits and services on government. The public is all the more demanding because the revolution of rising expectations makes today's luxuries tomorrow's necessities. Experience of satisfactory government services may also fuel the demand for still more services. As a result, claims on government services both proliferate and escalate. At the same time, pluralist democracies are also becoming more sensitive and accountable to public opinion. Politicians promise more and more at election time, but the more demands they recognize, and the more 'false expectations they encourage' (Brittan 1975) the less they are likely to deliver. As Crozier *et al.* wrote: 'The demands on democratic government grow, while the capacity of democratic government stagnates.' (Crozier, Huntington, and Watanuki 1975: 9). Government becomes overloaded and society becomes ungovernable. As a result, public opinion becomes increasingly cynical and disillusioned. Ultimately, it withdraws its support from the state, so undermining the system of government.

The survey evidence collected in *The Scope of Government* fails to confirm this diagnosis. While overload theory suggests the most active states with the highest public expenditures will come under the greatest pressure, the evidence suggests the reverse. Although there are too few cases to allow confident generalization, the heaviest demand for public services seems to be found in the least economically developed countries, which also display the weakest support for their governments. As Huseby shows in her chapter on 'Attitudes towards the Size of Government' in Volume iii, heavy demand and weak support seem to be related. The heaviest demand for services is found in the less well developed societies because they have the greatest social and economic problems. At the same time, high levels of unsatisfied demand for public services tend to undermine support for government. In contrast, the more developed states are best placed to satisfy demand, and their recent histories of stability and security have allowed them to build up a bank of political trust and allegiance which helps them survive short- to medium-term crises.

As a result, Borre argues in Chapter 13 of *The Scope of Government*, the most developed states seem to have the lowest levels of overload and are best equipped to deal with them. We will return to this theme later in the chapter. Meanwhile, the evidence collected in *The Scope of Government* suggests that overload theories are right to suggest a link between excess or unsatisfied demand upon government and dissatisfaction with that government. They are wrong, however, to suggest that this problem is to be found in an acute form in the advanced capitalist economies of the West.

There are three possible reasons for the failure of overload theory so far as mass attitudes are concerned. First, the theory tends to assume that citizens are insatiable consumers of public goods and that, under normal circumstances, demands upon the state will rise indefinitely. Demand for services is assumed to be irreversible (see e.g. Eichenberger 1977: 107). In contrast, survey data suggest that public opinion is not irreversible. For example, Borre and Viegas show in their chapter on 'Government Intervention in the Economy' that belief in government management of the economy appears to decline with increasing economic development. Support for government economic intervention is highest in Greece, Ireland and Italy, lowest in Denmark and Germany. In the same way, demands for government spending on some services seem to level off in wealthier nations compared with poorer ones. In short, the spiral of rising expectations of the public sector has been replaced—to some extent at any rate—by a spiral of falling expectations.

Secondly, the public agenda does not expand indefinitely. The public seems to constrain its agenda to a fairly constant number of matters. As new issues enter the agenda so other issues fall off. Perhaps the general public is capable of holding only a few issues in its mind at any one time. Perhaps it is sensible enough to realize that there can only be a few priorities. Whatever the reason, the number of issues on the public agenda does not keep on expanding as new issues present themselves, but appears to be limited to a fairly constant number.

Thirdly, overload and ungovernability theory argues that as modern pluralist societies tend to fragment into special groups and interests, so public opinion splinters into many issue publics which then bombard government with their incompatible demands. Theorists of postmodern society arrive at the same conclusion. In fact, there is little evidence of fragmentation of opinion and interest so far as state policy is concerned. As the figures in Table 4.3 show, opinion on eight major policy areas tends to cluster neatly into three general groups, one concerned with the welfare state, one with the environment and culture, and one with defence and law and order.

Other evidence presented in *The Scope of Government* confirms this conclusion. Roller uses factor analysis on opinion about twelve important problem areas and, again, finds three clear and distinct opinion clusters (see Volume iii, Table 3.2). Whatever the trends in post-industrial or postmodern social structure, these have not caused a decomposition of public opinion. On the contrary, opinion remains organized into a few main camps each of which is organized around a general policy position.

TABLE 4.3. *Attitudes towards spending in eight policy fields: Germany, Britain, and Italy, 1985*

The government should spend more on:	Factor 1	Factor 2	Factor 3
Old age pensions	0.79	−0.08	0.04
Health	0.72	0.07	0.14
Unemployment benefits	0.68	0.12	−0.13
Education	0.64	0.26	0.17
Environment	0.08	0.77	−0.14
Culture and arts	0.12	0.77	0.06
Law enforcement	0.05	0.16	0.84
Military and defence	0.08	−0.30	0.72

Notes: Entries are loadings on rotated factors (varimax rotation). Question: 'Listed below are various areas of government spending. Please show whether you would like to see more or less government spending in each area. Remember that if you say "much more", it might require a tax increase to pay for it.' Categories: spend much more; spend more; spend the same as now; spend less; spend much less.

Source: ISSP (1985), as presented in Vol. iii, *The Scope of Government*, Table 4.5.

A Legitimacy Crisis?

Although it originates in a different political tradition, legitimacy crisis theory arrives at much the same sort of conclusion as overload theory. There are different forms of legitimacy crisis theory but basically the argument is that the modern state is faced with contradictory demands. It must create the conditions for profitable business by investing heavily in infrastructure, while keeping taxes down. It must also legitimize itself and maintain the conditions of social order by providing welfare services (O'Connor 1973; Habermas 1975; Offe 1984). It cannot meet these contradictory demands and so it increasingly alienates both its capitalists and its workers. As a result, public opinion turns against the state, and legitimacy crisis results.

Notwithstanding the political protests of 1968, which provided the inspiration for the theory, mountains of survey data presented in *The Scope of Government* show little evidence of a widespread or growing disillusionment with the state and its services in the 1970s, 1980s, or early 1990s. Nor is there much evidence to support Offe's hypothesis of 'rational' opposition on the part of the higher and the lower income groups because of their particular tax–benefit position in the modern state.

A basic problem of legitimacy crisis theory seems to be that it underestimates the rather subtle yet hard-headed nature of public opinion. Citizens understand that a scarcity of resources is a basic condition of life, as Confalonieri and Newton show in their chapters on attitudes towards taxation in *The Scope of Government*. Consequently, public demands and expectations are tempered by realism. The public also understands that circumstances change. For example, had writers in the 1960s been able to foresee unemployment levels of the 1980s and 1990s, they would in all likelihood have predicted crisis and catastrophe. In fact, unemployment across Western Europe in the tens of millions has not had this impact. Times have changed and the goal of full employment, once thought essential for modern governments, is not currently regarded as realistic.

The public also realizes that governments, whatever they may promise, are limited in what they can deliver. Whether best described as 'cynical' or as 'realistic', modern public opinion is not necessarily disillusioned by the failures of politicians and governments. On the contrary, it has often (usually?) treated their rhetoric and promises with scepticism and a pinch of salt. Similarly, public opinion recognizes that some political goals may be incompatible and that there is a trade-off between them. The trade-off between unemployment and inflation is an example (Newton 1993: 165).

More fundamentally, the citizens of Western Europe have long believed that there is an incompatibility between freedom and equality, and have tended to divide themselves according to their preference for one or the other. The balance of opinion may well shift over time, as Roller (Volume iii, Chapter 7) and Thomassen (Volume i, Chapter 13) argue. But the public mood does not slide towards disillusionment, as legitimacy crisis theory seems to assume, because it cannot have everything it wants and has to sacrifice something for a higher priority. And lastly, the general public is able to distinguish between the limitations of democratic systems and of particular parties or governments. The failings of the latter do not necessarily contaminate faith in the former, at least in the short to medium term. We will pick up this theme again in the final chapters. Meanwhile, our conclusion is that public opinion seems to be both more subtle and flexible, but at the same time more hard-headed and realistic than theories of the legitimacy crisis assume. It is a curious fact that they seem to have seriously underestimated public opinion.

A Rational Choice Revolt?

According to some versions of rational choice theory (see e.g. Alt 1983; Pelzman 1980), increasing taxes combined with the thin distribution of public services results in public opposition to taxes and public services. In the early days of the welfare state relatively few people paid tax, and marginal tax rates were relatively low. Benefits, in contrast, were believed to be concentrated among the bulk of the lower income groups. As a result, the majority of voters benefited from public services and low taxes, and for self-interested reasons they supported the free-rider welfare state and its taxes. As more people were brought into the tax net and higher tax brackets, so they were inclined to calculate the balance of costs and benefits and change their mind. Informed by a rational, self-interested calculation, the majority mood shifted from support for an expansionist state towards a contractionist view favouring lower taxes and fewer services. According to this theory, criticism of the state, taxes, and of the welfare system is likely to be strongest among those with the highest incomes and the best education, because they will pay the highest taxes and understand what is going on. At the same time, the higher taxes are, and the more thinly benefits are spread, the more public opinion in general is likely to favour the contraction of the state.

By and large, the conclusions of *The Scope of Government* do not confirm rational-choice predictions, although it must also be said that they do not explicitly seek to test the theory. There is a clear but relatively slight tendency for the best educated and highest income groups to support the welfare state less strongly, although more noticeable is the relatively strong support across all income, education, and social groups. Nor do citizens seem to behave entirely in the rational, self-interested, and calculating way posited by rational choice models. Their attitudes seem to be informed, at least in part, by other considerations related to social justice, fairness, a wish to guarantee minimum standards for all, and a desire for a degree of social and economic equality (see Volume iii, Chapters 3–7). On the question of international government there is also evidence to suggest that ideal motivations such as peace, international co-operation, and unity contribute as much to support for the European Union, as self-interested economic gain (see Bosch and Newton in Volume ii).

Perhaps the clearest single example in the recent past is the fate of the Thatcher government's poll tax in Britain. As a per capita, flat-rate, and regressive charge the poll tax was widely criticized and opposed for its unfairness, a view shared as much by those who benefited from it as those who did not (Crewe 1988: 41–3). No doubt individuals, social groups, and nations vary in this respect, but survey evidence suggests that West European publics are not motivated only or primarily by hard-headed economic self-interest. This is mixed to some degree by a sense of the public interest and the public good.

A New Political Agenda?

Theories of welfare state backlash, government overload, and legitimacy crisis all argue that public opinion will change its expansionist mood to a contractionist one. A fourth approach argues not that public opinion will become contractionist, but that the nature of the public agenda will change. According to Inglehart (1990: 249–88) the law of diminishing returns means that the closer people get to material satisfaction, the less importance they attach to it, and the more they turn to the non-material benefits of quality of life and self-expression. These include such things as work satisfaction, self-realization, participation, and environmental protection. According to this theory, the very success of the welfare state has undermined itself—having solved many social problems of capitalism, support for the material goals of the welfare state is slowly draining away. Individualism, freedom, and self-fulfilment begin to replace collectivism, economic growth, and security as priorities. Younger, more affluent, and better educated people lead the way to postmaterialist politics.

From this there follows two possibilities. Either the old, materialist agenda is being replaced by the new, postmaterialist one, or the new has been added to, or fused with, the old to create a different agenda. The first theory of replacement has been called the 'proximity model' by Baker *et al.*, and the second the 'dominance model' (Baker, Dalton, and Hildebrand 1981: 343 n. 29). There is already some evidence in favour of the dominance model. In the first place, it seems that some of the new social movements, which are strongly associated with the new politics, have managed to combine items from the old and new agendas (Dalton and Küchler 1990). Secondly, some of the European Green parties have emphasized both environmental issues and the old themes of social and economic equality (Goodin 1992: 197). Third, as Offe (1985) has pointed out, the 'new' issues are firmly rooted in Western political theory of the last two hundred years and are integrated in the traditional and predominantly materialist agendas of established parties and interest groups. Fourthly, as Budge *et al.* have shown, some of the 'new' issues have been built into old party manifestos (Budge, Roberston, and Hearl 1987).

In Chapter 3 of *The Scope of Government* Roller tests the replacement versus addition hypothesis using the extensive Eurobarometer surveys which cover all the member states of the European Community. Her results show that, with one significant exception, the old policy agenda co-existed with the new from 1976 to 1991. Throughout the European Community in this period, over 90 per cent of respondents said that the issues of wealth, unemployment, and environmental protection were important or very important. Between 70 and 80 per cent said the same of social and economic equality, and of defending their national interests against the superpowers. About 60 per cent rated military defence as important or very important.

The exception concerns international security and co-operation. On the one hand, there is a gradual decline in the importance attached to military defence and to defending interests against the superpowers. This is not surprising given the decline of the Cold War and the eventual collapse of the Communist threat. On the other hand, there is also a gradual increase in the importance of giving aid to less developed countries. In this sense, one item of the old agenda fades, and one item of the new grows stronger. The pattern applies at the national level when individual responses are aggregated by country, and at the individual level within each country. In sum, the public agenda across Western Europe is not so much a new postmaterialist one, but a combined and modified new-and-old materialist and postmaterialist one. Public attitudes, beliefs, and values are evolving slowly, not suddenly changing or transforming themselves.

The Nature of European Attitudes about the Scope of Government

It is sometimes claimed that we live in a postmodern era of ideological meltdown. This claim relates to two different aspects of public opinion: its content and its organization. The matter of content has just been discussed. This section now turns to the topic of how West European public opinion is organized.

One widespread view of public opinion sees it as lacking, to a greater or lesser extent, in consistency, structure, coherence, information, and sophistication (see e.g. Neumann 1986: 22–9; Margolis 1979: 70–94; Butler and Stokes 1971: 140–64; Dalton 1988: 13–18). Converse (1964; 1970) refers to these aspects of public opinion in terms of 'non-attitudes' and 'doorstep opinion'. Another school sees public opinion as being, in some important respects at any rate, relatively organized, internally coherent and structured, reasonably consistent over time, based to some degree on a set of ideas or principles which form a basis of core beliefs, and rational (see e.g. Lane 1962; Rokeach 1973; Pierce and Sullivan 1980; Fleishman 1988; Feldman 1988; Dalton 1988: 27–33; Popkin 1991; Graber 1994). It is easy to over-simplify and exaggerate the differences between these two views, but the evidence presented in *The Scope of Government* leans towards the second view, in that it suggests opinion is relatively structured, internally consistent, persistent over time, and even, to a certain extent, subtle and sophisticated. We discuss each of these features in this section of the chapter.

We should make it clear at the outset that the argument which follows is, for the most part, based upon aggregate figures for public opinion, and that aggregate structure, stability, and rationality may conceal a good deal of individual incoherence, instability, and irrationality (Barber 1993). However, some measures are based upon the factor analysis of individual attitudes and they suggest a set of stable, integrated, and internally consistent attitudes.

The Structure of Mass Attitudes

It is said that as the division of labour becomes increasingly complex in postmodern or post-industrial society, as geographical and social mobility increases, as individualism triumphs, and as traditional communities, social groups, and organizations begin to decompose, so public opinion will begin to fragment into a large number and wide variety of 'issue publics'. Each small grouping will focus on only a few matters of immediate interest, with little overlap between them (see e.g. Converse 1964). The survey evidence across Western Europe does not support this conclusion. It suggests that mass opinion about the welfare state and the scope of government is structured and organized into relatively few attitude publics.

For example, Table 4.3 is based on ISSP data and shows that mass attitudes about spending on eight government services cluster into three groupings of related issues. The first concerns welfare matters (pensions, health, unemployment, and education); the second covers quality of life issues (environmental protection, arts, and culture); the third concerns security (law and order, and national defence). These three clusters of opinion appear clearly in Germany, Britain, and Italy.

A similar factor analysis of attitudes towards twelve policy issues covered by a Eurobarometer survey of 1976 also suggests three clusters of opinions in the member states of the EC (see Volume iii, Chapter 3). One centres on the old, materialist agenda of military defence and the protection of national interests against the superpowers. A second brings together four policy issues of importance to the new postmaterialist politics: income differences between the very rich and the very poor; resource differences between regions; more self-government for regions; and consumer protection. The third concerns the old materialist agenda of wealth and economic security, namely inflation, unemployment, and housing.

The ISSP and the Eurobarometer surveys ask questions about different policy issues so the three clusters found in each case are not identical. None the less, they have much in common. Both find that national defence and law and order go together, and both find that a number of issues related to welfare and economic security are grouped together. This suggests that public opinion in Western democracies is not fragmented into a wide variety of issue publics, but rather forms a few attitude groups which organize themselves around families of issues.

Persistence and Change over Time

Mass attitudes seem not to fluctuate widely or randomly over time. The point is made by comparing Political Action figures for 1974 with ISPP figures for 1985 and 1990, as shown in Tables 4.1 and 4.2 in this chapter. There is a good deal of consistency in responses over the sixteen-year period. This conclusion is supported by six Eurobarometer surveys between 1976 and 1991 which found that between 97 and 99 per cent of respondents in all countries rated unemployment as important or very important and put it at the top of the agenda every year. Four polls between 1976 and 1987 show that between 53 and 60 per cent rated military defence as important or very important, placing it at the bottom of the agenda in each year (see Table 3.3 in Volume iii).

There is a similar stability of attitudes over time with regard to government intervention in the economy. The ISSP surveys of 1985 and 1990 asked questions about eight different government policies ranging from wage and price control to reducing the working week and support for new technology and declining industries. The ranking of these eight is similar in the two years (see the chapter by Borre and Viegas in Volume iii). The ISSP surveys also asked about government control of communications and these, too, show stability over time. In both 1985 and 1990 more people supported the idea of revolutionaries being able to publish books than racists, and many more people supported the idea of newspapers being able to publish confidential economic plans than to publish confidential defence papers (see the chapter by Golding and Snippenburg in Volume iii).

This is not to say that public opinion never changes, of course, but that major fluctuations and long-term trends are usually explicable in terms of real-world events. For example, military defence gradually sank down the public agenda of most West European countries as the Cold War declined and eventually disappeared. At the same time, environmental protection has slowly gained in importance as our understanding of the issue has increased and as evidence about such things as endangered species or the ozone layer has accumulated. Support for government economic intervention increased during the first oil crisis (see the Borre and Viegas chapter in Volume iii).

These are not haphazard fluctuations to be explained by the vagaries of question wording, interviewer bias, response sets, or random responses. They are international patterns which are related to changing political, economic, and social circumstances in the real world.

Internal Consistency

The three clusters of public opinion which emerge from the ISSP (Table 4.3) and Eurobarometer surveys (Table 3.2 in Volume iii) make intuitive political sense. They are not statistical artefacts with little or no political meaning—the garbage in, garbage out problem. They form combinations of attitudes which make up more or less coherent, politically understandable, and politically consistent views about government services. In the ISSP survey, pensions, health, unemployment, and education are core services of the modern welfare state which form a common-sense grouping. In the Eurobarometer survey, unemployment, inflation, and housing also form a group of problems related to personal security. A concern for the environment, the arts, and culture belong together as postmaterialist policy preferences. Placing an emphasis on law enforcement and on military and national defence also makes political sense. That is, attitudes group around related policy matters which are easily recognized and labelled as concern with welfare, culture and the environment, and security.

The views of the individuals questioned are also internally consistent in the sense that those who think a given problem is important are also likely to say that it is a government responsibility (see Volume iii, Chapter 3). Similarly, there is a match between saying that a particular issue has high priority as a public service and expressing a willingness to pay taxes for it. For example, survey evidence reported in Chapters 3 and 4 of *The Scope of Government* show that the public rates the issues of unemployment and social and economic inequality higher than defence and law and order. Health care and provision for the elderly usually come right at the top of the list of government priorities (see also Table 4.2 in this chapter). When asked a priced question about taxes, mass surveys also show the general public are more inclined to spend their tax money on welfare than on defence and law and order (see Table 4.4). Rather than being random, mass attitudes about public policy seem to be relatively well organized and internally consistent.

Subtlety and Sophistication: Citizens are not Fools

The citizens of Western Europe also seem to be rather more sophisticated than many theories allow. They distinguish and discriminate between different kinds of public policies and programmes, choosing to support some strongly, others less strongly, and some not at all. For example, there seems to be robust support across most of Western Europe for a greater degree of income equalization. Many do not think their societies are yet equal enough, but this does not mean strong support for radical or total equalization. Rather, as Roller shows in Chapter 7 of Volume iii, the public seems to want a narrowing of existing income differences and greater equality of opportunity, not the complete equalization of society.

Similarly the public picks and chooses between services which it wants cut or protected. As we have just seen, in 1985 and 1990 there was a strong preference for spending tax money on welfare policies, less pronounced support for culture and the environment, and less still for law and order and defence (Table 4.4). Those who want more spent on one set of services are less keen on spending on others sets (see Table 4.3). This reinforces the earlier suggestion that mass attitudes

TABLE 4.4. *Attitudes towards government spending in five countries, 1985 and 1990*

	Germany 1985	Germany 1990	Britain 1985	Britain 1990	Italy 1985	Italy 1990	Austria 1985	Austria 1990	Norway 1985	Norway 1990	Mean 1985	Mean 1990
Welfare policies												
Spend more	50	69	83	85	76	81	43			71	70	78
Spend same	45	29	16	14	20	18	52			28	27	20
Spend less	5	2	1	1	4	2	5			1	3	2
N	966	2,635	1,427	1,115	1,463	950	864			1,360		
Order policies												
Spend more	8	6	16	11	13	13	9			8	12	10
Spend same	66	59	71	79	67	68	69			80	68	69
Spend less	26	35	12	10	20	19	22			12	20	21
N	979	2,664	1,436	1,128	1,477	961	862			1,431		
Culture policies												
Spend more	36	50	9	18	36	48	25			17	27	39
Spend same	61	48	74	74	59	49	70			74	65	57
Spend less	3	2	17	8	5	3	5			9	8	4
N	983	2,629	1,345	1,070	1,465	956	868			1,398		

Notes: Entries are percentages. Question: 'Listed below are various areas of government spending. Please show whether you would like to see more or less government spending in each area. Remember that if you say "much more", it might require a tax increase to pay for it.' 1 = spend much more; 2 = spend more; 3 = spend the same as now; 4 = spend less; 5 = spend much less. The variables are: (1) the environment; (2) health; (3) law enforcement; (4) education; (5) defence; (6) retirement; (7) unemployment benefits; (8) culture and arts. Variables (1) and (8) have been added together to form the additive index 'culture policies' and the categories recoded: 2–4 = spend more, 5–7 = spend same, 8–10 = spend less. Variables (2), (4), (6), and (7) form the additive index 'Welfare policies', and recoded: 4–8 = spend more; 9–14 = same, 15–20 = spend less. Variables (3) and (5) form the additive index 'Order policies' and recoded: 2–4 = spend more; 5–7 = same; 8–10 = spend less. The mean in each case includes only those countries surveyed in both 1985 and 1990 (Germany, Britain, and Italy).

tend towards internal consistency, though it does not, of course, suggest that they are always so.

Individuals do not either support or oppose the welfare state; they discriminate between different parts of it, and between different policy instruments. For example, strong and consistent support for social security programmes, including those for the unemployed, does not

TABLE 4.5. *Support for different socio-economic equality policies, 1987*

Dimension	Item	AU	GB	GE	NL	SW	IT	Avg.
Equality of opportunity	The government should provide more chances for children from poor families to go to university	80	84	87	85	81	90	85
Equality of result National minima	The government should provide a job for everyone who wants one	80	59	77	75	50	82	71
	The government should provide everyone with a guaranteed basic income	57	61	56	50	43	67	56
Redistribution	The government should reduce the differences in income between people with high incomes and those with low incomes	81	64	61	65	43	82	66
	People with high incomes should pay a larger proportion of their earnings in taxes than those who earn low incomes	86	77	80	73	82	79	80
Means index		77	65	71	66	51	83	69
N		972	1,212	1,397	1,638	987	1,027	

Notes: Entries for 'The government should. . .' items are percentages of respondents who agree strongly or agree. Entries for the second taxes item are percentages of respondents who say much larger proportion or larger proportion.

Source: ISSP (1987), as presented in Vol. iii, *The Scope of Government*, Table 7.2.

necessarily spill over into support for a guaranteed income (see Table 4.5). Perhaps the idea of a guaranteed income conflicts with other popular principles, such as the idea that people should work where possible, and that there should be differences of income based upon differences of ability and effort. At any rate, the general public distinguishes between different unemployment policies, strongly supporting some, weakly supporting or rejecting others.

The general public draws similar distinctions between different kinds of economic intervention, as Borre and Viegas show in *The Scope of Government*. Their evidence indicates stronger support for state ownership of natural monopolies such as electricity and public transport, than for competitive sectors like banking and the car industry.

V. O. Key once argued that 'voters are not fools' (Key 1966). This study draws the same conclusion. It is easy to exaggerate the subtlety and sophistication of public opinion, in reaction to the 'voters are fools' school of thought, but perhaps the safest thing to say is that citizens seem generally able to draw sensible and reasonably subtle distinctions between different kinds of principles and their application, and to follow them through in a not unsophisticated manner.

Writing about public opinion in the United States, Page and Shapiro (1993: 60; emphases in orginal) list a series of propositions, as follows:

that collective public opinion about policy is *real*; that it is *measurable* through survey research; that it forms *coherent patterns*; that it is generally *stable*; that when public opinion changes that it generally does so in *regular and understandable* ways; and that it nearly always changes in reasonable and sensible ways in response to objective events and to the new ideas and interpretations provided to it.

We have quoted this passage in full because our own conclusions are in almost total agreement, and because it became available to us only *after* we had drafted our own chapter. We take this to be an example of careful and systematic minds, armed with a great deal of empirical data, thinking alike.

Sociotropic versus Pocket Book Attitudes

The Beliefs in Government study does not explicitly confront the much discussed and complex debate about sociotropic versus pocket-book attitudes—that is, whether citizens seek to maximize their own interests or those of society and the public good. The question deserves a whole study and a whole book of its own (e.g. Lewin 1991). Our study, however, does throw some light on four aspects of the matter.

First, it is abundantly clear from the survey data assembled in *The Scope of Government* that the great majority of citizens in almost all West European nations support the welfare state. They do not like all welfare policies, but the great majority believe that their government should maintain minimum social and economic standards for all. They also seem to believe (or say that they believe, which is not the same thing) that they should pay their fair share of tax towards the costs of these services. Support for basic social security policies has not declined in recent decades.

Secondly, most citizens believe that the state should ensure a degree of economic equality. Roller's study of equality and the welfare state in *The Scope of Government* shows that the public does not believe in absolute equality, but belief in equality of opportunity is widespread, and most think that the distribution of wealth in their country is not as fair as it should be. The point is made again in Table 4.6.

Thirdly, although it is difficult to draw firm conclusions, most citizens seem to be prepared to pay taxes, or more taxes, in order to fund what they think are important public services. This view is contrary to the 'something for nothing' interpretation of mass opinion (see e.g. Sears and Citrin 1985). Some surveys have asked 'unpriced' questions of tax payers: asked if taxes are too high, most say they are; asked if they want more or better public services, most say they do. Hence, people want 'something for nothing'. More sensible questions asks respondents to say which, if any, services they would cut in return for lower taxes, or which if any services they would like to see improved and at what increase to their own tax bill. These sorts of priced questions elicit more sensible responses (see e.g. Peters 1991*a*). Moreover, as we have already said, there is a rough match between the services people believe are important, and the services they say they are prepared to pay more taxes for. Reviewing the literature with these qualifications in mind, Peters (1991*a*: 160) writes that 'citizens have demonstrated that they are not really as naïve about public finance as is sometimes assumed. Most citizens appear to recognise that if they want more services they will have to pay for them through taxes.' The evidence of *The Scope of Government* supports this conclusion.

Fourthly, it may be that some people express liberal ideas in principle, but favour interventionist politics to protect their own interests (see Free and Cantril 1969). In their chapter in *The Scope of Government*,

TABLE 4.6. *Attitudes towards issues of tax fairness*

(a) Government's responsibility to reduce income differences between rich and poor

	GE		GB		IT		AU	NO	IR
	1985	1990	1985	1990	1985	1990	1985	1990	1990
Should be	67	64	75	74	84	78	78	72	82
Should not be	33	36	25	26	16	22	22	28	18
N	1,048	2,812	1,530	1,197	1,580	983	1,580	1,517	1,005

(b) Government's responsibility to reduce income differences between those with high and low incomes

	GE		GB		IT		AU	SW	NO	IR	NL
	1987	1990	1987	1990	1987	1990	1987	1987	1990	1990	1990
Agree	61	56	64	57	82	70	81	43	56	69	65
Disagree	24	20	23	24	9	15	11	40	25	18	24
N	1,397	2,812	1,212	1,197	1,027	983	972	987	1,517	1,005	1,638

(c) People with high incomes should pay a larger share of their income in taxes than those with low incomes

	GE		GB		IT		AU	SW	NO	IR	NL
	1987	1990	1987	1990	1987	1990	1987	1987	1990	1990	1990
Larger	80	87	77	85	79	84	86	82	75	82	73
Same	19	12	22	14	20	15	13	17	24	17	22
Smaller	1	1	1	1	1	1	1	1	1	1	4
N	1,397	2,812	1,212	1,197	1,027	983	972	987	1,517	1,005	1,638

Note: Entries are percentages.

Sources: ISSP (1985, 1987, 1990), as presented in Vol. iii, *The Scope of Government*, Table 5.1.

Borre and Viegas refer to this as 'the hypocrisy of free-riders'—the mirror image of 'Mercedes Marxism' or 'arm-chair socialism'. However, their own analysis of ISSP survey data finds little evidence of such hypocritical free-riding. There is a clear and internally consistent set of attitudes which supports economic intervention, but no clear factor representing ideological liberalism, and hence no evidence that 'liberals' are likely to be interventionists when it suits them.

It would be foolish to conclude from this patchy and circumstantial evidence that citizens only and always follow their notion of the public good and the general interest, even less that their actual behaviour is determined by high-minded principles. At the same time, the evidence suggests that they do not always express selfish opinions, or always behave in ways which maximize their own economic interests.

The West European Pattern

There is a surprisingly large measure of agreement among the citizens of different West European nations about the proper scope of modern government, and the priorities that should be set for it. National variations are relatively minor; far more striking is the strong family resemblance in the national profiles of attitudes towards the scope of government, its responsibilities, its public services priorities, and towards issues of taxing and spending (see e.g. Tables 4.1, 4.2, 4.4, 4.5 and 4.6 in this chapter). There is a consistency of views across Western Europe on a wide range of other matters, including: ratings for important public issues; government responsibilities, issues of equality and redistribution; issues of social security; economic intervention; and government control of communications.

At the same time, there are also indications of some differences between social democratic and Christian democratic welfare states. In the Protestant and Anglo-Scandinavian nations of the north, where social democratic parties are strong, attitudes towards the scope of government are quite strongly correlated with the left–right variable and with party identification. In the southern, Catholic countries where Christian democratic ideology is strong, attitudes are less strongly correlated with political indicators such as voting and party identification.

What makes this consistency of attitudes all the more striking is that the same pattern is not found with such things as trust in government, political participation, beliefs in democracy, the efficacy of the citizen, or measures of political alienation (see Volume i, *Citizens and the State*). On such matters there is no consistent pattern stretching across Western Europe, but rather a varied set of trends which seem to be specific to particular nations at particular times. In this respect the findings of two Beliefs in Government volumes, *The Scope of Government* and *Citizens and the State*, stand in sharp contrast.

In spite of different forms of government, different forms of state services and provisions, different histories, economies, and cultures, there is a general West European view about public services and the welfare state. It is not too much to speak of a West European view, something which is relevant to the European Union in its attempts to form a common European welfare policy.

The Impact of Politics

The theories outlined in Chapter 2 of this book, and in the first part of this chapter, tend to ignore or to overlook politics. Wilensky's theory of the middle mass argues that changes in the industrial and occupational structure produce changes in public attitudes which result in welfare state backlash and tax revolt. Recent writing on postmodernism concentrates on changes in the mode of production and the economic system, which cause occupational, class, and social changes, which result in mass attitude change. The legitimacy crisis is caused by the economic contradictions of capitalism. Rational choice theory argues or assumes that individuals are motivated mainly by their own (usually economic) interests. Only overload theory explicitly claims that the problem is a political one, and therefore politically solvable (Brittan 1975). In the other cases, it is assumed that social and economic change is somehow automatically translated into attitudinal change about political matters, or else it is assumed that people respond to the economic imperative and that politics does not enter into the matter.

In contrast much of the evidence collected in *The Scope of Government* underlines the significance of government and politics. It suggests a two-way effect—an impact of politics, and an impact on politics.

The Impact of Politics at State Level

The effects of politics and political change on mass attitudes show at two analytical levels—the state and the individual. At the state level there are many indications of a political cycle caused principally by electoral swings and the alternation of parties in government. For example, in Germany and Britain during the 1970s and 1980s, shifts in opinion about the size of government (support for big government, or for rolling back the frontiers of the state) coincided with swings between left-wing and right-wing governments (see the chapter by Huseby in Volume iii). It seems that public opinion shifted in the light of experience: policies of incoming governments were provisionally accepted at election time, and later re-evaluated according to their impact. In this way, the public may tend towards cycles of opinion according to which party or coalition with what sort of policy is in power.

Thatcher's period of office in the United Kingdom provides a good example because she applied clear and radical policies over a relatively long period. As Huseby shows in *The Scope of Government*, before Thatcher's first election victory the British were relatively contractionist in their views about government, but by the time of her departure they were, if anything, more expansionist than before (see Crewe 1988 and Huseby in Volume iii). And as Borre and Viegas also show in *The Scope of Government*, public opinion was far more favourable towards privatization when she came to office than when she left.

Further evidence of politically induced fluctuations or cycles of popular opinion is to be found in Pettersen's chapter on security and the welfare state which suggests that vigorous conservative campaigns can cause shifts in public opinion, and perhaps election victory. However, this shift does not appear to last, and opinion tends to revert to its original state as the message fades away or as people gain experience of the policies in practice. Pettersen presents evidence of such political popularity cycles in Britain, the Netherlands, Denmark, and Norway (though not Sweden or Finland) with respect to pensions and welfare policies in the 1960–90 period.

In other cases politics seems to act as an intervening variable. For example, there is no clear or simple relationship between national affluence and support for policies to increase economic equality. In other words, Inglehart's argument that the most affluent nations will find economic equality less and less attractive seems not to hold for Western Europe, since support for economic equality has risen and fallen according to political events. Equality was an important political issue, even in affluent countries, during the wave of political protest in the late 1960s. This caused the direct link between affluence and equality to be broken during the 1970s, but as the impact of the 1960s' protests receded, so the issue of equality tended to sink down the political agenda in the more affluent countries, and a negative association between affluence and weaker support for equality re-emerged (see Roller, Chapter 7 in Volume iii).

In the same way Borre and Viegas in their chapter on economic management show that there is no clear relationship between attitudes towards government economic intervention in the economy and level of economic development. Rather, the terms 'economic intervention' and 'economic management' are interpreted in different ways in different countries according to their political history. In Italy, Austria, Spain, and Portugal government involvement in the economy, especially the nationalization of industries, was promoted by both left-wing and right-wing governments. In northern Europe, nationalization was more usually a programme of the political left. In this case, political factors intervene between attitudes towards government intervention in the economy and the level of economic development.

The examples presented here suggest that public opinion changes according to political influences which wax and wane in strength. There are also examples of long-term trends in opinion which are a direct response to changing political circumstances. The most obvious is the slow, persistent decline of national defence as a priority issue during the 1980s and early 1990s as the Cold War declined and then disappeared. International instability in the 1990s may cause the issue to rise up the agenda again. In this particular case, cause and effect are clear—political events caused political attitudes to change. It can scarcely have been the other way around.

In the case of public opinion about the environment the cause and effect relationships are more complex and probably run in two directions. The surveys show that the issue of environmental protection and control has gradually gained importance in the public mind during the 1970s and 1980s. This is probably because as evidence of environmental dangers has accumulated, so the issue has gained political importance. But it may also have worked the other way round as well—heightened political awareness has caused more research to be carried out and a larger and more sympathetic audience for the results of research.

The Impact of Politics at the Individual Level

The second level where political factors can be seen at work is in the analysis of individuals. In searching for explanations and in testing theories, *The Scope of Government* examines the relationship between opinion about government services and a range of social, economic, demographic, and political variables, including age, income, education, gender, employment, social class, materialist–postmaterialist orientations, left–right orientations, party preference, and party identification. In most cases the social, economic, and demographic variables have a weak association with attitudes, and even when statistically significant they are often substantively trivial. This is because sample sizes are often large, with a thousand or more being interviewed in each country, so that correlations as small as 0.06 may be statistically significant at 1 per cent, but still of substantively little interest. Though not notably strong, the class and political variables are usually more strongly correlated with attitudes than anything else. This is true of attitudes towards the size of government, taxing and spending, equality, and social security (see Chapters 4–8 in Volume iii). In all these cases, and in most countries and most years, the statistical associations between beliefs in government and political variables, such as left–right orientation and party identification, are usually stronger than any of the social, economic, and demographic variables. In the case of government control of communications, education is more strongly correlated with opinion about the rights of revolutionaries and racists to publish, but when it comes to newspaper freedom to publish, it is the party variable which sticks out again (see Golding and van Snippenburg, Chapter 10 in Volume iii).

As Pettersen states in Chapter 7 of Volume iii: 'Even if class politics and political preferences do not present us with a single and conclusive explanation of support for the welfare state, this dimension—often overlooked in the last decade of political science analysis—is clearly the best predictor of welfare preferences.'

Political considerations may also have a general impact on beliefs about the proper scope of government. The Beliefs in Government book on *Citizens and the State* (Volume i) finds no general or systematic increase in anti-government sentiments in Western Europe as a whole over the past two or three decades. On most indicators there is evidence of a growing alienation or disillusionment in some countries and in some years, but in other countries the trend is constant or shows signs of increasing satisfaction, trust, and contentment. The fact that there is no broad or systematic evidence of an overall growth of alienation and distrust may help to explain why *The Scope of Government* finds little support for a downward spiral of expectations about the proper scope of government. A population which retains faith in its system of government, and which believes it is reasonably democratic, is more likely to trust its government with a broad range of duties than a population which is alienated and distrustful.

This conclusion is supported by the finding that there is a link between satisfaction with the political system, on the one hand, and policy distance, on the other. Policy distance is the gap between the voter's preferred policies on a range of substantive matters (welfare, environment and culture, and law and order) and the policies of the government itself. The concept is useful because it applies to those on the far left who reject government policies because they are too right-wing, and to those of the far right who reject government policies as too left-wing. In other words, policy distance is a total measure of dissatisfaction with government policies. Borre uses this measure in his chapter on the scope of government and political support. He finds that, in seven out of eight countries, the greater the policy distance the lower the support for the political system; people who are estranged from government policies are also likely to express a dissatisfaction

TABLE 4.7. *Policy distance and satisfaction with democracy in eight West European countries, 1979–83*

	Near to government		At medium distance		Far from government	
	(3–8)	*N*	(9–10)	*N*	(11–12)	*N*
Germany	78	1,556	75	568	72	228
Denmark	73	1,354	70	562	63	271
Netherland	69	1,028	62	858	53	598
Great Britain	63	1,652	47	483	53	200
Ireland	57	1,472	52	494	49	316
France	55	826	47	867	43	551
Belgium	51	862	46	690	39	514
Italy	20	1,014	18	917	13	813

Notes: Entries are percentages who are 'very' or 'somewhat' satisfied with the way democracy is working in their country among those at each policy distance from government. The percentage base excludes missing data. Data for the three surveys for each country have been combined.

Sources: Eurobarometer, Nos. 11, 16, and 19, as presented in Vol. iii, *The Scope of Government*, Table 12.7.

with their political system (see Table 4.7). One might predict from this finding that when the policies change, usually because the government changes, trust in government and in public institutions would be restored to some extent among those for whom policy distance has been reduced. This is exactly what Listhaug discovers in his chapter on trust in institutions in *Citizens and the State*.

The Impact on Politics

The relationship between public opinion and government policy is clearly an enormously complex and variable one and we cannot begin to tackle the topic in a systematic manner here. However, one striking case appears in *The Scope of Government* which seems to present a clear example of public opinion change having a decisive effect on policy. In the 1970s, tax revolts in the West gained a good deal of media publicity. It seemed that anti-tax and welfare attitudes were quite widespread and growing stronger. With the help of hindsight we can see that the tax protest was neither deep rooted nor widespread. Nor was it all that it seemed. The notorious anti-tax Glistrup Party (or Progress Party) in Denmark is an example. In 1973 and 1975, 63 and 40 per cent respectively of its voters wanted *heavier* taxes on high incomes; they were not anti-tax, but wanted the tax regime adjusted so that middle and lower income groups paid less, and upper incomes paid more (Nielsen 1976: 149). This view of tax seems to have permeated Western Europe as a whole for the last decade and more.

Nevertheless, as a result of the tax protest, governments across practically the whole of the Western world moved quickly to change their tax regimes in quite radical ways (Pechman 1988). The reforms they implemented were generally similar: taxes were not reduced, but the burden was shifted from direct, visible and politically sensitive forms of taxation, such as income tax, to more indirect, less visible, and less sensitive taxes such as VAT/TVA; income taxes were often reduced; the highest marginal rates of income tax were brought down substantially; the number of tax brackets was reduced; there was a shift from individual and households taxes to business and corporation tax. In short, many Western states moved with unusual rapidity to implement basic changes, and this seems to have been a direct response to the 'tax revolt'.

We do not suggest that there is usually such a direct and simple relationship between public opinion and government policy. There is not. Nor do we suggest that the tax revolt was so strong and persistent that it could not be resisted by governments. On the contrary, it was not. But in this instance governments of all kinds moved quickly and decisively to change things. Perhaps the explanation is that governments are peculiarly sensitive to tax matters. If so, it suggests that public opinion can have a direct and powerful effect on matters which are close to the pockets if not the hearts of their governments.

Conclusions

In 1980 one of the few systematic and comparative studies of public opinion about welfare (Coughlin 1980: 153–4) argued that:

It is fair to conclude that despite the presumed fiscal crisis of the welfare state, the taxpayers revolt, runaway inflation, and other scenarios of doom and gloom, the American people, like their West European counterparts, are not quite ready to abandon the commitments of providing the benefits and services of the welfare state . . . As we have seen repeatedly throughout this study, some types of social welfare are deeply entrenched in popular attitudes, and are likely to survive whatever the developments over the next few years.

The present study amply confirms this conclusion, not just so far as welfare is concerned but also on a wide range of other government services and activities. The core services of the welfare state—health, education, housing, and provision for the old, the ill, and the unemployed—are almost universally (usually more than 90 per cent) regarded as government responsibilities. A rather lower percentage— but still a large majority of around 65 per cent—believe this to be the case for minority rights, gender equality, economic equality, and assistance for industry. There is little evidence that support for public services is crumbling; on the contrary, it seems to be resilient.

To be accurate, what most of the statistical material produced in *The Scope of Government* shows is that support for public services and the welfare state in the late 1980s and early 1990s remained at a high level. The data for this period are relatively good and plentiful. Information about earlier decades is thin and patchy. Therefore, we cannot show that support has not declined, although it was so high in the 1980s and 1990s that it is difficult to see how it could have fallen appreciably from even higher levels in the 1960s and 1970s.

To this extent, the predictions about government overload, legitimacy crisis, and rational-choice revolt are not borne out by the data we have.

There is little sign of a welfare state backlash, tax revolt, legitimacy crisis, or general disillusionment with public services. That is not to say there has been no change, but change is not necessarily decline. The public agenda has not remained constant over the decades. West European publics now place less importance on defence than during the Cold War, and they believe in less government regulation of the economy. Equally, environmental matters have increased in importance in the public mind. These are matters of change, not decline.

It is important to distinguish between fluctuations and trends in mass opinion. Fluctuations are relatively short term, lasting from a few months to a few years They may be quite sudden and steep, but iron themselves out in the long run. Trends last for decades or generations and show long-term continuity. Theorists have been tempted to generalize—or rather to over-generalize and over-interpret—fluctuations in order to anticipate trends. In this chapter we have tried to sort out the trends from the fluctuations and draw the appropriate conclusions about long-term change.

Changes in mass attitudes have been slow and limited in the 1970s and 1980s. There have been shifts in public priorities but these have not resulted in a widespread rejection of the old attitudes and agendas. Rather the old has been modified and the new has been incorporated. The result has been stability, continuity, and adaption, rather than fundamental or wholesale change.

This may help to explain why the much discussed issue voting of the 1970s and 1980s has not had the effect of disrupting traditional voting patterns in many West European nations. It may also help explain why the single-issue, new social movements of the 1970s and 1980s have not had as large an impact on traditional party systems and voting patterns as some predicted. The incorporation of the new agenda into the old, and the relatively close association of new issues with party identification means that neither issue voting nor the new social movements have been successful in breaking the mould of orthodox party politics. They have shifted policy agendas but they have been less successful in by-passing the old party and pressure group systems.

Perhaps the general conclusion is that theories of change might concentrate less exclusively on what are undoubtedly enormous pressures for change in modern society, and look also at the enormous pressures for continuity and stability. If there is merit in this suggestion, then the paradox is that theories of change have concentrated too much on change, and too little on obstacles to change.

5

International Government

The history of the Western world over the past few centuries could be written as the history of the development of nation states and of conflict and competition between them. The history of the last fifty years could be written in terms of the growing power and importance of international or supranational governments and agencies such as the UN, NATO, COMECON, the IMF, the World Bank, GATT, the G7, OPEC, and so on. In many ways the European Union is the most innovative, experimental, and far-reaching of these. Among the regional supranational governments of the globe it is the most powerful, and the one which is setting the pace and direction for others. In short, international or supranational government adds a new, growing, and increasingly powerful dimension to modern government, particularly in Western Europe.

Developments in the past twenty or thirty years have been so startling and so rapid that the future of the nation state itself is in doubt, at least in its present form. Some writers claim that we increasingly live in a global village and a borderless world (Ohmae 1989) which is beginning to bypass and undermine nation states (see e.g. Dogan 1994). Others argue that, in some respects, the nation state is as vibrant as ever (see e.g. Sharpe 1988, 1989; Hoffman 1966). Still others argue that the West European nation state has been rescued by the European Union (Milward 1992; Wallace 1994). The purpose of this chapter, however, is not to discuss the future of the nation state and international government in Western Europe, but to ask what citizens feel about international government, and how and why their feelings have developed in this way.

The chapter is divided into four sections. The first examines attitudes of support and opposition to three agencies of international government which are most important to West Europeans—the UN, NATO, and the European Union. Is public opinion internationalist, or is it more parochial and nationalist? Does the general public welcome international government, or does it oppose it as the most recent and possibly the worst form of big government? How has opinion developed or changed over time, and do past trends help to inform us about the present, and possibly the future, basis of opinion?

The second section considers the problems of mass ignorance of international affairs. Do people know what they are talking about when they answer survey questions about international affairs? Are they ignorant, random, and inconsistent? Are their views on international affairs based upon prejudice and stereotypes?

The third section considers the structure of mass opinion about international politics. Like the previous chapter about the scope of national government, it asks whether aggregate public opinion about international politics tends to be rather formless, contradictory, volatile, and lacking in sophistication, or whether, on the contrary, it shows a degree of structure, consistency, stability over time, and perhaps even a grasp of world events and trends.

The fourth section discusses the bases of mass opinion about international attitudes. Are they simply reflections or echoes of élite opinion? Does the public take a pragmatic view, seeing international government as an instrument of economic self-interest and security, or does it take a more idealistic view which focuses on international peace, co-operation, and unification? Is public opinion simply a reflection or an echo of élite views? Or is it rather built upon a growing sense of European citizenship and trust between people? Does national pride encourage or inhibit 'Europeanism'? The chapter draws heavily on Volume ii of the Beliefs in Government project, i.e. *Public Opinion and Internationalized Governance*. For the sake of convenience, this is often abbreviated to Volume ii.

First, however, the chapter looks at levels of support for international government among the populations of Western Europe, and at the ways in which these have changed since the early 1950s.

Support for International Agencies of Government

As Table 5.1 shows, West European public opinion about international affairs generally distinguishes between matters relating to (1) the

TABLE 5.1. *Structure of attitudes towards the EC, NATO, and UN, 1989*

Variables	Orthogonally rotated factors		
	I	II	III
EC membership	0.76	0.06	0.03
Unification of Europe favoured	0.69	0.00	−0.02
Benefit of European integration	0.69	0.04	0.12
Regret if EC were dissolved	0.62	0.02	−0.16
Confidence in EC decisions	0.50	0.26	0.32
US military presence in Europe	0.03	0.75	−0.07
Opinion on NATO	0.05	0.83	0.09
NATO still essential	0.03	0.79	0.03
EC or NATO responsible for defence	0.09	0.59	0.19
Strong national defence	0.05	0.54	−0.39
UN doing a good job	0.02	0.16	0.82
Variance explained	28.9	16.8	8.4

Note: Entries are factor loadings, pooled data.

Source: Eurobarometer, No. 32, as presented in Vol. ii, *Public Opinion and Internationalized Governance*, Table 16.6.

European Union, (2) NATO, and (3) the UN (see also Ziegler 1987). This three-fold division will be used as an organizing principle for the first part of this chapter.

European Integration and the European Union

Between them the United States Information Agency (USIA) and the Eurobarometer surveys of the European Commission have produced the longest and richest run of data on international attitudes among West Europeans. The USIA surveys started in 1952 and ran until 1976. They cover West Germany, Italy, France, and the UK. (For details of the USIA survey and their results 1952–1963 see Merritt and Puchala 1968.) Answers to the question 'Are you in general for or against making efforts towards uniting Western Europe?' show strong and increasing support for unification throughout the period in Italy, West Germany, and France. In the 1950s more than 60 per cent approved of efforts to unite Western Europe; by the mid-1970s it was usually closer to 80 per cent. Support was initially high in Britain (78 per cent in 1954), fell to low levels after two failed attempts to join the EC, but rose again in the 1970s.

In 1970 the Eurobarometer surveys started asking an almost identical question about European unification: 'In general, are you for or against efforts being made to unify Western Europe?' (Very much for/only to some extent/ against/very much against). The question was asked irregularly from 1970, but from 1978 it was asked every year in all member states. The Eurobarometer confirms the USIA studies. From 1976 to 1994, average support (excluding 'don't knows') for the idea of West European unification in all member states of the EC did not drop below 70 per cent, and in the late 1980s it was often over 80 per cent (see Figure 5.1).

It is one thing to favour the abstract principle of European unification, perhaps quite another to support the EC. To gauge public opinion about the EC itself the Eurobarometer survey asks three further questions:

(1) 'Generally speaking, do you think that [your country's] member-ship of the European Union is a good thing, a bad thing, or neither good nor bad?' This question has been asked continu-ously since 1973 and is labelled the 'membership' question.

(2) 'Taking everything into consideration, would you say that [your country] has on balance benefited or not from being a member of the European Union?' This question, asked continuously since 1983, is labelled the 'benefit' question.

(3) 'If you were told tomorrow that the European Union had been scrapped, would you be very sorry about it, indifferent or relieved?' This question has been asked continuously since 1981 and labelled the 'dissolution' question.

It should be noted that the benefit question does not ask about economic benefit but about any kind of benefit—cultural, environmen-tal, peace and security, for example. Quite possibly many people answer it in terms of economic benefits, however. We should also note that the European Economic Community transformed itself into the European Community and then to the European Union, but for the sake of simplicity and brevity we use the current title throughout this chapter, unless a survey question or quotation specifically refers to another title or point in time.

To summarize: although there are variations between countries and over time, most people in EU member states have expressed approval for the idea of European unification and for membership of the EU during the 1970s and 1980s. Support for membership fluctuates between 50 and 70 per cent, between 45 and 60 per cent believe that their own country benefits from membership, and between 40 and 50 per cent

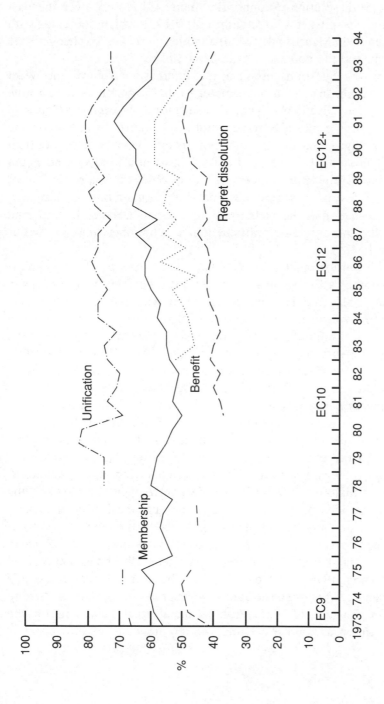

FIGURE 5.1. *Support for the European Union, 1973–94*

Notes: EC-10 includes Greece; EC-12 includes Spain and Portugal; EC-12+ includes the former East Germany.

Sources: Eurobarometer surveys, 1973–94.

would regret dissolution. Support has increased slowly over the past two decades, in spite of a large slump after 1991 which coincides with the debates over Maastricht, the difficulties with the Exchange Rate Mechanism, and the collapse of the Soviet bloc.

Other survey questions confirm the internationalism of the West European public. In the Eurobarometer of 1975, members of the nine EC nations were asked: 'Are you, yourself, for or against the Common Market developing into a European political union?' In one sense the question is vague because it does not specify what sort of political union, but in another sense political union of any kind is a stringent test of internationalism. None the less, absolute majorities were expressed in favour in six of the nine (Italy, Luxembourg, Germany, Belgium, France, and the Netherlands). Only in Ireland, Britain, and Denmark did those against political union outnumber those in favour (Inglehart 1977*a*).

The 1987 Eurobarometer survey also asked: 'Are you for or against the formation of a European government, responsible to the European Parliament?' This too is a vague question which begs the issue of what sort of government with what sort of powers, but it also poses a form of political unification going far beyond the state of affairs at the time. Answers vary between countries, but in Italy, France, Belgium, and Luxembourg there were absolute majorities in favour, and in Spain, the Netherlands, Portugal, West Germany, Ireland, and Greece those in favour easily outnumbered those against. Only in Britain and Denmark did those against outnumber those for. In the twelve member states as a whole, 49 per cent were in favour of a European government, and 24 per cent were against (Inglehart and Reif 1991: 10).

Although there are variations between countries, and fluctuations over time, a majority of citizens in the twelve member states of the EU favour the idea of European integration and the European Union. A majority also supports the idea of political unification with a form of European government (unspecified) responsible to a European parliament. The pattern of support has generally been maintained since the early 1970s, and even further back in France, Italy, and West Germany. This suggests fairly widespread and relatively strong support for the idea of unification as an abstract idea, and for the European Union as a practical form of international government.

Support for NATO and the UN

Compared with European unification and the EU, support for the United Nations and for NATO is less clear and certain, but still favourable on balance for most of the post-war period. The USIA surveys show qualified but general support for the United Nations. In 1956, for example, more people in France, West Germany, Italy, and Britain thought the UN was doing a good job than a bad one and, with the exception of France, more believed it had justified its existence than not. In all four countries large majorities thought the UN should go beyond merely discussing and investigating international problems and should be involved in solving them. Similarly, majorities believed that the UN should have its own armed force, and large majorities believed the UN should enforce international control of the Suez Canal and maintain a peace-keeping force in the Middle East (Merritt and Puchala 1968: 408–9).

Opinion polls conducted by Gallup International suggest a similar qualified and variable support for the UN in the 1970s and 1980s. In 1974 more people felt that the UN was doing a good job than a bad one. In 1985 this situation was reversed in three out of the six nations surveyed, but in 1989 the same question asked in eleven West European nations shows a balance of opinion in all of them believing that the UN was doing a good job. As Everts says in Chapter 16 of Volume ii, to the degree that people are willing to make a judgement on the performance of the UN, it is very positive.

Support for NATO also varies between countries and across time, but once again the balance of opinion in Western Europe has been favourable since the mid-1950s. According to the USIA surveys conducted between 1955 and 1960, most of those who had an opinion on the matter in France, West Germany, Italy, and Britain favoured their country's membership of NATO, and more believed it had done well than badly. Many more in all four countries believed that NATO had contributed 'somewhat' or 'a great deal' to West European security than that it had done nothing or endangered it. More believed it would be better to keep NATO than scrap it, although in France and West Germany only 22 and 25 per cent respectively had an opinion one way or the other (for detailed results of the USIA surveys on NATO, see Merritt and Puchala 1968: 323–60). In Volume ii Everts assembles statistics which show, despite variations between countries and over time, continuing support for NATO across Western Europe during the 1970s, the 1980s, and into the 1990s.

There are different forms of international co-operation for different purposes, but a basic distinction may be drawn between military or 'hawkish', and non-military or 'dovish' internationalism. In Europe the hawks support NATO rather than the EU, and the doves prefer the EU to NATO. Alternatively, some people may want both military and non-military international co-operation, whereas others may want neither. Out of this Everts creates a typology of (1) integrationists, who favour military and non-military co-operation, (2) non-military partners, who favour the EU but not NATO, (3) military allies, who favour NATO, but not the EU, and (4) isolationists, who oppose NATO and the EU.

Eurobarometer surveys in 1980, 1989, and 1991 in EU countries show that integrationists are the largest category. In 1991 they formed half the respondents. The next largest category is made up of those favouring economic partnership (about a fifth). Military allies and isolationists are the smallest, with less than 10 per cent each. The 'undecideds' and 'don't knows' declined in numbers to a fifth in 1991. Most significantly, perhaps, those favouring either military or non-military co-operation, or both, increased substantially between 1980 and 1991. Although it is early days to generalize about the new Europe, it seems that the European public is leaning more towards international co-operation of both a military and a non-military kind.

Mass Ignorance and Prejudice

The previous chapter argued that aggregate public opinion about the scope of government and the welfare state should not be dismissed as ignorant and unworthy of serious analysis, but the same claim cannot be extended automatically to public opinion about international affairs. There are good reasons for treating this with caution, even profound scepticism. Most people are not deeply involved in politics, even less in international politics, which are often remote, complex, and difficult to understand. The general public has little first-hand experience or knowledge of foreign affairs, and depends upon the mass media for information. Many agencies of international government are comparatively new and changing. It would not be patronizing to suggest that mass opinion about international affairs is rather ignorant, random, and volatile. As Almond (1950: 69) has said: 'Foreign policy attitudes among most

	Military co-operation	
	Favourable	Unfavourable
Favourable	Integrationists	Non-military partners
	49%	18%
Unfavourable	Military allies	Isolationists
	8%	5%

Non-military co-operation appears as the vertical axis label.

FIGURE 5.2. *Military and non-military co-operation in the EU, 1991*
Note: 'Undecideds' and 'don't knows' total 21%.
Source: Derived from Table 16.6 in Vol. ii, *Public Opinion and Internationalized Governance*.

Americans lack intellectual structure and factual content. Such superficial psychic states are bound to be unstable.'

Knowledge of the UN, NATO, and the EU

In her chapter on territorial aspects of the EU in Volume ii, Westle presents Eurobarometer figures showing that over 80 or 90 per cent of EU citizens know that their own country is a member, and that about two people out of three in the ten member nations in 1985 knew that Spain and Portugal had applied to join. However, in the same volume Niedermayer and Sinnott show that smaller percentages were informed about such things as the European Parliament, the President of the Commission, and the Council of Ministers. Another recent and detailed study of the European Parliament finds that knowledge about it is not widespread (Hofrichter and Klein 1993).

USIA surveys in 1956 reveal a similar mixture of knowledge and ignorance about the United Nations. Most in France, Italy, and Britain (not West Germany) knew their own country was a member, and large majorities in all four countries knew that the United States and Russia were also members (Merritt and Puchala 1968: 407–8). In 1989, however, only 41 per cent could pick out the name of the UN Secretary-General, and only a quarter could name a UN agency or body such as UNESCO or UNICEF (Everts in Volume ii).

Knowledge of NATO is considerably less widespread in Western Europe. In France, West Germany, Italy, and Britain substantial minorities of between about 20 and 40 per cent had not heard of NATO, and another 10 per cent or so did not know whether their own country was a member, or else said it was not. In some cases the 'not awares' and 'don't knows' add up to more than 70 per cent of the sample (Merritt and Puchala 1968: 338–60). In later Eurobarometer surveys large minorities of up to 45 per cent could not answer questions about NATO (Everts in Volume ii). In sum, public knowledge of the EU, the UN, and NATO, is still very thin and patchy, although it seems to be spreading. Significant minorities of Western populations, even majorities, seem not to be armed with even the most basic information.

There are two main reasons why this level of ignorance means treating mass surveys on international affairs with caution but not rejecting them outright. First, it is not the *level* but the *pattern* of ignorance and opinion which matters most. If the surveys did not show a relatively large proportion of 'don't knows' and 'not answereds', our social science scepticism would be aroused immediately. But people do admit their ignorance by giving 'don't know' or 'not answered' responses, and for the most part, those who do answer are generally able to give factually accurate answers. For example, asked about their trust in foreigners, about one in ten give a 'don't know' answer about the Americans, British, Germans, and French, but close to a third are unable to answer questions about Luxemburgers, Portuguese, and Chinese (Inglehart 1991: 152). Similarly, in the USIA questions about NATO in the 1950s and 1960s, between 18 and 54 per cent of British, West Germans, Italians, and French said they had not heard of NATO. The factual accuracy of the answers of the rest was good: the largest single group knew that the United States was a member and that the Soviet Union was not, and few did not know either way (Merritt and Puchala 1968: 338–60).

The pattern of ignorance also generally makes sense. For example, it is usually higher among poorer nations, among less-well-educated individuals, and those with lower levels of political interest. Ignorance about the EU is more widespread among the newer member states than the older ones (see the chapters by Everts, Niedermayer and Sinnott, and Westle in Volume ii). Ignorance about international affairs seems to be falling as education improves and mass media penetration grows. That is, ignorance is often patterned in a predictable and understandable way. It is not random or meaningless, as it would be if many people gave haphazard substantive answers based upon ignorance or chance. The pattern lends some credibility to mass surveys rather than undermining them. Because of this, some analysts treat 'don't know' responses as evidence in their own right (Merritt and Puchala 1968: 115–27; Wessels, Chapter 4 in Volume ii).

The second reason for not dismissing surveys of mass opinion about international affairs concerns the difference between factual information and what might be called 'opinion information'. The first concerns textbook information about names, dates, places, or institutions. The second involves impressions and opinions about general matters. For example, in their research on mass opinion about the European Parliament in Volume ii, Niedermayer and Sinnott find that factual information is generally quite poor. At the same time, they also find that most Europeans have a clear understanding of the European Parliament's 'democratic deficit'. They conclude that 'no matter what way one looks at the data, it is evident that there is a persistent public sense of a democratic deficit . . . It is not surprising . . . The simple fact is: there is one.' In other words, in spite of the lack of detailed factual information about the European Parliament, most people have some appreciation of the overall picture. Citizens may not have a high level of information about politics, but they may still be able to make sensible, even rational, political judgements (Graber 1994).

The general public did not have detailed information about the Maastricht Treaty or the Exchange Rate Mechanism, but a general awareness of these problems seems to have caused a sharp drop in support for the EU. Again, the public is not informed about the details of NATO but, nevertheless, the proportion of people saying that it was 'essential' after the collapse of the Soviet bloc fell steeply. In this sense the survey evidence suggests that those who express an opinion have a general and fairly realistic appraisal of international affairs, although they may well lack factual information. With this in mind we can go on to the next step of the analysis.

The Nature of International Attitudes

In the previous chapter it was argued that aggregate public opinion about the state and its public services tends towards organization and structure, internal consistency, stability over time, and even a degree of subtlety and sophistication. This is not to say that the person in the street is a fully formed ideologue, but it does mean that West European public opinion about government and its activities is rather cogent, systematic, and consistent, perhaps surprisingly so.

Public opinion about international affairs is a good test case for this claim. The remoteness of international affairs, the complexity of many issues, the relative newness of such organizations as the UN, NATO, and the EU (compared with national states and structures) and changes in them, suggest that ordinary citizens may find it difficult to build up information about them, even less understand or express sensible opinions about them. For this reason, early writers often assumed that public opinion about foreign affairs was comparatively disorganized, unstable, and rather random and inchoate (Everts and Faber 1990). More recent theories, which focus on the amount of international news, the cognitive mobilization of the public, and improved education, tend to take a different view (see e.g. Inglehart 1991).

Structure

The previous section showed that popular opinions about military and international affairs are included in a cluster of attitudes which cover domestic law and order, and national defence. This cluster, in turn, is part of a broader group of attitudes which relate to what have been labelled the 'old' or materialist and the 'new' or postmaterialist agendas. In other words, mass attitudes towards international affairs do not stand alone but are, in general, integrated into broader structures of opinion.

When we look more closely at attitudes towards international affairs we find that they are also organized into clusters or groupings of opinion. For example, Table 5.1 uses factor analysis of the responses to eleven questions about international affairs and shows that they cluster neatly into three factors which together explain 54 per cent of the variance. The first centres on the EU and European unification. The second involves defence questions about NATO, the US military in Europe, and national defence. The third revolves around the single question in the survey dealing with the United Nations. These results confirm an earlier study of 1980 Eurobarometer data by Ziegler who found two main factors which he labelled military and non-military co-operation (Ziegler 1987). The two studies by Ziegler and by Everts show that West European public opinion about international affairs is structured and organized; responses tend to be patterned around particular and distinct families of issues.

Internal Consistency

The two studies also indicate that public opinion is internally consistent in the sense that it makes political sense to group European unification together with the EU, and to group national and European defence together with NATO and the American military presence in Europe. The United Nations stands slightly apart from these two. In other words, the three clusters suggest a degree of internal logic in mass attitudes towards international affairs in which opinions about like issues are grouped together in a consistent way.

Westle's chapter in Volume ii on the territorial expansion of the EU presents evidence pointing to the same conclusion. She shows that those who believe that the entry of a new country into the Union will benefit their own country, or the EU as a whole, tend to favour the new membership. Those who anticipate costs or problems are less enthusiastic about broadening membership, while those undecided about effects were unlikely to express an opinion one way or the other. Since the future effects of widening the Union cannot be known, a relatively large proportion of EU citizens are unwilling to express an opinion about it. Once again, this suggests an internal consistency of attitudes: those who don't know, tend to say so; those who see benefits, recommend expansion; those who do not, oppose it. This is elementary and trivial, but that is precisely the point: the polls suggest that mass opinion is internally consistent and logical.

Persistence and Change over Time

As the previous sections show, the Eurobarometer surveys find a stability of attitudes about military defence over rather long periods of time. Four surveys between 1976 and 1987 put the issue at the bottom of a list of popular priorities, substantially lower than unemployment which headed the table on each occasion. Similarly, attitudes of support and opposition to the EU among its member states show a fairly high degree of patterned and long-term stability. Countries with a relatively high level of support in the early 1970s (notably West Germany, France, Belgium) generally maintain it into the late 1980s. Countries with relatively weak support (notably Britain and Denmark) also keep their pattern. Support for the EU is consistently higher among the older member states than the newer ones, although the newer ones are tending to close the gap as time goes by (see Table 5.2).

The stability of mass attitudes is maintained at even fairly detailed levels of judgement and opinion. At irregular intervals the Eurobarometer presents respondents with a long list of public problems and asks them to say whether they think they are better decided by the national level or jointly within the European Union. Responses generally persist over an eighteen-year period between 1974 and 1991. (See Sinnott's chapter on policy orientations and subsidiarity in Volume ii.) Development aid, pollution control and environmental protection, and energy supplies are regularly assigned to the joint EU level. The reduction of regional inequalities, consumer protection, and regional self-government are regularly assigned to the national level. Responses tend to be consistent over time even at quite a detailed level.

It does not follow that public opinion on international affairs never changes, but that it does so in response to external circumstances, not in a random fashion. Table 5.2 shows that support for European unification has increased slowly over the past two decades, but rather faster in the newer member states as they get accustomed to membership. Over

TABLE 5.2. *Indicators of support by length of EC membership, 1970–89*

	1970	1975	1980	1985	1989
(a) Unification: percentage supporting 'very much'/'to some extent'					
EC-6	74	74	76	81	82
EC-10	—	69	72	77	78
EC-12	—	—	—	74	78
(b) Membership: percentage who regard it as a 'good thing'					
EC-6	—	67	64	69	69
EC-10	—	59	53	60	65
EC-12	—	—	—	60	63
		1983	1986	1989	
(c) Benefit: percentage claiming to have 'benefited'					
EC10		52	55	59	
EC12		—	46	59	

Source: Eurobarometer, No. 32, as presented in Vol. ii, *Public Opinion and Internationalized Governance*, Table 5.1.

shorter periods of time there are greater fluctuations in support. For example, enthusiasm for the EU declined sharply after Maastricht and the ERM difficulties. Likewise, the collapse of the Eastern bloc was followed by a sharp fall in numbers saying NATO was 'essential'. Similarly, the numbers favouring the exclusion of Great Britain from the EU rose steeply between 1976 and 1984 during which time Mrs Thatcher had underlined Britain's status as *The Awkward Partner* (George 1990). In 1990 a third or more of EC citizens (including Germany) had no opinion about the impact of German reunification on the EC or European integration, but after the event this uncertainty had decreased considerably, as Westle finds in her chapter on expansion of the EU in Volume ii. These shifts of opinion were not volatile or groundless, but were created by changing circumstances which caused public opinion to shift in an understandable manner.

Sense and Sophistication

Although relatively high proportions admit ignorance or are unable to answer questions about international affairs, those who do express opinions are sometimes quite sensible, possibly even subtle. In his essay on policy orientations and subsidiarity in Volume ii, Sinnott shows that citizens discriminate between different types of public issues when they assign them to national or international government. Scientific research, Third World aid, environmental protection, and foreign policy are consistently ranked at the international end of the continuum. Standards for education, health and welfare, data protection, cultural policy, and the press are consistently ranked at the national end. There is, of course, a certain common-sense grounding for this apportionment of tasks. Likewise, the ability to distinguish between NATO matters of national and European defence, on the one hand, and European unification on the other, suggests an ability to discriminate between different sorts of international issues with different sorts of implications for different organizations. So also does the public reaction to NATO and the end of the Soviet threat, and the reaction to the EU after Maastricht and the ERM failure.

We must be careful not to exaggerate the sense and subtlety of public opinion in these matters. The claim is certainly not that ordinary citizens are well informed, or that they can articulate an elaborate and consistent ideology. At the same time, survey evidence suggests that aggregate public opinion is reasonably well organized, fairly

consistent internally, quite stable over time, and to some extent discriminating and able to react sensibly to changes in international affairs.
Those who do not know answers to questions generally say so, and the
factual accuracy of those who do answer is within tolerable limits.

The Bases of Public Opinion about International Affairs

If ignorance, randomness, inconsistency, and volatility cannot explain
international public opinion, what does? The literature seems to offer
four main types of explanation: (1) élite opinion leadership, (2) economic self-interest, (3) national interest, and (4) a growing sense of
European identity and trust. These are not mutually exclusive explanations. We will consider them in turn in the next few sections of this
chapter, concentrating on their ability to explain attitudes towards the
European Union.

Élite Opinion Leadership

Some writers view public opinion about international affairs largely as
the creation of political and economic leaders (see e.g. Rosenau 1961).
According to Deutsch, such opinion does not 'bubble up' from the grass
roots, but rather 'cascades down' from the highest élite levels until it
eventually reaches ordinary people and is absorbed by them (Deutsch
1968, 1972). Lindberg and Scheingold (1970) argued that public
opinion in the 1960s provided little more than a sort of background
factor, a 'permissive consensus', which allowed élites to press on with
their European project. Perhaps mass opinion displays some of the
features of organization, consistency, and coherence precisely because
it simply reflects the views of political and economic élites?

Other writers argue that public opinion pushes élites on some international issues. According to Inglehart, postmaterialists in the general
public tend to set the pace on matters of international integration and
co-operation (Inglehart 1990; but see also Janssen 1991). Among other
things the formation of public opinion about international affairs may
have been encouraged by a huge increase in the sheer volume of
low-cost news and information, the improved education standards of
the population, and increasing levels of cognitive mobilization.
Consequently, some writers are now of the view that public opinion
can and does play a significant role in shaping foreign affairs. (See

especially Sinnott's chapter on integration theory in Volume ii, and Aldrich *et al.* 1989.)

It is exceedingly difficult to put these 'élite pull–mass push', or 'bubble up–cascade down' theories to the test. They require good time-series data on both élite and mass opinion, and the disentangling of many causes and effects. It is also possible that the early stages of European unification were élite lead, while public opinion now plays a more important role. The recent series of referendums in Denmark, France, Austria, Finland, Sweden, and Norway suggests this possibility.

One reason for suspecting that the 'élite pull' theory is incomplete is the fact that mass international opinion tends towards a degree of internal consistency, sense, and coherence. It seems unlikely that mass opinion would display these features if it were mainly a reproduction or reflection of élite opinion. This, however, is circumstantial evidence, and we need something more substantial.

Political parties are likely to be crucial in the processes of mass opinion formation and mass pressure. The classical function of parties is to aggregate and articulate the opinions of their members and supporters—a bottom-up process. At the same time, parties may also 'cue' opinion on complex and remote matters about which members and supporters might otherwise have vague opinions—a top-down process. As a result, opinion about the EU tends to cluster around parties and party families. Many of the chapters in Volume ii show a close correspondence between party variables and EU support, and how West European party families tend to cluster in this respect.

Do party members create party policy or do they follow the policies of party leaders? Wessels's research in Volume ii tries to answer this question by tracing the cause-and-effect relationships between party manifestos and party follower opinion at different times before and after elections. The results of his work suggest both cascade and bubble-up effects, but the strongest causal pathway runs from the pre-election opinion of party followers to their opinion at election time, and on to their post-election opinion. Party followers have an opinion about the EU before their party election campaigns swing into action, and their party then reinforces these views. In short, public opinion seems to have a life of its own—it does not simply follow or reflect the opinion of party élites, although following and reflecting seems to be a smaller part of opinion-formation process.

Economic Self-Interest

The élite pull–mass push model dominates among theories explaining mass attitudes towards international affairs. However, it may not hold under certain circumstances, particularly when powerful forces involving self-interest, especially economic self-interest, are concerned, or when the old forces of nationalism and national self-interest are concerned. Therefore we turn to economic self-interest as an explanation of public opinion, either as a determinant in its own right, or as a factor which can negate élite influences.

It would not be surprising if economic self-interest was the motivating force behind support for the EU. At the same time, it would be worrying for the EU if it was. Instrumental or specific support might well dry up in hard economic times; diffuse support is more likely to ride out economic storms, being rooted in more basic values and ties of loyalty and trust (Easton 1965; 1975).

The Eurobarometer surveys show that citizens see the EU in both specific and diffuse terms. They see it as having both material and ideal goals. Asked 'What things in your opinion bring the countries of the European Union together?' exactly equal numbers (41 per cent) answer in terms of the economy and in terms of world peace (Eurobarometer, No. 27, 1987: 19–33). Large percentages believe that the EU has a major economic role and should play a more important one in trade, currency, and taxation decisions. At the same time, it is also viewed as an important international organization which should play a major role in peace keeping, international co-operation and integration, environmental protection, social justice, and the equalization of resources (see e.g. Eurobarometer, No. 24, 1985; No. 31, 1989; and No. 32, 1989).

Although European citizens clearly see the economic role and purpose of the EU, it is difficult to find evidence of strong links between their economic situation and levels of EU support. Attempts to uncover statistical associations in any given year between national economic conditions and levels of support for the EU in different member states generally fail (see Bosch and Newton in Volume ii; see also Zeus 1990). Nor do economics seem to explain fluctuations in EU support in different nations over time. Time-series regression analysis provides little evidence that yearly fluctuations in such things as unemployment, inflation, economic growth, or trading relations within and outside the EU, are related to attitudes towards EU membership or European integration. Short-term variations over a few years are sometimes associated with economic growth and decline (Inglehart and Rabier 1978: 74; Handley 1981: 360; Dalton and Eichenberg 1991: 13), but over a longer time span three non-economic trends stand out.

First, there has been a slow and gradual overall increase in support levels from the first Eurobarometer surveys up to 1991. Secondly, there was a rapid rise in support levels in Spain, Greece, and Portugal just before and immediately after they joined. And thirdly, the sharp slump in support between 1991 and 1994 seems to have been a reaction to Maastricht, the failure of the ERM, and possibly to the collapse of the Soviet bloc. Since the pocket-book implications of Maastricht, the ERM, and Soviet collapse will take some time to materialize, it seems more likely that the drop in EU support is a response to the more immediate political implications of these events.

We may also look for the significance of economics on EU support at the individual level. Once again, the research of Bosch and Newton in Volume ii finds that there seems to be little connection between enthusiasm for, or opposition to, either European integration or EU membership and a variety of individual economic characteristics such as income, class, employment status, and economic optimism. In some ways farmers and fisherman form an group which is an acid test of the relationship between economics and support for the EU because the lives of both are so strongly affected by EU economic policy and expenditure. In the period from 1973 to 1990, however, the EU views of farmers and fishermen were usually not significantly different from those of other occupational groups in their own countries.

In short, there is not much evidence that economic considerations have a big impact on attitudes towards Europe. Economic factors do not seem to be closely associated with national variations in aggregate support for the EU at any given point in time, nor with variations in aggregate support over a period of years, nor with differences in individual support.

Europeanism and Nationalism

'Appealing though the idea of a united Europe is,' writes Milward (1992: 446), 'the strength of the European community does not lie in that abstract appeal. It lies in the weakness of the nation state.' In spite of this robust view, the relationship between nationalism and popular support for the EU is a puzzle. The simplest theory is that nationalism and 'Europeanism' are incompatible and that older and prouder nations will be more resistant to the EU than younger and less nationalistic ones. The theory founders at the outset. Table 5.3 shows that there is no relationship between the percentage saying they are 'very proud' of their nation, and support for the EU. Nor does any such relationship appear when national pride is measured in terms of the percentage saying they would be prepared to fight for their country.

The opposite idea, that people have to be secure in their national identity before they can risk identification with Europe (Hoffman 1966: 864) does not work any better. Countries with apparently strong national identities such as Britain can have low levels of EU support, or like France they may have quite high levels. Conversely, countries with a weaker national focus, such as Belgium, can have high levels of support.

A third possibility, which tries to combine these two theories, also fails. It suggests that to identify with the EU and with European government, people need to have a well developed but not an especially strong sense of national identity (Hoffman 1966). According to the figures in Table 5.3, the paired comparisons of Luxembourg and Britain, and Denmark and the Netherlands do not fit the theory at all well.

Perhaps these are the wrong measures of national identification and pride. Another indicator might be the Eurobarometer question, 'On the

TABLE 5.3. *National pride and support for EC membership, 1985*

	'Very proud of their nation'	'Willing to fight for their country'	'Satisfied with democracy'	Support for EC membership
GR	72	76	60	47
SP	64	69	58	67
LU	62	67	74	85
GB	54	61	55	39
IR	53	45	50	57
IT	45	38	27	79
FR	42	57	46	70
DK	40	63	74	36
NL	34	52	61	85
PO	33	65	39	61
BE	26	36	59	68
GE	20	33	72	62

Notes: Entries are percentages.

Source: Inglehart (1990).

whole are you very satisfied, fairly satisfied, not very satisfied, or not at all satisfied with the way democracy works in [your country]?' Those satisfied with national democracy might be inclined to reject the EU because of its democratic deficit, and those dissatisfied might turn to the EU to compensate for national deficiencies. Alternatively, people satisfied with their national system might tolerate the democratic deficiencies of the EU, whereas two levels of democratic inadequacies may be too much to accept. Once again, however, a glance at Table 5.3 shows that neither hypothesis works well. Satisfaction with national democracy is associated with strong EU support in the case of Luxembourg, but weak in the case of Denmark. Few Italians are satisfied with their democracy but support for EU membership is comparable to Luxembourg where satisfaction with democracy is high. There seems to be no relationship between enthusiasm for the EU and beliefs about democracy at home.

For this reason Martinotti and Stefanizzi, in their chapter 'Europeans and the Nation States' in Volume ii, argue that the root causes of internationalism vary from one country to another according to national situations and experience. In the Netherlands, Luxembourg, Ireland, and Portugal most people both approve of EU membership and are satisfied with democracy in their country. In Italy, and to some extent in the former East Germany and Greece, most are dissatisfied with the national system of democracy and seem to turn to the EU to compensate. In France, Belgium, and Spain, opinion is divided between two main groups: the first are satisfied with democracy at home and support the EU; the second look to the EU to compensate for the failings of democracy at home. And, lastly, in Denmark, West Germany, and Britain, public opinion is divided between two main groupings: the first are satisfied with democracy at home and support the EU; the second are satisfied with national democracy but disapprove of EU membership. No single explanation works across nations for even a majority of countries; support for the EU seems to be contingent on national circumstances.

European Citizens?

Nations are built upon the foundations of shared identity, common culture, and a sense of political community. These in turn are often (not always) based upon a common language, history, religion, community, a set of shared expectations about citizenship, and a common loyalty both to other citizens and to the state.

As an international or supranational organization the EU may find it specially difficult to build a European identity and consciousness. Not only is it made up of a dozen nation states, some very old, but it is divided by different languages, cultures, and histories. It has a northern and predominantly Protestant grouping of countries which faces the Atlantic, and a southern, Catholic group which faces the Mediterranean. It has been riven by conflict and war for many centuries, even within living memory.

Yet creating supranationalism in Europe in the 1980s and 1990s may not be quite the slow and difficult process that nation building was in earlier centuries. The mass media are a new and powerful element in the equation. Western Europe increasingly sees itself as an economic entity in the competition for world trade. It has a high population density, a high level of interaction, and it is laced together with one of the globe's most elaborate and advanced communications systems. The memory of the Second World War may be a driving force behind the creation of political efforts to prevent any such thing ever happening again. It remains a matter for empirical investigation, however, whether West Europeans are beginning to develop a sense of common identity.

Duchesne and Frognier investigate this matter in their chapter on European identity in *Public Opinion and Internationalized Governance*. In spite of fairly widespread enthusiasm for the EU, they find that relatively few people seem to regard themselves as 'European'. They are much more likely to identify with their nation, city, or locality. Indeed, only a small percentage say they belong to Europe before they belong to their country, region, or town. There is no indication that older nations are more likely to generate a sense of European identity than the younger ones, nor is there a positive or negative association between a sense of European citizenship and a sense of national pride— as there is no relationship between EU support and national pride.

It must also be admitted that it is notably difficult to measure a sense of European identity, or to capture it within the framework of a mass survey with closed ended questions. People have multiple identities and what sparks a sense of belonging to one or another is likely to depend very much on particular circumstances which cannot be captured readily by a formal questionnaire. Quite possibly this is an aspect of personal identity which is not best handled by mass surveys. Nevertheless, for what they are worth, the mass surveys do not suggest that a sense of European identity or citizenship is strongly developed in EU member nations.

Trust

Trust is the expectation that the behaviour of others will be friendly not harmful, and distrust the expectation that it will be harmful or unpredictable or both (Pruitt 1965). Since trust has been picked out as a particularly important basis on which to build common political action (Deutsch 1952; Inglehart 1991: 145–85; 1988), we can ask whether high and increasing levels of trust between West European nations forms the basis of popular support for the European project. The question can be answered by analysing responses to the Eurobarometer question: 'Now, we would like to ask about how much you would trust people from different countries. For each country please say whether, in your opinion, they are in general very trustworthy, fairly trustworthy, not particularly trustworthy, or not at all trustworthy.' The question was put to samples of citizens in all the member states of the EC in 1976, 1980, 1982, 1986, and 1990, although with some minor word changes at different times and in different countries.

In his chapter in Volume ii on trust between Europeans, Niedermayer finds that citizens of all twelve member states collectively place more trust than distrust in the people of all other member states (see Table 5.4). In 1990, EU citizens believed the most trustworthy people were Luxemburgers, Danes, Dutch, Belgians, and Germans. They believed the least trustworthy were the Greeks, Portuguese, British, and Italians. However, though feelings of trust are stronger than feelings of distrust, they do not overwhelm them. At the same time, comparison shows that EU citizens do not find their own fellow nationals a great deal more trustworthy than all other EU citizens. By these standards, trust between Europeans seems to be quite high.

Perhaps a better comparison is between the trust Europeans place in each other, and the trust they place in non-Europeans. The 1980 Eurobarometer found that West Europeans place much more trust in other West Europeans than in Russians, Japanese, and Chinese. Significantly for the earlier argument about ignorance, 29 per cent gave 'Don't know' answers for the Chinese (Inglehart 1991: 152).

Niedermayer finds that levels of trust within Europe rose between 1976 and 1990 (see Table 5.5). On the three-point scale, the aggregate score of the EC nine (the members in 1973) rose from 1.55 in 1976 to

TABLE 5.4. *Development of trust among the peoples of the European Community, 1976–90*

	1976	1980	1986	1990
Belgians	1.84	1.90	1.82	1.96
British	1.57	1.72	1.64	1.62
Danes	1.93	2.00	1.98	2.01
Dutch	1.94	1.97	1.94	1.97
French	1.54	1.60	1.63	1.83
Germans	1.68	1.76	1.75	1.84
Greeks	—	1.45	1.50	1.55
Irish	1.33	1.60	1.60	1.67
Italians	1.22	1.27	1.47	1.61
Luxemburgers	1.90	1.97	1.91	2.03
Portuguese	—	1.38	1.50	1.59
Spanish	—	1.42	1.53	1.72

Notes: Entries are EC-9 means. The figures are derived from the Eurobarometer question: 'Now, we would like to ask about how much you trust people in different countries. For each country please say whether, in your opinion, they are in general very trustworthy, fairly trustworthy, not particularly trustworthy, or not at all trustworthy.' A three-point scale was derived from these responses in which 0 indicates low levels of trust, and 3 high levels.

Sources: Eurobarometer, Nos. 6, 14, 25 and 33, as presented in Vol. ii, *Public Opinion and Internationalized Governance*, Table 10.2.

TABLE 5.5. *Levels of trust among nine member states of the EC, 1976–90*

	1976	1980	1986	1990
Level of trust (means)	1.55	1.63	1.66	1.75

Notes and source: See Table 5.4.

1.75 in 1990. The USIA surveys also asked trust questions in their surveys of the big four European nations in the 1950s and 1960s, and although they are not directly comparable with the Eurobarometer questions, it is significant that the USIA responses suggest less trust in the 1950s and 1960s than the Eurobarometer surveys in the 1970s and 1980s. It would seem, therefore, that levels of trust have gradually risen in Western Europe since the 1950s.

We should not place too much reliance on these figures. The very notion of measuring trust is problematic, and the Eurobarometer idea of capturing it on the basis of a single question which is then collapsed into a one-dimensional, three-point scale is riddled with potential problems. Even if one could measure its varied qualities and nuances, the relationship between trusting attitudes and trusting behaviour may not be close. Nevertheless, the relatively high and increasing levels of trust which members of the EU place in each other may help to explain why they support the EU and the idea of European unification.

Summary

It has been argued that mass opinion about international relations is too poorly informed to be taken seriously. International affairs are remote, often abstract and complex, so public opinion about them is likely to be guided by large measures of ignorance and prejudice. In this sense, it forms a good test case for the conclusion of the previous chapter that aggregate mass attitudes towards domestic politics are reasonably well structured, coherent, consistent, stable over time, and even subtle and sophisticated, up to a point.

The evidence suggests that public opinion about international affairs is not a prime example of the non-attitudes or doorstep opinions, for two main reasons. First, although the level of public information about international politics is by no means high, those who do not know enough to answer questions are inclined to exclude themselves by giving 'Don't know' or 'No response' answers. Those who do respond are generally able to give factually correct answers when asked to do so.

Secondly, although the general level of textbook knowledge about international events and organizations is not good, respondents seem to have a reasonable grasp of the main issues. Most European citizens do not know much about the structure and operations of the European Parliament, for example, but they understand that it suffers from a 'democratic deficit'. To use the terms of the previous chapter, they may not have 'factual information', but they are able to express 'opinion information'. Popkin (1991: 212–18) draws a similar distinction between what he calls 'textbook knowledge' and 'low-information rationality' or 'gut rationality'.

It can also be shown that large-scale and long-term shifts in public opinion about international affairs seem to be a response to events in the real world. Among other things, support for NATO dropped steeply after the collapse of the Soviet bloc (and then picked up again), and enthusiasm for the EU also declined sharply after the Maastricht troubles and the failure of the Exchange Rate Mechanism. Both

Maastricht and the ERM were difficult, technical issues, but the general public understood their general significance and reacted accordingly.

In short, public opinion on international matters, like public opinion on domestic politics, is not to be dismissed lightly. Whatever may have been the case in the early post-war years, we do not now find strong evidence to support Almond's (1950: 69) assertion that foreign policy attitudes lack intellectual structure. If anything they seem to show the sort of low-information, gut rationality discussed by Popkin.

One piece of evidence supporting this view is that factor analysis of mass survey responses to a set of questions about international affairs reveals an underlying structure and coherence. People take up the same sorts of policy positions with respect to different aspects of the EU, and they have a different set of policy positions with respect to NATO and US military deployment. The United Nations forms a third opinion set. In dealing with mass attitudes, therefore, there are empirical grounds for distinguishing between these three areas of international affairs.

Support for the EU, NATO, and the UN seems to be relatively high across Western Europe. There are substantial differences between nations, but support has also risen slowly and steadily over the past twenty years or so, particularly support for the EU. There is little evidence that West Europeans as a whole oppose international government as just another, possibly the worst, form of big government. On the contrary, public opinion no longer forms the 'permissive consensus' described by Lindberg and Scheingold (1970). There is a substantial weight of opinion in favour of international co-operation and integration, and in the long term this seems to be growing.

In the scholarly literature the main explanation for public opinion on foreign affairs is that it is largely the creation of internationally minded political élites—it is élite pulled rather than mass pushed. Although this is a notoriously difficult field of research, the chapters in *Public Opinion and Internationalized Governance* reveal rather little evidence to support the theory, at least in recent times.Wessels, who focuses on the question, finds evidence of both élite pull and mass push, but stronger statistical evidence to show that opinion 'bubbles up' from the masses, rather than 'trickling down' from élites.

It is possible that élite influence can be minimized by powerful intervening considerations, of which political parties are likely to be the most important. Significantly, Wessels finds that opinions about the EU cluster fairly tightly around political parties, in the sense that party programmes and party supporters take up much the same position with respect to the EU. Indeed, an association between political variables, particularly party variables, and attitudes towards political issues is one of the themes that runs throughout all the volumes of the Beliefs in Government project. In the case of EU support, however, Wessels finds that while opinion clusters around parties, the campaign efforts of parties reinforce the pre-existing views of their supporters rather than creating them.

Public opinion is neither a reflection nor a direct creation of parties; it has a life of its own. It is significant that in both Britain and Denmark, where party élites are deeply divided about the issue and unable to give a clear lead, public opinion is also relatively unenthusiastic about the EU. Which is cause and which effect, however, is a different question. USIA survey data show that British support for European unification was high in the 1950s, but declined after two failed attempts to join the EC, since when neither the main political parties nor the public have regained the strong consensus of the early years.

Élites may also have less influence over non-élites where the latter have first-hand experience of, and a direct interest in, political issues. In such instances, so the theory goes, citizens will act in their own self-interest, especially their own economic self-interest, since these are the most personal and the most powerful motivating forces. In other words, the influence of élites is less likely to prevail where people can see what is in their own immediate economic interest. Unfortunately, the theory fails to find much support in *Public Opinion and Internationalized Governance* which can supply rather little evidence of a systematic association between support for the EU and economic considerations—neither individual economic self-interest nor national economic interest.

The previous chapter found (patchy and circumstantial) evidence of sociotropic attitudes about the scope of government and the welfare state. The same seems to be true of attitudes towards the EU which most people see as both an economic organization and in more idealistic terms as a means for achieving peace and international co-operation. This, perhaps, explains why there is no close association between economic variables and support for the EU which is both affective and instrumental, specific and diffuse.

In this respect the EU is clearly seen to have a symbolic and ideal role as an agency of international or supranational government, and as such it seems to stand in contrast to, or even in competition with, the interests of nation states. Consequently, it has been argued, weak

nationalism is a precondition for the development of strong internationalist attitudes. However, some argue the reverse and claim that a
strong sense of national identity is a 'springboard' for internationalism. Once again, the evidence seems not to fit the theory. There is no
simple, clear, or direct association between measures of support for
European integration and the EU, on the one hand, and measures of
nationalism, national pride, or pride in national democracy, on the
other. Martinotti and Stefanizzi (Volume ii) find that both strong and
weak nationalism are associated with support for the EU, depending
on different circumstances in different countries. Nationalism and
Europeanism are not incompatible in principle, although they may
be in some countries, at some times, and in certain circumstances.

What makes the matter more puzzling is that growing support for
the EU and for European integration does not seem to be associated
with a developing sense of European identification. The great majority
of people say they belong to their country, city, or locality before
Europe, and the proportion thinking of themselves as Europeans first
is still very small. At the same time, there is evidence of a growing
sense of trust between Europeans, and mutual trust is said to be a
cornerstone of democratic co-operation. It is not clear which is cause
and which effect—are Europeans more inclined to co-operate within
the EU because they increasingly trust each other, or does trust grow
out of the practical experiences of co-operation, or both?

Whatever the answer, the evidence of *Public Opinion and Internationalized Governance* suggests a continuing cultural diversity
within Europe, but a growing political homogeneity. People continue
to identify with their nation, region, or locality. They continue to see
those from other nations, regions, and localities as different, but, more
importantly, they appear to feel increasingly able and willing to trust
and co-operate with them. What seems to matter is not a common or
uniform European culture or identity, but a growing sense of being
able to do political business with people who are different. In this
sense, current attempts to build up a common culture of European
citizenship, successful or otherwise, are largely irrelevant to European
political integration. What counts much more is the creation of a
common set of rules for handling cultural diversity, including a
capacity to trust others even though they are acknowledged to be
different.

Perhaps this is not surprising. Some nations, such as Switzerland
and the Netherlands, are characterized by cultural pluralism and by

peace and democratic stability. The co-operative nature of their government and politics is built upon a common understanding of the rules of the democratic game. We will take up this crucial matter of the rules of the democratic political game in the next chapter.

6

Citizens and the State

The Problem

After more than four decades of debate about liberal democracy it seemed for a while as though the world had come to at least a tacit agreement that the end of history (Fukuyama 1992) had indeed arrived. With the downfall of the Communist regimes of Central and Eastern Europe in 1989 all acceptable alternatives to the democratic constitutional state seemed to have been exhausted. And yet this impression probably owed more to the immediate shock of political events than to informed reason. Fukuyama's original article in *The National Interest* of 1989 soon provoked objections in the same journal, and these were followed by a thorough-going critique (Anderson 1992). On logical grounds alone, it is not possible to argue that all states will ultimately end as liberal democracies, and, in any case, the end of history argument does not claim that reverse transformations are not possible. Indeed, this would be inconsistent with evidence from the past and with Huntington's (1991) theory of the three waves of democratization.

However, a different point is being made here. There is some virtue in the idea that there is no serious alternative to the constitutional democratic state based upon individual rights and cultural, social, and political pluralism. But precisely for this reason the collapse of undemocratic regimes in Europe and elsewhere makes it all the more important to compare the various ways liberal democracies have organized themselves over the last two centuries or so. To do so is to discover whether some democracies have been noticeably more successful in coping with problems, producing favourable outcomes, and involving people in decision-making.

The breakdown of authoritarian and totalitarian regimes of both the left and the right may in fact already be making its mark on the way pluralist democracies look at themselves, although we cannot yet tell whether the precipitous decline of satisfaction with democracy in most EU member states since 1991 (Commission of the European Communities 1993*a*: 24) is part of a long-term trend. This decline, it should be added, is not only likely to stimulate public discussion about democracies in OECD countries, but may also lead to a new emphasis on research about differences in structures, procedures, and outcomes within developed democracies. We shall return to this point in the final chapter.

Following Dahl (1989: 220), polyarchies are treated as the present-day variant of democracy. They extend basic rights to virtually all their adult citizens and operate with constitutional and procedural arrangements which permit opposition and a change of governing élites. While there is no guarantee that polyarchies cannot return to totalitarian or authoritarian rule, the evidence suggests that a period of uninterrupted democracy, plus additional conditions such as the peaceful change of two governments (Huntington 1991: 266–7), is enough to consolidate democracy.

Since 1945 our sense of the specific conditions in which democracies thrive has been sharpened by contemplation of the totalitarian paths taken by Germany and Italy, the Second World War, and the terrifying experience of the holocaust. This has three major implications. First, while there are reasonably clear criteria of what democracy is and is not (Powell 1982: 2–7; Lijphart 1984: 37–40; Dahl 1989: 213–43; Vanhanen 1990: 17; Huntington 1991: 5–13), there are varying degrees of democracy. To phrase it differently, democracy is a variable, not a constant. In this respect the passage of time is a crucial factor since democracies may move on the democratic continuum. The concept and standards of democracy themselves may also change—what was regarded as democratically acceptable forty years ago, may not be so now. Secondly, democracy is a set of formal and informal rules which define the framework for the interactions between individuals and corporate actors. In other words, democracy is a process, and political outcomes are always the result of an exchange involving elements of the institutional (macro), the intermediate (meso), and the individual (micro) levels of socio-political organization. They can, therefore, only be fully understood if all levels of the system are considered simultaneously. Here, incidentally, lies the basic rationale of the need for *comparative* research which allows us to take account of macro-variables, at least in principle. Thirdly, while the nation state is a meaningful unit of analysis, if only for reasons of international law, it increasingly operates within an environment which is wider than national boundaries.

If one is willing to accept Dahl's concept of polyarchy as an institutionalized system of pluralistic competition which includes practically all members of the state and grants them basic rights, then the topic of this chapter immediately comes into focus—that is, the relationship between citizens and the state. The idea of making citizens of all adult members of the state, of giving them rights as well as duties, and allowing them to participate politically can be traced back through the medieval city of Italy to the Greek *polis*. What is sometimes forgotten, however, is that the Greeks were not inclusive but rather granted rights of full citizenship to only a small and privileged fraction of the population. In addition, citizenship was usually not open but ascribed by inheritance. While these limitations may have been necessary at the time, they became less and less necessary as the modern territorial state emerged. For it developed its own instruments of spatial integration, even though initially these were also designed to reflect élitist interests. Mainstream political science seems to agree that the idea of *representation* both preserved and transformed the classical idea of democracy. At the beginning of the nineteenth century it was impossible for a political philosopher such as James Mill to conceive that the people of Britain—or any comparable state—could participate, *en masse*, in government (Stimson and Milgate 1993: 902). Consequently, a system of representation had to be set up in which those defined as citizens with economic, legal, and social rights (Marshall 1963: 65–127) would elect representatives.

In such a system much turned on the definition and criteria of citizenship and voting rights, and it is understandable that a debate raged in the nineteenth century about these matters. Moreover, James Mill insisted that representation would only work if a common cognitive and emotional foundation for the political community and its interests could be created. With his emphasis on knowledge through education, he reiterated a theme which was also central to conservative republican thinking about democracy: the need for virtuous, responsible citizens (Dahl 1989: 24–8).

While it may be true that the idea of representation has saved democracy as the guiding ideology of the modern state, it is also true that the representative principle has caused a great many citizens to become structurally divorced from participation in day-to-day decision-making. Here lies a source of strain in contemporary democracies between states and their citizens. In itself, this is not a serious normative issue. People should and could participate in all public affairs were it not for the scale of the modern territorial state, which makes it impossible. Rather the problem lies in the notion that immediate and direct democracy without formal organization—and this includes representative organizations—is *a priori* inconceivable and unreal (Böckenförde 1991: 382–7; see also Budge 1993: 136–55). Other thinkers of the radical postmodernist school argue that representation *as such* is not possible because 'what is really interesting cannot be represented: ideas, symbols, the universe, the absolute, God, the just, or whatever. Representation is alien to what postmodernists value: the romantic, emotions, feelings. According to the sceptical postmodernists, representation is politically, socially, culturally, linguistically, and epistemologically arbitrary. It signifies mastery.' (Rosenau 1992: 94).

Not to side with either of these two extreme options is to accept the challenge to examine, over and over again, and in each new set of conditions, the balance of direct and indirect links between the citizen and the state, and to make it an *empirical question* which institutional arrangements optimize this balance in terms of creating and maintaining system legitimacy. In doing so, one need not be as sceptical as Sartori (1987: 113–14) who believes that 'real' citizen participation is impossible in the modern territorial state, because of inherent élitism and insuperable practical difficulties. Sartori argues that real participation works only in very small groups. (For a counter-example, see the concept of the planning cell developed by Dienel 1991.)

In the chapter that follows we discuss some of the core elements of the relationship between the state and its citizens before turning to the theoretical and empirical nature of the relationship.

The State

Long historical processes of change, development, and differentiation have embedded the concept of the state deeply in European political thinking (Sartori 1987: 53). In this context the state embraces that set of political institutions which is continuously concerned with the creation, implementation, and reinforcement of decisions related to the authoritative allocation of values in a given society.

The specific institutions of the state represent fixed structures with a highly ambivalent character. On the one hand, they are only one element of power-sharing in society which makes democracy possible at the outset (Rueschemeyer, Stephens, and Stephens 1992: 63–6). On the other hand, the enormous concentration of state power—what Weber terms *Gewaltmonopol* (coercive monopoly)—means that the control of the state and its power has also commanded attention from political thinkers. Montesquieu's solution to this problem of concentrated power was the separation of the executive, legislative, and judiciary, a typical example of the logic of internal division which provided a means of controlling the power of the almighty state *at the institutional level*. Even now the secret of a good and efficient constitution lies in its ability to balance these powers in a sophisticated and flexible manner.

Vanhanen's analysis places a balance of powers at the centre of his analysis of the conditions favouring the emergence of stable democracies: 'The process of democratization seems to follow the same basic rules in all countries. Political systems tend to democratize when important power resources become widespread and they tend to remain non-democratic as long as important power resources are concentrated in the hand of the few' (Vanhanen 1990: 194). The independent variables in Vanhanen's analysis are indicators of the *societal dispersion of power*; his central dependent variable concerns how election results show a spread of votes between more than one party. In other words, in his treatment of democratization he finds it sufficient to concentrate on *political* power-sharing within the legislative branch of government. In doing so, he recognizes with others (Castles and Wildenmann 1986; Katz 1987) that modern parliamentary democracies are based upon parties.

Vanhanen's approach to democratization is appealing because it is simple and straightforward. It also sufficed at a time when the important questions concerned why some countries did not become democratic although, in principle, they might well have done so, and vice versa. But, as the perspective shifts towards an examination of the details of different democratic arrangements *from the inside,* it is no longer enough to take the vote as the sole political input. Indeed, it will no longer suffice to concentrate on the input dimension at all.

Two examples will illustrate the point. In party democracies, the separation of power between the executive and the legislative may narrow, or even vanish almost completely, if the same party controls both branches of government. This is so even if the non-partisan part of the bureaucracy continues to be wedded to the idea of the neutral implementation of legislative decisions. In addition, even the judiciary is not completely independent, considering that in countries such as the United States and Germany, the selection of judges for constitutional courts is to some extent a partisan matter. The same applies to the filling of élite positions in the public media. As a result, party penetration of different institutions of the system tends to bring together those things which were designed to be independent.

The second example comes from federal systems in which there is a vertical separation of powers between federal and state government. In these systems there is a need for integration of policy and effort which produces a set of new bureaucracies, which Scharpf and his co-workers (1976) aptly identify in terms of *Politikverflechtung* or policy linkage. An example in the German case is provided by the constitutional obligation of the *Länder* to create equality of living conditions. Of course, some sort of vertical integration between federal and state government must be maintained, but the point is that the bureaucratic links which meet this need are not always accessible to the public or even to parliamentary control.

The more differentiated a political system becomes the more likely its decision-making capacities are to be hampered. Scharpf (1985) has coined the term *Politikverflechtungsfalle*, or policy-linkage trap, to describe this phenomenon. This *structural* problem contributes to the complaint, so often voiced in modern Western democracies, that political decisions are either not made, or require an inordinate amount of time and effort to make. If this feeling is then aggravated by the belief that the political decision-making process is no longer accessible to the general public, then a threat to the legitimacy of the system cannot be ruled out.

Nevertheless, the divisions and internal differentiations of modern democracies are among their major hallmarks. Following a distinction drawn by Easton (1965; 1975) between the objects and the modes of political orientations, recent political science has found that citizens do indeed distinguish between politicians as office holders, and the offices they hold. (For good summary statements and empirical analysis, see Fuchs 1989, and Westle 1989.) Although comparative analysis is somewhat hampered by lack of data, it also emphasizes that a particular strength of democratic systems is their ability to separate the partisan level from a non-partisan one.

The separation between authorities and regime (the third Eastonian level of political community need not concern us here) reflects perfectly the central logic of democratic politics: pluralist competition for government is institutionalized on the authority level, but is regulated by the non-partisan procedures and rules on the regime level. Regarding political authorities, Luhmann (1986: 75–88, 167–82) points out that all functionally differentiated systems organize their subsystem communication through basic bipolar codes. In politics this code is that of the government and opposition. If one shares Luhmann's view of the essential importance of such codes, then the question for any democracy is how well it meets the demands of clarity created by its code at the level of political authorities. One conclusion, for example, might be that the systems which Lijphart (1984) calls majoritarian are well equipped to satisfy expectations created in the public mind by the government–opposition code (Powell 1989). That is to say, voters who are able to choose between parties which are capable of forming governments on their own, and which have clearly defined programmes, should be more satisfied with their political system than those where coalition government does not produce such a clear-cut set of electoral consequences and where government policy is the result of coalition bargaining.

When we argued earlier that the internal structures and procedures of democracies should be compared with greater theoretical sophistication and in more empirical detail, this idea also entailed the notion of functional equivalents. Rarely have modern democratic systems been designed on a blackboard or to a blueprint. Perhaps the post-war constitutions of Germany and Japan are exceptions. Nevertheless, different systems achieve similar democratic qualities through the use of varied institutional arrangements. Therefore, it may be that there are functional equivalents to the mechanisms created by majoritarian systems to achieve voter satisfaction. In the case of Switzerland, with its national multiparty coalition governments, the far-reaching plebiscites at cantonal and local level come to mind.

The whole logic of Luhmann's coherent argument about the operation of bipolar codes rests on various implicit or explicit considerations, only three of which need be discussed here. First, the principle of the alternation between government and opposition depends on the willingness of the general population to accept government policies whatever the colour of the party or parties in power. Even though these policies can be enforced by the legitimate coercive monopoly of the state, it is a popular willingness to accept them which matters and, as Huntington (1991: 266–7) rightly argues, this cannot be taken for granted. For this reason he requires that at least two peaceful changes of government are achieved before democracy is consolidated. In other words, citizens are willing to accept the *regime* even if they do not like the government or its policies. (See Klosko 1993: 354–6, for an interesting twist of this argument in the context of a critique of Rawls 1971.) However, if the institutions, values, and norms of the regime are doubted, then the stability of the whole political system is called into question. At the very least it is possible that citizens who did not vote for the government will not regard themselves as bound by its decisions.

The second point is that the binary government–opposition code has an explicit political meaning which is reflected in the political programmes of the parties forming the government and the programme of the government itself. The programmes of the parties and of the government are not necessarily congruent (Klingemann, Hofferbert, and Budge 1994). Luhmann (1986: 169–74) recognizes the need for a link between those who exercise political power to create binding decisions, and the programme from which such decisions are derived. In his view, political power and political programmes can be brought together by secondary binary codes. He names two; conservative versus progressive, and contractionist versus expansionist views of the state.

Empirical research has shown (Fuchs and Klingemann 1989) that both secondary codes are embedded in a general yardstick which is known as the left–right dimension. This is not to say that the dimension applies equally well to all political systems (in the United States the equivalent is the liberal–conservative dimension), or that it covers the whole of the political agenda or all voters. Nevertheless, it is the only abstract principle which helps organize coherent political programmes, on the one hand, and the belief systems of mass publics, on the other.

The problem, however, is that the left–right schema owes its existence very much to the sort of social and political situation in which emerging industrial societies were dominated by class cleavage. This is still clearly reflected in the present-day meaning most people attach to the schema (see Fuchs and Klingemann 1989). But the left–right binary subcode has gradually been losing its grip both *within and between party electorates*. It has done so as a result of voter dealignments, changing social conditions, an increase in issue voting, the politicization of the electorate, the internationalization of government, and the emergence of new (and often international) issues, such as the environment and international security. This has created confusion within the electorate when it comes to making programmatic choices between parties and governments, and it will no doubt continue to do so in the future. There are two obvious consequences of this development. First, ties between parties and their supporters will become progressively weaker. Secondly, there will be a greater tendency for people to turn from the vote and to opt for issue-specific forms of political involvement. We will return to this later in the chapter.

The third point about Luhmann's argument concerns the growing internationalization of government, which may be said to be a two-sided phenomenon. The first refers to the global trend towards the internationalization of the political agenda—peace-keeping, the environment, trade, economic development, international aid, migration, security. Secondly, the growing powers and scope of the European Union and the growth of the international political agenda both operate to lessen the accountability of national governments. As such they represent another potential threat to the legitimacy of national authorities and—in the long run—to democratic regimes in general.

The blurring of accountability of governments to their people can be remedied in various ways. However, in the context of the European Union, the problems of *Politikverflechtung*, or policy linkage, between up to four levels of government (European, national, regional, and local) may be severe. Besides, the democratic deficit of the European Parliament may be even more problematic. But there is more even than this to the accountability problem. In the 1960s and 1970s analysts and politicians alike seemed to assume the state should extend its reach further and further. The consequence, as we saw in Chapter 4, was the unprecedented growth in the scope of government, especially its social expenditures between 1950 and 1970. The latter accounted for much of the increase in the state's share of GNP (Flora 1988: xxii) which approached the 45 per cent level by about 1980.

At that time many expected this share to continue rising. As economic growth continued so it was anticipated that the state would continue its journey from social state to all-embracing welfare state (Luhmann 1981). As we have already seen in Chapter 2, some writers argued that this would result in public waste and increasing citizen dissatisfaction. Depending on their normative position, some predicted a crisis of ungovernability (Rose 1980) or a crisis of legitimacy (Offe 1972).

As it turned out, neither of these crises materialized. Instead, the structural economic problems of OECD nations in the 1990s forced them to manœuvre unhappily between the Scylla of financial contraction and the Charybdis of trying to stimulate economic growth and employment. With these financial problems came increasing pressures from the electorate, although the political context changed drastically. There now seems to be a general agreement in OECD nations that solutions to some of the most pressing economic problems cannot come from the state. New agents are now held responsible for curing economic ills, including private sector economic élites, trade unions, and even individuals.

It is not clear in 1995 how this situation will develop. The scarcity of resources caused by structural economic stagnation in Western Europe seems to have created an awareness of the *specifics* of the conditions under which the state can or cannot grow. Similarly, as Volume iii of Beliefs in Government shows, it has raised the question in the public mind of priorities for public policy—or to put it a different way, of how the state should grow or contract. Two consequences of the situation are already visible.

First, the revolution of rising expectations has been halted as far as both individual wealth and public benefits are concerned. Contrary to the claims of the 'crisis of legitimacy' school, they have been reduced, sometimes to below previous levels. Quite apart from a rising number of poor people, large minorities seem to be experiencing a falling standard of living, and this for the first time in three or four decades. At the same time, this seems to have been accommodated without impairing general allegiance to the democratic system. Secondly, the state and especially local authorities are now looking hard for ways to economize on services by privatizing and turning to market competition. Public investments in things like sport, culture, and leisure have been cut, or even abandoned, and turned into individual responsibilities.

It is too early to see how the economic problems of citizens and of the state will be resolved, but there is one aspect of the matter which deserves special attention here because it concerns the matter of government accountability. Voting studies have tried to discover whether people vote more on past experience (retrospective voting) than future expectations (prospective voting), but research has generally been inconclusive on the matter (Kiewit and Rivers 1985). However, it seems that this is not due to a lack of aptitude or assertiveness on the part of most citizens. Indeed, in the preceding two chapters it has been argued that mass survey evidence for West European citizens shows them to be able to make sensible judgements about government and politics. Rather it seems that the degree to which voters are unwilling to hold governments clearly accountable for their past economic record is a sensible response to the difficulties of telling what the outputs and impacts of government policy are.

This is neither surprising nor irrational behaviour on the part of voters. After all, comparative policy research has been notoriously weak at measuring the effects of policy, its successes and failures. As long as the connection between government programmes and policy outputs and impacts is not reliably demonstrated it is understandable that voting behaviour will be necessarily based upon frail judgements. Needless to say, this kind of situation—*ceteris paribus*—is likely to create voter frustration.

Recent studies (Putnam 1993; Lijphart 1994; Klingemann, Hofferbert, and Budge 1994; see also Sharpe and Newton 1983) have emphasized how much politics matter for policy outcomes. Findings of this kind should stimulate more research. Indeed, if there is anything at all to classical democratic arguments about accountability, and the ability of citizens to 'vote the rascals out', political outputs should be a more important focus of research. There are difficulties, however. While some policy output measures form reasonably reliable and objective yardsticks by which to judge government performance, others are highly contestable, and none are beyond dispute and different interpretations. Nevertheless, the *comparative* evaluation of outputs across democratic polities should carry considerable weight, as indeed they increasingly do in scholarly research and, to some extent in the mass media, among politicians, and in political parties. The reasons for this development are many, but three should be mentioned here.

First, the ability of open societies to observe and evaluate themselves has been made easier by modern techniques of data collection and compilation, including survey research. In addition, the comparative treatment of data, including those relating to government outputs, has been made easier by the increased communication between countries and by the attempts to standardize both objective and subjective indicators. Secondly, media technology has made it possible to internationalize the news, and to make it cheap, easy, and fast to communicate. As a result audiences can make their own comparisons across countries, including comparisons of government performance. Thirdly, and probably most importantly, OECD countries have followed similar paths of development in recent years, and are now confronted by common problems with common origins and consequences. This has led to a substantial convergence of opinion among governments, parties, and mass publics about how to assess the important problems of the day. Political controversy no longer rages over what the issues are or what the goals should be, but over the best means to achieve an agreed agenda. In the term coined by Butler and Stokes over twenty years ago (Butler and Stokes 1969: 189), the emergence of *valence politics* in OECD countries makes it easier for mass publics to compare their own countries with others in the OECD group. Thus, it encourages people to look at the experience of other countries, including the party composition of governments, as a way of trying to understand their own government's performance.

We have looked at the state first in this chapter because of its 'black box' nature. That is, many aspects of the state's decision-making processes are obscured from the public and becoming more so. This is just as true for those who participate directly in the decision-making process. When contrasted with the classical, blueprint model of an open democratic society, this situation must make the relationship between state and government, on the one hand, and citizens, on the other, a problematic one.

The problem used to be less acute in earlier political times when universal electoral participation was still not fully achieved, when the state had not been transformed into the all-embracing welfare state, and when the vote was thought to be the proper and most democratic way of linking citizens to the political system. In those days voter options were well defined yet limited and constrained by institutional arrangements like electoral laws and the oligopolistic structure of competitors in the political market. Besides, electoral participation demanded relatively little from citizens in terms of involvement and information. As a result, voting was thought to be important because it endorsed the democratic rights of citizens and, at the same time, changed or reinstated governments—the ultimate sanction in the power game of politics.

State–citizen relations have not operated in this simple way for some time now. The objective circumstances of both have changed, and so also have the subjective feelings of citizens. Though sometimes unnoticed, state and government bureaucracies have grown vastly in size, complexity, reach, and power. New institutions have changed the composition of the democratic state and, not least, shifted the balance of power between legislatives and executives in favour of the latter. It is no accident that the judiciary is assuming a more influential role in the legislative process, one example being the major *institutional* role played by the European Court in fostering European integration. And last, the eclipse of communism requires a closer scrutiny of the way in which democracies function and the outcomes they generate. This is the state side of the state–citizen coin, which the Beliefs in Government project has not examined, except in a contextual fashion.

But there is also the citizen side of the coin, and citizens too have changed both in their objective life situations and in their subjective views of the political world. We can speak of these changes with a great deal of authority as a result of the Beliefs in Government research.

Citizens

According to conservative republicanism, the democratic citizen is a virtuous citizen who is wedded to the commonwealth of the people. This normative claim made most sense in a political system where all citizens had an equal say, and where numbers were small enough to permit everyone to participate. In the city state who was and was not a citizen was a matter of controversy, but in modern democracies the idea that universal adult suffrage should be granted to all adult members of a nation has laid the issue of 'who are the people' to rest.

While the idea of a virtuous and benevolent citizenry has never been relinquished, at least explicitly, the fathers of the American Constitution were sufficiently aware of human frailties to design a constitution around them. Their system of institutional checks and balances tried to minimize the potential impact of those who failed to live up to the ideal. This made it easy to deny citizens formal political rights only in exceptional circumstances such as mental illness or grave criminal offence: the rest were permitted and encouraged to perform whatever constitutional rights their system granted them. It is easy to forget that this crucial requirement of modern democracy was established less than a hundred years ago in some European nations, more recently in others, and has not yet been achieved in many parts of the globe. As a result, it is not surprising that the right to vote—the big political equalizer—is regarded as an important condition for system consolidation in the newly established democracies, and as both blessing and obligation for citizens.

At the same time, a brief look at past writings also shows a strong thread of scepticism about the political wisdom of the average citizen. This was probably most pronounced among the critics of modern mass society (notably Ortega y Gasset) whose doubts were fuelled by the rise of authoritarian and totalitarian governments in some democracies in the twentieth century. It was further encouraged by social science research in the late 1940s onwards which seemed to provide hard empirical evidence about the shortcomings of voters. (For an outstanding and influential example, see Converse 1964.) As a consequence, arguments about the role of élites for stabilizing democracy gained currency. One influential argument in this school of thought was Schumpeter's notion of democracy as a form of government in which the mass of ordinary citizens were restricted, more or less, to the role of choosing between competing élites.

That élitist theory came under heavy fire from proponents of participatory democracy (Pateman 1970) is now history. This version of democracy, based on Rousseau and John Stuart Mill, views political participation not only as a means of arriving at decisions, but also as an end in itself which develops the democratic personality. There is no need to discuss this particular perspective in any detail here (it has been considered in a more critical fashion by Sartori 1987: 111–14), but we will consider two specific aspects of participatory democracy requiring attention.

We have already pointed out that Schumpeterian democracy is minimalist. It requires only an electoral system and a party system which enables voters to make a choice between competing parties for the purpose of choosing a government. At the same time, voters are required to have that minimal level of information necessary to make the choice, and to exercise their voting right.

When political cleavages were relatively few and simple in twentieth-century democracies (Lipset and Rokkan 1967; Lijphart 1984), voting decisions were also relatively easy. The political world was clearly organized and people belonged to one of a few classes, groups, or *Lager*. Issues were unequivocally divided between the left and right (Downs 1957; Bartolini and Mair 1990: 65), and the intensity of political feeling was enough to encourage high voting turnouts.

With the breakdown of old cleavages and the emergence of new conflicts, the transparency and simplicity of politics has come to an end. The enormous increase in individual wealth in OECD nations since the 1950s (Lane, McKay, and Newton 1991: 48–63), the educational revolution, and the development of new media technologies, particularly television, have all weakened traditional politics and its parties. What are the consequences of these changes?

On the one hand, Bartolini and Mair (1990) have shown that this process has not produced the increased voter volatility predicted by some of the theories discussed in Chapter 2. This is all the more surprising since the reduced policy distances between parties discovered by Bartolini and Mair make volatility more, rather than less, likely. They attribute the outcome to a decrease in institutional incentives favouring volatility and even to a small increase in the degree to which the electorate is anchored by the parties. The latter point is important because it emphasizes the organizational and ideological role of parties and of party–interest group links, a point to which we will return in the next chapter because it is also a central conclusion of the Beliefs in Government research programme.

It is a different question to ask how long stability of party–voter relationships will last. The decreasing distances between parties found by Bartolini and Mair (1990: 193–211, 302–7) may be understood in terms of attitudinal data about party dealignment. (For the German case, see Dalton and Rohrschneider 1990.) The claims made for value change which now date back twenty years in the social science community seem to have found a clear expression in the growth of Green parties, as Müller-Rommel has shown (1993: 163–5). The question for research must be, therefore, how long parties in general, particularly traditional parties, will be able to maintain a stable following among voters.

One part of the answer to this question concerns the adaptability of parties to the issue of the environment as a new political concern (see especially the chapter by Roller in Volume iii). The strains placed upon the parties of the traditional left by the emergence of postmaterialism and the Greens is clearly visible in the conflict between the old and the new left. At the same time, the growing ideological heterogeneity of party followers and the rise of issue voting casts serious doubt on the ability of voters to express *specific* preferences through the vote, and about the ability of parties to aggregate these preferences into a coherent programme.

Research on the 1960s and 1970s shows that rising mass scepticism about political parties was not the only source of public doubt about contemporary government and politics (Crozier, Huntington, and Watanuki 1975; Lipset and Schneider 1987). At that time, the movement of opinion across organizations and across countries suggested that there must have been more general factors at work which reached beyond the specific issues of party politics and party government—factors that impinged on the way individuals reacted to their political world.

However, the general trends of the late 1960s and 1970s did not continue into the 1980s. Listhaug and Wiberg's chapter in Volume i shows that confidence in institutions during that decade was a mixture of stability in some countries, and increases and decreases in others. Certainly confidence in social and political institutions did not generally continue to decline. It is tempting to conclude that the decline of the earlier period was the result of a general change in the political outlook of people and—behind that—of the spread of television.

Because the trend in television ownership was fairly inconspicuous at first, systematic research on the impact of this truly revolutionary innovation was rather neglected. One of the rare studies at the time was undertaken by Elisabeth Noelle-Neumann (1988) who conducted a controlled field experiment on the impact of newly acquired television sets in Germany in 1966–7. The somewhat shaky statistical basis of this research (only 336 households were studied) would probably have doomed it to oblivion long ago, had it not been for the way it documents remarkable changes in people's orientations after they had acquired a television set.

First, those who had acquired television became more interested in politics. Secondly, and more importantly, their views about politics changed depending on patterns of newspaper readership. For regular readers of newspapers the 'political' character of politics was emphasized—it was seen to be more complex and more difficult to understand. Casual newspaper readers, in contrast, saw politics as easier to understand, more stimulating, and more entertaining. If one adds to this Ranney's conclusion that television has the effect of compressing time and making political events move faster, then it is at least plausible to argue that television has had a substantial impact on the electorate's view of politics and, most likely, on the political process at large as well.

Lack of comparable research makes it risky to generalize such findings to other times and nations, but in the West German case the conclusion that television causes an increase in political interest is corroborated by other work (Noelle-Neumann and Köcher 1993: 617–18; Berg and Kiefer 1992: 166). Dalton (1988: 23) has also shown an increased political interest in France, Britain, and the United States, and although the increase is less clear than in Germany, it seems to be associated with television. The question, however, is what are the meanings and consequences of this increase in political interest.

As early as 1977 Inglehart (1977*b*: 291–2) spoke of the rising levels of cognitive mobilization of Western electorates and attributed this to the spread of education and the media. Nevertheless, the question is whether better education and growing media penetration are sufficient to account for the higher levels of mass political sophistication.

There is little reason to question the logical connection between education, media coverage of the news, and mass political knowledge, but the situation is more complex than this. In the first place, it is useful to distinguish between political facts or information, on the one hand, and political knowledge on the other. The term 'political knowledge', as used here, entails an ability to understand and integrate facts into a coherent, general scheme. Education and information are necessary but not sufficient conditions for political information. There is a lot of research on political information, much less on political knowledge, which makes it difficult to study the subject properly. However, Noelle-Neumann (1988: 230) does not find evidence of rising levels of political knowledge in Germany, and her findings fit well with Neumann's (1986: 170–8). He sees the US electorate as more or less permanently separated into three distinctive political strata: the apoliticals, about 20 per cent of the total; the mass public, about 75 per cent; and the activists, about 5 per cent. Although Neumann does not elaborate on the point, it seems that there is little movement between strata, so that across time the proportion in each remains fairly constant. Consequently, while political learning may occur and the *level* of political sophistication may increase, this will not change the overall *distribution* even if the information gap between groups is altered. In some ways this is reminiscent of the knowledge gap hypothesis originally formulated by Tichenor, Donohue, and Olien (1970). This says that the more information available in society, the proportionately greater the amount absorbed by those with the resources to do so, and the greater the knowledge gap between them and those without these resources.

The tensions caused by the growing complexity of the modern world and by the increasing amount of knowledge necessary to deal with it is not easily coped with by most citizens. It is a problem which will be resolved mainly through social differentiation and an increasingly refined division of labour. The important role of experts, specialist committees, and interest group specialists speaks to this point. It is impossible even for legislators to command the knowledge necessary to make enlightened decisions across the wide array of topics they have to deal with.

This argument must not be misread to mean that the average voter has no way of assessing political matters. We have reiterated at various points in this book V. O. Key's dictum that voters are not fools, and provided evidence to support the view. But it must also be said that this depends on the kind of low-information rationality (Popkin 1991), which, for lack of close or regular contact with the political world, necessarily thrives on information provided by the mass media.

The inevitable political division of labour which information overload induces leads us straight back to the dilemma of representation which was discussed earlier in the chapter. An important qualifying element which we may now include, however, concerns the observation that increasing cognitive mobilization and politicization may combine to produce selective engagement in different modes of political action.

For much of the twentieth century most political participation by most people has been confined to voting and to activities, such as campaigning, related to elections. The long battle for equal voting rights made the ballot box an important symbol of democracy. But there was more to the vote than symbolism. Even if modified and moulded by the electoral rules of the game, the electorate determined which parties and élites formed the government until the next election. In this sense, high turnout was rightly regarded as an indicator of the legitimacy of the exercise.

In the 1920s and 1930s the 99.9 per cent votes in authoritarian and totalitarian regimes injected a note of caution into interpretations of high voting turnout. In democracies, however, there was never any doubt about the meaning of the vote: to change or maintain governments. Not least in the context of the legitimacy crisis debate in the 1970s, it was also suggested that a long-term decline in voting might signal the crisis of democracy that many social scientists, especially on the political left, were looking for. But even in the early 1970s no such general fall in turnout could be detected (Dittrich and Johansen 1983). And more recent work by Topf in Volume i which extends research into the 1990s has failed to find evidence of a general fall in turnout rates across Western Europe on the whole. Equally, there is also no evidence to suggest that increasing levels of cognitive mobilization have caused voting rates to increase. Of course, this is retrospective analysis which may overlook the possibility of future change. Meanwhile, however, it seems that the 1970s and 1980s were marked not so much by turnout change, but by more general trends which formed what has been called a participatory revolution (Kaase 1982).

Inglehart was the first to notice what he called 'the silent revolution': a secular shift in the value preferences of mass Western publics away from the traditional concerns with physical security and economic well-being and towards non-material matters such as self-realization and political participation. Later research showed a fairly pervasive trend of this kind which was mainly of a generational nature (Inglehart 1990; Inglehart and Abramson 1994). However, because of the ranking measurement procedures used by Inglehart, it seems most likely that he has missed the most important ingredient of value change: the 'old' materialist values were not completely displaced by the new ones, but rather were added to them in a process of value synthesis (Klages 1988: 112–47). In fact, if a rating rather than a ranking procedure is used, the largest group of voters in West Germany (44 per cent) were high on both materialist and non-materialist values (Maag 1991: 116). Research using the Eurobarometer surveys and reported in Volume iii suggests that the same sort of change has occurred across member states of the European Union. It seems that one core element of the process of value change over the past two decades or so has been the integration of traditional and modern values.

Much of the criticism of Inglehart is based on the claim that he considers not values but political issue preferences. While this may be a major shortcoming for some purposes, it turns out to be an advantage for political scientists. This is because the Inglehart measures relate directly to politics and political policies and hence to the potential conflict between the 'old' and 'new' political agendas (Baker, Dalton, and Hildebrandt 1981).

The intellectual appeal of Inglehart's speculations (in the early 1970s they were little more than that) made his measures a logical choice for the Political Action study. As it turned out, the strong relationship between postmaterialist values and positive attitudes towards unconventional political behaviour, as well as the behaviour itself, made it clear that these were not a passing phase. In fact, we have argued in Chapter 3 that direct, highly visible, and unconventional forms of participation have become one of the most pervasive trends in political behaviour in OECD countries.

Initial criticism was directed at the decision of Political Action to study not just behaviour but *attitudes towards political action* (Budge

1981). Later this decision delivered rich returns. It allowed research to observe the growing *repertory* of different forms of political action, and at the same time it sharpened awareness of the ways that different contexts convert preparedness for action into action itself. The distinction between a potential for action (favourable attitudes) and action (behaviour) also provided a fresh focus on political mobilization. At the same time, it created a theoretical bridge between research on political participation and on the new social movements (Dalton and Küchler 1990).

From the beginnings, research was concerned with different dimensions of participation, although this was as much a matter of theory as empirical research. Initially, writers like Milbrath (1965) saw only one dimension because they concentrated on elections and campaign participation. Later work suggested four dimensions; voting, campaigning, communal activities, and particularized contacts (Verba and Nie 1972; Verba, Nie, and Kim 1978). The Political Action study (Barnes, Kaase, *et al.* 1979) extended these notions from institutional participation to direct action. It argued that there are two broad aspects of political behaviour—conventional and unconventional. Both were assessed empirically by Guttman scaling techniques because of the underlying theoretical logic of asking how far a respondent was willing to go on each of these dimensions.

More recent research (Uehlinger 1988; Parry, Moyser, and Day 1992) has not disproved the Political Action approach but has further refined it (as suggested by Muller 1979 some time ago). The single dimension of direct action has now been separated into three subdimensions: problem-specific direct action which is legal; civil disobedience (illegal direct action which does not involve physical violence); and political violence. We have already argued that research shows that the distinction between attitudes towards political action and political action itself is both theoretically meaningful and empirically valid. Analysis of the twelve EU countries (Kaase 1992) indicates that a *preparedness* to turn to legal direct action has spread widely in public opinion, although there is a wide gap between attitudes and action. This finding speaks both to the broad legitimacy these modes of participation have achieved, and to the fact that there is no direct bridge between a mode being in the repertory and being actually used. But there can be no doubt that the citizens of OECD democracies have now added uninstitutionalized ways of influencing politics to their use of electoral powers. The repertory of political action has expanded.

One of the problems here is that there is no clear-cut line dividing legal political action from civil disobedience in democratic polities. The definition of both is surrounded by ambiguity and the distinction is culturally specific. As a result, the expansion of the political repertory has caused tensions and conflict, a state of affairs which is aggravated by an increasingly subjective definition of political reality on the part of some activists (Blumenthal *et al.* 1972: 71–95; see also Kaase and Neidhardt 1990: 41–55).

As a consequence, modern society will have to confront the problem of political groups which move between legal and illegal action to make their voice heard. While this is a formidable challenge to modern democracy, the quantitative, though not qualitative difficulty is eased by the fact that a willingness to contemplate direct or illegal action is not spread across the whole population. Rather, the tendency is strongest among the young, the better educated, those on the left, post-materialists, and the politically active (Kaase 1992; Parry, Moyser, and Day 1992: 223–4). The behaviour of this section of the population might be counterbalanced by the capacity of established organizations (parties and trade unions) to mobilize traditional politics (Verba, Nie, and Kim 1978). However, if the capacity of these organizations to mobilize continues to decline, then the chances are that direct political action of various types will have a bigger impact on the political agenda and political decisions.

Empirical research on this topic is inconclusive because decision-making is not easily examined. The study by Verba and Nie (1972: 299–33) indicates that participation at the community level does matter, but because the agenda of activists differs from that of other citizens, there is a tendency for outcomes to be biased. A later study by Parry and his colleagues (1992: 264) does not reach quite the same conclusion. Nevertheless, we should keep in mind the fact that the willingness to consider or actually to use a wider range of political action is not distributed equally among all members of modern society. The consequence may be inequality of political influence.

Citizens and the State

The relationship between the state and its citizens is a *dynamic* one. The pervasive growth of state expenditure and public employment in the post-war period has increased the amount of state–citizen interaction, even though this still consumes only a minuscule part of daily life. Unfortunately, research on citizen encounters with public bureaucracies has been sporadic, and comparative studies over time are particularly lacking. What research there is suggests that most contact concerns a specific problem, such as unemployment (Katz *et al.* 1975: 21), and, therefore, a specific problem group. In addition, it is an open question whether citizens see their various contacts with local, regional, and national government as contacts with the state at all, and whether these contacts have a *general* impact on the way they see the state. Finally, and most importantly, research on the quality of life has shown time and time again that politics is of peripheral importance compared with other areas of life (for German research, see Glatzer and Zapf 1984: 199; for the EU countries, see Commission of the European Communities 1993*a*, A48).

This turns out to be a mixed blessing for the state. On the one hand, the distance between most citizens and politics makes them less vulnerable to the vicissitudes of political life. This helps to explain the relatively high levels of political satisfaction which we have found in the Beliefs in Government research. While people tend to attribute their successes to themselves and their failures to others, the distance between the citizen and the state makes it unlikely that failures in people's personal lives will be blamed too quickly on the latter, as against institutions which are more closely integrated in the everyday life of citizens. Thus the dominance of the private over the public helps to buffer the political system from the effects of short-term, personal, and idiosyncratic dissatisfactions.

On the other hand, it is exactly this distance which encourages stereotyped perceptions of politics and which makes people dependent upon the media, which tends to be negative in its reporting (see Kaase 1994: 230, on the German case). This may explain why the Eurobarometer studies find that people are substantially more satisfied with their personal life than with public affairs and the way democracy works in their country (Commission of the European Communities 1993*b*: 1–36). More than seventy years ago, Lippman (1922) wrote about how the media might influence public perceptions of politics in this way. It seems that the gap between personal and public satisfaction is now so consistent in different countries at different times that the explanation cannot lie in the changing performance of governments in particular countries and at particular times.

On occasion, spectacular events send shock waves through a political system which affect political sentiments for a time, after which politics

return to 'normal'. Such phenomena are different from long-term underlying shifts of attitudes. For example, we have observed in various parts
of this book that some critics of late capitalism anticipated an irreversible revolution of rising expectations which, because the state could not
sustain it, would result in a legitimacy crisis and the loss of democratic
allegiance. As we have seen in Chapters 3 and 4, the Beliefs in Government research has shown that this was not the case, at least until 1990.

But this is itself a perplexing finding which needs explanation. We can
point to two possibilities. First, dissatisfaction may have been focused at
the level of political authorities, thereby deflecting it from the level of the
democratic regime. Secondly, political parties have changed to accommodate the rising expectations of citizens. For example, the participatory
demands of women have resulted in female quotas for leadership positions. Furthermore, parties have changed their platforms in response to
new demands and issues (Klingemann 1986; Budge, Robertson, and Hearl
1987; Laver and Budge 1993; Klingemann, Hofferbert, and Budge, 1994;
Klingemann and Volkens 1995). In sum, parties, in common with other
organizations and institutions, are like living organisms which change in
order to cope with new pressures in their environment.

To the best of our knowledge, there is no comparative literature
which documents in detail the changes in state structures and procedures over the past forty years. While it seems reasonable to assume
that they have occurred, it is also difficult to assess the extent to which
they are a response to internal or external stimuli, and what role citizen
demand has played as an external stimulus.

The minimal hypothesis which the Beliefs in Government research
sustains is that changes in public attitudes and beliefs seem to have
resonated with state actors and agencies (see Chapters 4 and 5). Nevertheless it remains true that longitudinal evidence linking states and
citizens is not available, so the impact of one on the other cannot be
systematically examined. We must also be wary of circular reasoning
which assumes that the continuing high levels of state legitimacy must
be due to change and flexibility of both states and citizens. Given the
limitations of present evidence, therefore, it seems best to treat the
mutual interdependence of state and citizens not as a conclusion but
as a hypothesis guiding future research.

In our earlier reflections upon the state we emphasized the central
role of the government–opposition mechanism in the generation and the
management of political conflict. Curiously, the ungovernability thesis
about pluralist (or hyperpluralist) politics treats this same mechanism as

the driving force behind the rising spiral of expectations, which, because they cannot be satisfied, end up draining the system of its legitimacy. This seems to be based upon a rather mechanical conception of politics which overlooks two important points: parties are not fools, and voters are not fools. With growing recognition of the scarcity of resources, the populations of West European democracies have grudgingly accepted the fact that public priorities must change, even perhaps that real personal incomes will stagnate or fall for a while.

This may yet create severe problems for West European political systems. For example, the recent decline of economic performance in EU member states coincides with a rather spectacular decline in political legitimacy in those countries (Commission of the European Communities 1993a: 24, A14). Although we are unable to establish a causal link between economic stress and political legitimacy, we can note a similar occurrence in 1982 in West Germany before the Schmidt socialist–liberal coalition fell apart after a poor economic showing. However, a similar performance on the part of the Thatcher governments in Britain did not have the same political impact, and it should also be noted that the German trend reversed itself in the mid-1980s. In other words, as we have already noted, changing economic circumstances do not necessarily have a direct and immediate impact upon political attitudes. The connection between the two is often politically mediated, and as a result, what may seem a long-term trend initially, may turnout to be only a period effect later on. These are themes which present themselves time and time again in the Beliefs in Government research. Not surprisingly, therefore, Inglehart and Abramson (1994) argue for the operation of period effects in their article dealing with the decline of postmaterial orientations in the European Union since 1990.

However, it is an open question whether Western Europe will return to economic growth soon. Problems of high unemployment, particularly among the young, the globalization of markets, and of world competition with low-wage economies, are aggravated by the scarcity of raw materials and by environmental pollution. The developments were not foreseen by the advocates of postmodernism and postmodern politics. Their extrapolations from the past to the future give the politics of individualism and hedonism a central place which is now challenged by economic circumstances and by the political philosophers of communitarianism. This philosophy is interesting because it requires an entirely new relationship between the individual and the state. We will return to these problems in the final chapter of this book.

7

A Crisis of Democracy?

The Same Old Song and Dance?

A century is a short time when measured against the span of Western civilization since ancient Egypt or Mesopotamia. It may be long enough, though, to allow us to draw some valid conclusions about the conditions favouring or threatening the stability of democracy.

When analysing the spread of liberal democracy since the 1970s, Huntington (1991: 17) observes that countries which adopted democratic rule just before or after the First World War were particularly vulnerable to authoritarianism or totalitarianism. He also points out that one important threshold which working and stable democracies must cross is the transference of power through at least two free and peaceful elections. In a comparative study of stability and change between the two world wars, Berg-Schlosser and De Meur (1994) also emphasize the role of democratic tradition in maintaining democratic rule. As a consequence, one might argue, talk of democratic crisis in OECD nations is unwarranted, if only because they have strong democratic traditions and a long series of peaceful transfers of power by election. It is an altogether different question whether, as Offe (1993: 816–17) speculates, these nations are unusual in world history in possessing all the characteristics favourable to liberal democracy.

The largely uneventful, quiet days of building modern democracy in these countries lasted from the end of the Second World War until the mid-1960s, when the civil rights and student movements challenged established authority. At that time, demands for a new agenda and an expansion of political participation originated in small and well-resourced groups, and then spread, as we have seen, to a much wider public. However, these demands were not based upon a desire to change the fundamental rules of the political game. By the 1980s, as Sniderman (1981: 141) put it, 'time [had] witnessed the eclipse of alternative conceptions of a political order in America'—and, one might add, in other OECD countries as well.

Sniderman's claim was made at a time when communism was still regarded as a real challenge to liberal, pluralist democracy (Kielmansegg 1988). Perhaps it was no surprise, therefore, that the academic and intellectual left took the rising levels of political conflict in these countries to presage the imminent collapse of capitalist democracy, a development hailed expectantly by advocates of state socialism. However, since democracy did not break down, and as evidence about its durability began to accumulate (Fuchs 1989; Westle 1989), the theme more or less disappeared from the political science agenda, at least in its 1970s version. It has re-appeared in different guises since—most recently, perhaps in the form of 'civil society' theory which has re-emerged from a detour through Central and Eastern Europe. In this guise, however, it has taken on a very specific political and theoretical meaning in the context of the critique of the totalitarian state.

We have already argued that the exhaustion of the 'communist alternative' seems to be creating a new sensitivity towards the *specific* conditions in which polyarchy thrives, and towards the *different* institutions and procedures associated with it. This new emphasis squares well with current political reflection and debate within these countries about their own ideological and procedural principles. The current discussion is many sided, varied, and complex and we cannot claim to do it full justice here. Nevertheless, a few general observations are pertinent to this book and to the Beliefs in Government project generally.

The emergence and institutionalization of a political order designed to safeguard individual rights of freedom and equality is epitomized in the modern democratic state. Market democracies seem to have an unbeatable advantage over other systems in creating wealth and for securing the allegiance of their citizens to the state by the allocation of scarce resources through market and quasi-market mechanisms. At the same time, the ever-present problems of social inequality and poverty, which gave rise to socialism in the first place, have been contained by the modern welfare state to a degree acceptable to a majority of the population, at least. It is exactly this combination of achievements which gives both meaning and substance to claims to have balanced the demands of political equality and individual freedom: negative freedom in the sense of a reduced level of threats to everyday life, and positive freedom in the sense of freedom which empowers individuals to organize their own lives.

Of course, a wealth of research on the quality of life shows that overall satisfaction with life, as well as satisfaction with specific aspects of it, is much less dependent on objective and external factors than internal and subjective ones. Once a basic level of health and security is sustained, people turn to personal and subjective standards in order to evaluate their material and spiritual circumstances. This is why the capacity of reference groups to anchor the individual is important.

This anchoring mechanism allows a great deal of individual flexibility and security. It permits individuals to adjust, within limits, to deteriorating circumstances without immediate threat to their personal identity. (It should be noted in passing that this is precisely why the 'law of rising expectations', relied upon so heavily by the 'crisis of democracy' theorists, turned out to be not too law-like after all.) What is required for individuals is a set of yardsticks and reference objects with which to locate themselves in their social context. However, with the almost complete disappearance in Europe of totalitarian and authoritarian options, in which ordinary citizens were seen to fare so poorly, an important yardstick by which to judge the success of Western democracies may simply have vanished into the blue.

The collapse of communism may, therefore, have deprived Western democracies of easily understood and intuitively appealing comparisons. If this loss is to have an impact it is likely to show up, first of all, in the self-perceptions of the West. In other words, as we have argued before, the loss may well be made good not just by comparing democracies with other systems, but also by comparing different nations and their achievements within the family of democracies.

Much of this is speculation, of course, and it is further complicated by the indeterminacy of the present situation. On the one hand, lack of viable options may strengthen the liberal democracies. On the other, the disappearance of the immediate enemy may also lower identification with democracy and reduce the willingness of individuals to accept decisions and outcomes which are personally unfavourable to them. Political apathy or diffuse protest may result. But this is a simplistic interpretation which overlooks the complexity of interactions between institutional, structural, organizational, and individual factors. While it may be trivial and obvious to make this point, the ease with which crisis theories project selective perceptions of the past and present into the future makes it necessary to repeat it none the less. It also induces a due sense of modesty and caution in any attempt to speculate about the future course of democratic development. Nevertheless, we maintain that such speculation can profit from an informed analysis of the status quo.

Therefore, in what follows we will look back at Beliefs in Government and other research in order to identify potential trends. Of course, we are critically aware that our own evidence and much other empirical evidence on the matter is restricted to the micro level of the individual citizen. To a great extent this is due to the highly developed methodology of survey research and to the fact that individuals, as a unit of analysis, are more readily accessible to researchers than many other elements in the political system.

The Foundations of the Democratic State: Some General Thoughts

From the earliest days, reflections on the state have circled around its double-sided nature: the hegemon or Leviathan which must hold sufficient coercive power to guarantee peace and security; and the hegemon which, because of its very concentration of power, threatens the freedom of those who live under its rule. Once the concepts of freedom and equality were established both in principle and rules guiding everyday political conduct, it was agreed that the state could be defined as that organization with a monopoly of the legitimate use of coercive force. That is, the state could exercise its powers only on constitutional and legal grounds and on condition that its legitimacy was recognized by free and equal citizens.

The constitutional democratic state emerged at a time when traditional forms of authority were giving way to rational-legal forms. As part of this process, the foundation of political legitimacy also shifted from the transcendental (mainly religious) and the traditional (ruling dynasties) to an agreement about rules governing the conduct of politics—what Luhmann (1969) calls '*Legitimation durch Verfahren*', or the procedural, rather than the substantive, dimension of politics. Agreement was now built around acceptance of the rules of the game, rather than its particular outcomes.

Once Rousseau's theory of the common will was rejected, the inevitability of political conflict, and how to manage it peacefully, became the principle on which the institutions of the modern democratic state were grounded. The institutionalization of conflict became, in turn, the basis of what is now labelled pluralist society. Ever since de Tocqueville's reflections of democracy in America, the role of public and private associations in the operation of pluralist democracy have been accepted. These associations not only form the fabric of social integration but also the means by which individual inequalities of resources can be counterbalanced by collective resources. Parties and interest groups are particularly important in this respect. At the same time, the collective organization of interests is also an important counterweight to the centralized power of the state. This has become all the more important since the secularization of society has gradually eroded the religious and traditional basis of authority and changed the conditions of legitimacy.

Part of the vacuum left by the secularization of society has been filled by agreement about the rules governing the conduct of everyday political life. Nevertheless, this narrowed substantially the emotional basis of commitment to the system. Pluralists tried to cope with this problem by arguing that there had to be at least one area of agreement about politics which constituted the basis for the peaceful resolution of political conflict. In liberal thinking the essence of the agreement concerned the constitutional rights of individual citizens which could not be legally denied. This high principle is set out in Article 79 of the German Constitution, for example, and in a Bill of Rights or its equivalent in other nations. In turn, the rights of individuals have to be supported by corresponding institutional arrangements.

Exactly what these institutional arrangements should be is a difficult normative question, and empirical research on it has been plagued by substantive and methodological difficulties. In dealing with the political philosophy of John Rawls, Klosko (1993) has pointed to the fact, well documented by research, that abstract democratic principles do not always work perfectly in practice. Even worse, he points out in reference to a study of Kuklinski *et al.* (1991) that thoughtful consideration of the principles may not enhance but undermine their general acceptance. One might conclude that consensus about the fundamentals of modern democracy is narrow and fragile, even with an increasingly well-educated electorate. This seems to show itself most clearly in controversial matters such as affirmative action politics in the United States (Kuklinski *et al.* 1993)

These considerations flow from the fact that there is no easy or direct translation of procedural into substantive principles of action. Recent sociological research (such as in Beck 1986) suggests the even more basic problem that processes of social dealignment and differentiation are now creating free-floating individuals who are no longer fully integrated into society, and hence no longer share the common set of beliefs which such an integrated society is capable of generating.

At the moment, the arguments of Beck and other critics of postmodern society have not been addressed by systematic, comparative research, certainly not time-series research, and they remain a matter of intelligent speculation. Nevertheless, there is some evidence in the Beliefs in Government research which supports this speculation. First, Thomassen, in his chapter 'Support for Democratic Values' in Volume i, finds partial evidence that 'support for individualist aspects of democracy has increased while at the same time support for collectivist aspects has decreased'. Secondly, Scarbrough, in her chapter 'Materialist–Postmaterialist Value Orientations' in Volume iv, finds clear evidence of a trend towards postmaterialism, with its increasing emphasis on individual fulfilment. Thirdly, the form of postmodern politics discussed by Gibbins and Reimer in their chapter 'Postmodernism' in Volume iv (see also Crook, Pakulski, and Waters 1992) draws heavily upon the notion of individuals who are detached from the organized politics of parties and pressure groups, and who turn either to the more ephemeral politics of new social movements, or to highly particular, issue-specific, and spontaneous forms of individual action.

As early as the 1950s, social scientists wondered about the social and political consequences of individualization, though they called it atomization and isolation (Kornhauser 1960). Little evidence could be mustered to support the claim at the time. On the contrary, there was rather more research to show that individuals were able to overcome the socially destructive forces of industrial and economic change by rebuilding their communities, and with them a strong sense of individual and community identification (Wilmott and Young 1960; Gans 1967; Newton 1969: 100–11; Bell and Newby 1971: 131–85). Even today, the evidence for postmodern individualism, including that found by the Beliefs in Government project, is incomplete, to say the least. Besides, it is also questionable whether the evidence that has been found is not biased in favour of postmodern theory. For example, in an earlier chapter we argued that Inglehart's method of studying value change may be seriously flawed because it is more likely to find evidence of value change than synthesis. Similarly, contrary to the logic of individualization, Scheuch (1993: 158–68) presents data for

Germany between 1953 and 1991 which show that membership of voluntary organizations has increased substantially over time.

This is well supported by the comparative and time-series analysis of Aarts, in his chapter on intermediate organizations and representation in Volume i, who found no evidence that intermediary groups are beginning to break down. At first sight this contradicts the seminal work of Streeck (1987), but the two findings may be reconciled if one considers Streeck's point (1987: 477–82) that organizations try to maintain their membership by using such things as selective incentives. Although the evidence about political parties suggests that there is no general trend common to Western societies, research on voluntary organizations and intermediary associations does not suggest a growing atomization of individuals. What it does suggest is relatively stable memberships over time, but changes in the motivation underlying group membership and in the types of organizations people belong to.

This conclusion is corroborated by a West German study which examined informal support networks as an important element of social integration. The study finds, on the one hand, that traditional social groups have maintained much of their importance. On the other, it also finds that, together with the proliferation of life-styles, 'the most important component of whatever loss of community there is, is an increasing need for individuals to become active in the construction of stable and reliable support relationships within the environment' (Diewald 1991: 252; our translation).

The trend towards a form of society which is both individually fluid but also organized and integrated is well represented by the steep growth of single person households in countries such as Denmark, Germany, and the Netherlands. This is one of the most interesting trends in contemporary society. It has important economic consequences because it raises the question of how to satisfy the growing demand for single person housing, the cost of which is often high. The second consequence is that continuous welfare state intervention in the housing market in many parts of Western Europe has neutralized market mechanisms, thereby reinforcing state responsibility for housing and, as a result, politicizing the whole issue. In countries such as Britain, a different process has produced a similar result. Here the Thatcher governments forced a state withdrawal from housing by making local government sell its domestic property to tenants. As a result of this and other economic measures, a rapid rise in homelessness (especially among young, single persons) and poverty has caused a re-politicization of the housing question. This comparison suggests that countries respond to the problems of individualization in different ways, but it remains an issue with far-reaching consequences in all of them.

Related to the process of individualization in the West, but perhaps even more challenging for OECD nations is the variation in birth rates in different regions of the globe. Already the OECD nations are incapable of sustaining their present populations themselves. Miegel and Wahl (1993) have spelled out the potential *political* impact of this situation in some detail, arguing that it may well have some fairly momentous implications, including a possible structural cleavage between the young and the old.

Falling birth rates are the result of a complex causal chain, but there is little doubt that they involve factors such as individualism, hedonism, and the growing desire of women to make careers for themselves outside the home. Indeed, these are all the legitimate rights of individuals and intrinsic freedoms of modern society. Nevertheless, they also create problems for democratic polities. For example, one of the difficulties with the decision of many women, especially those with a better education, to take up a career is the slowness with which society responds to the need for alternative child-rearing arrangements.

Another problem is violence among hitherto 'normal' groups like middle-class schoolchildren and motorists, steeply rising levels of crime, and, not least, an apparently never-ending history of corruption among top politicians in many established democracies. Empirical evidence about these things is notoriously shaky, but the feeling people have about them contributes to the sense that modern society is losing its firm moral basis.

The examples of household size, birth rates, working women, crime, and corruption are intended to demonstrate the continuing processes of individualization and their political implications. However, we do not wish to repeat the vision of doom which has so often accompanied past conjecture about the future of democracy. On the contrary, we have argued before that democracy is more resilient and adaptable than many previous writers have recognized. Nor are we arguing that Western democracies have not faced serious problems in the past, any more than we claim that the present difficulties are without precedent. On the contrary, the topics have been taken up because they help us to understand why some of the traditional concerns of democratic theory, such as the good citizen, are surfacing again in the new guise of communitarianism. This emphasizes attachment and obligation to the community, mainly to the local community but also to society at large (Bell 1993).

This is not new. Long before the collapse of the Soviet system writers such as Etzioni in his book *The Active Society* (1968) and John Rawls in his *Theory of Justice* (1971) reflected upon the moral and institutional foundations of modern democracy, and more recently Michael Waltzer (1992) has done the same in discussing civil society. These writers deal with the inherent problems of modern society such as poverty, prejudice, racism, inequality, and political extremism and look for solutions of an individual, organizational, and institutional nature. It is a condition of the human predicament that these, and similar problems, will continue to challenge the imagination of the citizens and élites of society.

What is new, however, is a conjunction of two circumstances. First, the collapse of communism now makes it more likely that Western societies will scrutinize more closely their different ways of dealing with these problems, and will compare their varying successes. Secondly, this is happening at a time when pluralist democracies seem to be suffering from a weakened sense of ideological commitment and integration (Waltzer 1992: 190).

While it may be correct that the growing feeling of political dissatisfaction in contemporary societies is the result of a lack of clear-cut political alternatives, this is only a more acute version of an old problem. At the turn of the century Max Weber pointed to a progressive *Entzauberung* (disenchantment) with the world which was associated with religious and ideological secularization. In contemporary society this problem is epitomized by the tensions which inevitably arise from a loss of universal values and a relativist conception of 'the good', both of which are intrinsic properties of liberalism and political pluralism.

Durkheim's concepts of mechanical and organic solidarity, like Toennies' *Gemeinschaft und Gesellschaft*, point to the effects of modernization which change the way society is held together. While these are neutral concepts which can be related easily to contemporary ideas about differentiation and individualization, they are also often used with a sense of loss and regret which assumes that 'the good old days' have come to an end.

It was twentieth-century totalitarianism, with its demands for social and ideological conformity, which created the current instinct to reject total commitment to a political philosophy, whatever its origins and nature. The terrifying histories of left-wing and right-wing totalitarianism have highlighted the need to protect individual rights and freedom at all costs—even that of a segmented and poorly integrated society. Yet this is also a matter of emphasis since individuals do not survive alone in any society. They require the protective shield of supporting social networks.

In an extreme form, one argument is that the only integrating force in contemporary society consists of the ever-present conflict which derives from a pluralism of norms, values and life-styles which we now take for granted (Dubiel 1992: 106–18). But since this conflict produces both winners and losers the question arises of why the losers accept unfavourable outcomes. The answer seems to be that the rules of conflict resolution are seen as *fair* by a large majority of citizens. There must then be institutions which not only create the rules in the first place, but also ensure that losers abide by them. The only corporate actor with the capacity and the resources to do this is the legal, democratic state. It comes as no surprise, therefore, that even such a convinced liberal as Michael Walzer emphasizes the need for a strong state to cope with pluralist diversity (Walzer 1992: 193; see also Göhler 1992).

The built-in antagonism between the quest for a strong state and a type of liberal democracy which maximizes individual rights can be solved, liberals argue, by enhancing the role of individuals in political decision-making (Walzer 1992: 189–96). This is a theme which has gained post-war currency, starting with Pateman's (1970) writing on participation and continuing with public and scholarly debate alike. Sartori (1987: 111–15) is rightly critical of 'participationist' writings, and questions the underlying logic of asking for more participation without specifying the 'how, what, why, and where' of it. He suggests that participatory democracy basically means referendum democracy, and claims that the general population cannot make such a system work because of its political ignorance. Rather, participatory democracy requires a set of institutions capable of producing a population which is sufficiently sophisticated and knowledgeable to make sensible decisions (Sartori 1987: 115–20).

We shall return to this theme a little later in the chapter, but before doing so it is necessary to make three preliminary points. The first concerns the amount of consensus necessary to guarantee rational and non-violent decision-making, the outcomes of which are accepted even by the disadvantaged. At one extreme, there is the essentialist philosophy which claims that human history reveals a universally valid set of values and principles concerning the dignity of human life (Nussbaum 1993). This approach has been challenged because of its potential affinity with totalitarian thinking, and also because there are no rational grounds for the enforcement of a single moral code. At the other extreme, liberal ideology argues that diverse interests preclude the possibility of universally valid prescriptions for social and political conduct.

Neither extreme is ideologically satisfying and neither catches empirical reality. Apparently, however, there are some codes of conduct which a majority of citizens regard as reasonable or tolerable at any given times, even though the codes may change over time. Given the lack of transcendental or absolute foundations for such beliefs, it may be plausible to look—as Klosko (1993: 355–6) does—for functional equivalents in the institutions of pluralist democracy. In this respect we may use Easton's concept of the *political regime* because in principle the regime is divorced from everyday political conflicts which are contained within the binary government–opposition code of political authorities.

The boundaries between the regime and authority levels of the political system, however, are fluid in both theory and practice, and therefore the proper relationship between the two should be a focus of continual debate and discussion. For example, modern democracies are increasingly fusing the elements of executive and legislative power which were rigidly separated in classical liberal constitutional theory. Other examples concern inter-governmental relations and decision-making within federal systems, and decision-making in international or supranational government such the European Union. In both cases lines of accountability are broken, with resulting difficulties and confusion for the public. Even within Britain, where multiple levels of government are not an acute problem, the principle of democratic accountability has become blurred, confused, perhaps even avoided, by the multiplication of 'quangos' (quasi-autonomous non-governmental organizations) and 'egos' (extra-government organizations) (see Weir and Hall 1994).

The second problem to be considered concerns the role of the state and the ways of expanding the political influence of its citizens. Much writing, including that in Volume iii, shows how the social state (*Sozialstaat*) was transformed into the welfare state (*Wohlfahrtsstaat*) between 1950 and 1980 (Luhmann 1981: 7–11), and how the expansion has now been halted. But even if the frontiers of the modern state are rolled back somewhat, the wide scope of government which remains will continue to justify the claim that citizens have too limited a role in political decision-making.

In this matter a lesson may be learned from the broadening of the franchise in the last century. Although the process was slow and cautious it was invariably accompanied by warnings about how giving the vote to the masses would dilute the quality of the electorate and damage the quality of political life (see Hirschman 1991). It is not surprising that similar doubts are now expressed about the idea of extending citizen influence beyond that exercised in formal voting rights.

Nevertheless, there are weighty arguments in favour of this. In the first place, substantial parts of the electorate have become detached from traditional communities and social contexts, and from the parties and interest groups which are rooted in them. In the second place, the diversification of life-styles and beliefs makes it more and more difficult for modern parties to produce programmes with broad appeal. Citizens are therefore right when they claim that the vote is an increasingly inadequate way of expressing *specific* policy preferences. Thus modes of political participation beyond the formal vote need to be used.

The empirical evidence collected in Volumes i and Volume iv shows that many people in the 1990s have drawn the conclusion about the need to go beyond the vote in order to exert political influence. But a major problem with this development, and one which shows clearly in the research, is that different strata or groups are not equally inclined to participate in this way. The concern which follows (Verba *et al.* 1993: 314) is that the preferences of the active and the inactive differ substantially. Therefore, selective use of the wider political repertory brings the old issue of political equality back in. The problem is aggravated by periodic shifts in citizen political involvement, as analysed by Hirschman (1982).

The challenge is all the more important since, to repeat Sartori's point (1987), it is impossible to involve all citizens in all political decisions. It is not even possible to involve all in the important ones, setting aside the problem of how we are to separate important from unimportant in this respect.

Kaase and Barnes (1979) argue that it requires imagination to create institutional arrangements capable of balancing the need for participation and the need for stable and orderly democracy. On the one hand,

the demand for political equality and participation are at the centre of
the democratic creed; on the other, it is necessary to avoid the extreme
ebbs and flows of political mood and fashion. Little more than experiments at the local level, such as the planning cell (*Planungszelle*)
invented and refined by Dienel (1991) and his associates (Zilleßen,
Dienel, and Strubelt 1993), have emerged to fill this need. At the local
level there are also experiments in many parts of Western Europe with
decentralized local government offices, walk-in information centres,
user-friendly bureaucracies, and consumer satisfaction questionnaires.
The relative scarcity of innovation in this field is due less to the
stubbornness of political élites and their desire to hold on to power,
than to the structural difficulties of creating institutions and practices
which extend the capacity of citizens for political participation. What is
required is an intelligent and practical discussion of the options and
their limitations, but this is exactly what is lacking in liberal democracies at present. Small wonder that feelings of political frustration
seem to surface every now and again among élites and masses alike.

Liberalism, Democracy, and the Clash of Civilizations

Strains in modern democracy arise from the fact that individualism has
pushed the liberal creed to the point where a sense of community,
common purpose, and a sense of responsibility towards society and
its politics have been eroded. The strains are not yet strong enough to
call the ideology of liberalism into question, but they do raise questions
about the limits of liberalism.

At first sight the question seems to be a *contradictio in adjecto*. If
individual rights are the epitome of liberalism, on what grounds can
these rights be limited? The truism that individual rights are qualified at
the point where they impinge on the rights of others does not help much
because it does not solve the difficulties of sorting out individual rights
in specific circumstances. Nor does it answer the question of how to set
policy priorities. In this respect we must beware of the dangers of
historicism and learn from experience that each discussion of the
subject is embedded in a particular historical period. Indeed, philosophical debate about the foundations of liberalism suggest that it is
not possible on *a priori* grounds to claim that liberalism is the one
value system based on universal truths. While some think this a great
loss, others such as Rawls (1985) and Rorty (1990, 1991) reach the

conclusion that a liberal democracy based on Western concepts of freedom of justice is both possible and worth striving for.

This is linked to Fukuyama's 'end of history' argument, not because liberal democracy has triumphed for ever, but in the sense that it should always be an *empirical question* whether there are other types of political system which can provide more freedom, justice, security, economic well-being, and spiritual satisfaction than liberal democracy. This, in turn, implies some sort of competition within liberal democracies, and between them and other forms of polity. In the case of the former, further research may corroborate Lijphart's (1994) finding that, over the long haul, consensus democracy is superior to majoritarian democracy on almost all counts. However, it may turn out that, so far as a balance of many qualities is concerned—economic, social (community and belonging), spiritual (religion), and political (authoritarian–democratic)—the performance of other countries such as the four little tigers of South Korea, Singapore, Taiwan, and Hong Kong may be superior to the OECD nations. These are countries that seem to have found a way to harmonize economic growth with religious beliefs, such as Confucianism, and with some variant of political authoritarianism.

In the not too distant future, however, it may become apparent that economics does not drive the behaviour of nations in the same way. This is where Huntington's (1993) speculations about the future of international conflict fit in. We do not intend to join the ranks of Huntington's critics (see the September/October 1993 edition of *Foreign Affairs*). Rather, the point should be made that the spread of democracy to Central and Eastern Europe from about 1990 must not necessarily be read as showing the universal appeal of liberal democracy. These are European countries that share a European culture and traditions. Huntington's emphasis on the *cultural* dimension of politics—primarily the religious—suggests that liberal democracy, as a system built on rational secular authority, may remain what it always has been: an option for a minority of nations which have developed under very specific economic, ideological, cultural, social, and political circumstances (Parekh 1993).

This will not necessarily cause problems, but two issues may arise. First, liberal democracies could be threatened if the clash of cultures takes a military turn—hence the concerted effort to prevent the proliferation of nuclear weapons. Secondly, the globalization of production and commerce may challenge the economic dominance of the OECD nations. Europe's inability to compete with the low wage economies of Asia and the Pacific and the erection of customs and other barriers against economic competition in some of those countries hint at the challenges which the OECD nations face. This is an additional reason why economics in these countries will continue to matter for democracy.

Economics and Democracy

Seymour Martin Lipset's discussion of the relationship between economic development and democratic stability has been much challenged and modified ever since he published *Political Man*. One of the most important qualifications of the thesis is Vanhanen's (1990: 13), who addresses the puzzle of why some countries with high levels of economic development have not become democracies. He writes: 'My answer to this question is simple: the level of resource distribution, not the level of socio-economic development or modernization, is the causal factor behind the process of democratization.' In other words, in addition to the central principle of formal political equality, discussed earlier, we must now add the further condition of economic equality for the development of democracy. In recent years there has been an undue emphasis on freedom, and too little discussion of equality (both formal and substantive) as another essential principle of democracy.

Nevertheless, the empirical evidence that, *in general*, economics in the form of an open, competitive market economy matters decisively for the emergence and maintenance of democracy is overwhelming as Helliwell (1994) shows in his study of 125 nations in the 1960–85 period (see also Diamond 1992). Revisiting the topic, Lipset (1994) himself has re-emphasized his earlier position, but also included a set of other factors such as institutional arrangements (electoral laws), the structure of party systems, historical contexts, modes of transition to democratic rule, and not least, political culture. All these have to be considered in addition to the economic dimension when explaining the transition to, and consolidation of, democracy. Refining the theory in this way owes much to the analysis of case studies which deviate from the standard economic model (Diamond 1992). They are necessary to avoid economic determinism and to understand the complexity of different pathways to democracy (see Rueschemeyer, Stephens, and Stephens 1992).

Postmodernism and Postmaterialism

As time goes by, and as more countries fall into the category of liberal democracy, the importance of economic performance for establishing and maintaining democracy tends to slip from sight. It is easily taken for granted because the OECD nations have experienced economic growth over a fairly long period now, and because opinion leaders—both academic and others—have been generally privileged with job security and good incomes. It is no chance that the postmaterialists of the modern world are disproportionately found in reasonably well-paid jobs in the media, academia, and the public sector. It is also among these groups that the debate about postmodernism rages.

We have dealt with the subject already in the previous chapter and will not return to it in any detail here. However, it is notable that when postmodernists address the topic of politics at all, two general themes can be detected. On the one hand, politics is regarded as an activity best abandoned, if possible, because it interferes with the potential freedom of individuals to develop themselves. For the 'postmodern sceptic' (Rosenau 1992: 139–44), politics is inauthentic. Postmodernists who take this view see little point in discussing the nature of political institutions or in considering empirical evidence about the performance of liberal democracies. It should also be noted, in passing, that shying way from observable socio-political reality and systematic research results is also a feature of some liberal political thinkers like Rawls and Walzer.

On the other hand, postmodernists of the 'affirmative' kind (Rosenau 1992: 144–55) are more likely to discuss concrete political matters. When they do so, especially the activists among them, they clearly emphasize non-institutionalized modes of participation and 'doing things for themselves'. It is no surprise, therefore, that what little research there is on the matter shows that postmodernists are usually also postmaterialists.

In general, politics are not a matter of great importance for post-modernists, but even more notable is the systematic neglect of economics, and the tendency to take economic growth and affluence for granted. Perhaps this is not surprising, given the discussion of economics and democracy in the previous section. In addition, much of postmodern theory wishes to eradicate the subject–object distinction because it implies a structural relationship of control. In its place postmodernists wish to separate the public (the political) from the private, and exclude the public from further consideration. This view further obscures the nature of politics. This is the approach to life of postmaterialist prototypes who are deeply involved in the individual and the private, although they are not necessarily non-political at the same time. Given this private and apolitical disposition, the question is, what impact will the spread of postmodernism among the mass public have on liberal democracy? Postmodernist thinkers themselves assume that it will grow because they do not think that serious economic troubles will return. The fact that economic matters are once again high on the agenda in contemporary Europe is not, of course, at all consistent with this view.

The second theme, already touched upon in the previous chapter, concerns the ageing populations of Western democracies. There are national differences in Western Europe, but the current size of birth-giving age groups and their rates of reproduction are currently insufficient to maintain the population, setting aside the effects of immigration. Therefore, the size of the working population will shrink while those on pensions will increase. The problem will worsen as life expectancy rises (Miegel and Wahl 1993: 78).

As a result, the combined effects of demographic change and of global production, trade, and employment make it unlikely that materialist concerns will lose their power in the Western world. Consequently, the mechanics of a postmaterialist take-over, as laid out by Inglehart (1990: 66–104), are subject to substantial doubt. There is no question that the corner stone of his argument concerning the value preferences of age cohorts is well based empirically. If, given the underlying model of generational change, younger cohorts are more postmaterialist than older ones, then the overall balance of society will continue to shift towards postmaterialism. There were substantial dips in postmaterial attitudes in 1977 (the oil crisis) and between 1980 and 1982 (economic crisis), but Inglehart argued these were period effects since all cohorts showed these changes. He suggested that as the economic situation improved so each cohort would return to its 'normal' level of postmaterialism. As subsequent research proves, he was right.

Since 1990 the Eurobarometer surveys show an even larger dip in postmaterialism, most likely reflecting the economic problems of the late 1980s and early 1990s. Once again, it is an empirical question whether we will see a return to previous levels of postmaterialism, and whether the younger cohorts will exceed the levels of older cohorts. If our analysis is correct, though, EU member nations in the year 2000 and beyond will continue to be afflicted by economic strain and, therefore, neither will occur. The claim here is that the political agenda of EU nations will *not* be *increasingly* dominated by postmaterialism.

There is more than sheer economic reasoning underlying this conclusion. As long ago as 1975 in the British part of the Political Action study, Marsh pointed to the fact that a rank preference for postmaterialist values does not automatically imply that economic issues do not matter. Rather, he showed that despite the emergence of postmaterial issues, economics continued to loom large in the public mind. This finding squares with the point made by Klages that developed societies are not moving towards an exclusive emphasis on postmaterialism, but towards a synthesis of material and postmaterial values. It also squares with the findings presented in Chapter 4, which show that the population of Western Europe has modified, but not turned away from its concerns with the material matters of the welfare state, economic security, and economic equality.

In sum, while new values undoubtedly surfaced in the 1960s they have not replaced a concern with economic well-being. Both objective and subjective factors suggest that economic problems and concerns will remain a concern in the public mind. What does this mean for democratic legitimacy?

The Legimacy Question.

Legimacy, that is the free consent of the population to the institutions, procedures, norms, and values of their system of government, is not only a question for democracies. Undemocratic systems of government may be seen as legitimate by their populations no less than democratic ones. This is why some argue that popular legimacy is not enough, and that there should be other tests of the quality of a system of government. This raises all sorts of difficult normative questions about what sort of test might be applied, of course. Nevertheless, the matter of popular legitimacy remains, including whether and to what extent the population feels a sense of loyalty to its system of government, on what this is based, and what particular aspects of the system it appreciates most.

In dealing with this it seems sensible to recall the defining characteristics of democracy—inclusive citizenship and the institutionalization
of political diversity—and to ask whether these command consent from
Western populations. The term 'legitimacy' is generally conceptualized
as consisting of supportive attitudes and favourable evaluations of the
political regime, that is, the non-partisan institutions, procedures,
norms, and values of the polity. Thus legitimacy is a micro concept
which concerns *individual* beliefs about macro features of the political
system.

Unfortunately, empirical research has been slow to devise indicators
of this notion of legitimacy and there is less longitudinal and comparative evidence on the matter than one would like. Fuchs, Guidorossi, and
Svensson, in their chapter 'Support for the Democratic System' in
Volume i, however, use the Eurobarometer question about satisfaction
with democracy to show that claims about the legitimacy crisis in late
capitalist societies were largely mythical. Unfortunately, the questionnaire data do not make it possible to distinguish between diffuse and
specific support, or between support for authorities and regimes, so it is
not possible to probe deeply into the matter of legitimacy. However,
more specific studies (Muller, Jukam, and Seligson 1982; Fuchs 1989;
Westle 1989) show that the mass public can and do make such
distinctions, a finding which has important implications for the
dynamics of modern politics.

In the previous chapter we discussed the central role the government–
opposition mechanism assumes in these dynamics. In a comparative
analysis of six democracies Weil (1989) empirically validates this
point. He shows that an ineffective opposition (caused by polarization, fractionalization, oversized government coalitions) has a negative
effect on *regime* legitimacy, while government performance has no
effect, or at most an indirect and interactive effect. Government
performance affects political authorities in the sense that it is related
to government turnover.

However, if government performance is persistently poor over an
extended period of time, even if the governing parties and coalitions
change, it is probable that support for the regime will begin to decline.
Since OECD countries change their governments after elections at
irregular intervals, and since their economic performance has generally
been satisfactory or good, perhaps we can take a relaxed view of the
legitimacy problem. On second thoughts, however, the grounds for
optimism are not quite so strong.

The first cause for concern is voter de-alignment from established political parties. While it can be shown that parties are not helpless victims of this trend, but can take positive action to keep their supporters and even win new ones, there are limits to their capacities. If the groups, organizations, and communities in which they are rooted begin to decline then their capacity to recruit is also undermined. Besides, the shift from position politics to valence politics also complicates their task, as does the rise in issue voting. There are also mounting constraints on policy-making imposed by limited resources, by the courts, and by international government (especially the European Union), all of which make it difficult for parties and oppositions alike to form clearcut programmes and policies for which they can be held accountable. The apparent tendency to form oversized coalitions may be one consequence of these factors.

The second concern, which may be causally related to the first, is the growth of anti-party sentiment which threatens the core functions played by parties in democracies. Although the terms 'anti-party' and 'anti-politics' are sometimes used in a vague way, a comparative study of thirteen nations between the 1960s and 1990s shows a trend since the 1980s for a decline in party membership and an increase in voting for anti-system parties (Poguntke 1994; see also Aarts's chapter in Volume i). Country-specific differences, especially in voting turnout, suggest cautious generalization, but none the less the trend seems to exist.

An apparent dissatisfaction with parties is likely to be extended to politicians and other élites, although the lack of comparative élite studies makes it difficult to be sure. In addition, the electoral support given to protest parties suggests a dangerous disenchantment with traditional politics. So too does the electoral support for 'non-parties', that is parties without a broad programme, an inexperienced leadership, or much of an organization. However, these have often been rather short-lived in the past, and we cannot tell how long they will last now.

Finally, the extension of the political repertory to include non-institutionalized forms of participation is also a potential threat to political legitimacy. Although it encourages more grass-roots involvement, it also encourages over-commitment and political disappointment (Hirschmann 1982: 92–120).

Such considerations lead us back to the 1950s and 1960s idea of a *civic* culture, which offers the *potential* of political involvement beyond the vote, but basically relies upon the vote, and which is based upon a relationship of trust between rulers and the ruled. It also keeps a crucial area of private life separate from the public and the political. If it is backward to value this kind of civic culture then we must face up to the problems of the current system in a different way. We have shown that much of the new political activism is disproportionately concentrated among the middle and upper class, thereby opening up an extra avenue of influence for them. This challenge to political equality must be counter-balanced by institutional measures in the short run, but by greater substantive social and political equality in the long run.

Up to this point the legitimacy question has been treated as a prime concern of the nation state, but the dual processes of the internationalization and the regionalization of government will raise the issue at these levels as well. The problem is that decisions are increasingly taken above (the EU) or below (quangos and egos) the national level by forms of government which are not directly legitimated by popular vote. This is less of a difficulty in federal systems such as Germany, Austria, and Switzerland, but in other countries the question may well become a controversial matter. It is difficult to know how lack of a clear and acceptable European constitution will affect national governments, but it seems reasonable to suppose that a semi-sovereign European parliament will both help weaken the role of national parliaments, while suffering from a democratic deficit itself.

The Future of Democracy—a Recurrent Theme

In this book we have tried to crystallize the most important findings of the Beliefs in Government project, and, at the same time, locate them in the continuing debate about democracy. The many weaknesses and the important insights in this literature suggest two general conclusions. First, as research has accumulated on the subject, the more it has become clear that different nations have been directed by a great complexity of factors down different pathways towards democracy. Secondly, the Beliefs in Government project shows that underneath the stability of modern Western democracies there have been some truly pervasive changes. Citizens have become more educated, more politically involved, and more active. At the same time, they have also become more individualistic, more self-centred, and more wedded to the specific interests of their immediate group than the concerns of the polity as a whole. Intermediary political structures have also changed in various ways. As the class struggle and its ideological concerns have waned so intermediation has become less monolithic and more varied. People are members of a broad variety of associations, most of them non-political, but capable of mobilizing politically as the need arises. Traditional parties and interest groups—especially churches and trade unions—struggle hard and reasonably successfully to maintain their role, but they face a formidable challenge from many varieties of new social movements. In the past these have been primarily on the left–wing of politics, but they have been so successful that they are now threatened with right-wing imitators and rivals.

Although Beliefs in Government has not studied political institutions, other research has shown how these have changed in important ways since 1945—referendums, more political personnel directly elected, decentralization, more open government, less élitism. In part, these developments are the result of rising demands for political rights and influence. At the same time, the growing network of decision-making, involving government and non-government organizations and national and international organizations, means that decisions are increasingly removed from the parliamentary realm into areas that are not under public control or even scrutiny. This raises serious questions about legitimacy. It also raises questions about whether the political system can perform its most prominent and responsible task—the authoritative allocation of values.

Nevertheless, in the competition between liberal democracy and other forms of government, liberal democracy has come out a clear winner as the communist states of Central and Eastern Europe slowly and painfully turn to democracy, just as the authoritarian regimes of southern Europe did before them. But this is not yet the end of the story. The debates between liberals and communitarians, and between modernists and postmodernists continue and however they may turn out, they certainly sharpen our sense of the inherent weaknesses of liberal democracy. In particular, they point to the loss of shared community and the continuing inequalities between citizens. This is why competition between different types of democracy, and between democracies and other political systems, will not disappear from the world's political agenda.

Beliefs in Government has documented how the political orientations of citizens in up to sixteen West European countries have developed since the early 1960s, which is the earliest the time-series data will allow us to study the process. These were years of unprecedented economic growth, of a revolution in educational achievement, changing world views, exposure to new ways of life through foreign travel and the mass media technology of television. But in these years people also became aware of the high environmental price paid for economic growth, a burden which will be carried by generations to come.

The political agenda of the future will be influenced increasingly by international trends, forces, and considerations; national perspectives on democracy and decision-making will become less and less adequate for an understanding of its logic and outcomes. In this sense, Beliefs in Government has documented an important era in Western politics, but one which seems to have come to a close in the early 1990s.

APPENDIX: PROJECT PROPOSAL FOR DECISION BY THE GENERAL ASSEMBLY OF THE EUROPEAN SCIENCE FOUNDATION ON 2 NOVEMBER 1988

Introduction

In May 1987 the ESF Standing Committee for the Social Sciences sponsored a Conference on Political Science Research in Europe which was held at the European University Institute, Florence, Italy. The conference was chaired by Professor Jean Blondel in his capacity as chairman of the Government and Law Committee of the UK Economic and Social Research Council and was attended by representatives from 15 ESF member countries. The purpose of the conference was to discuss research priorities in political science with a view to possible collaborative efforts and the strengthening of links between research councils and academic researchers. From the perspective of the European Science Foundation, a particular concern was to identify research work on particular topics that could benefit greatly from being studied at the European level. The research topic of 'Beliefs in Government' was prominent among the recommendations arising from the conference concerning topics that held strong potential for fruitful research collaboration. It was felt that a substantial number of academics were undertaking research on this topic in individual countries using electoral survey and public opinion data. There was a strong case for linking leading scholars in this field to reinterpret their data and research findings, and to assess the compatibility of the nationally collected data for comparative analysis at the European level.

As a result of its discussion of the conference recommendations the Standing Committee for the Social Sciences agreed to hold an exploratory workshop on 'Beliefs in Government' as an early activity of its new programme for its third mandate (1988–92). Professor Max Kaase (University of Mannheim, FRG) and Professor Kenneth Newton (University of Essex, UK) were invited to consult widely and to prepare a proposal for a scientific programme which would focus on the secondary analysis of existing data. The present proposal has emerged from these consultations which included a final workshop held at the ESF in late September 1988. The research programme was planned to commence from January 1989.

Summary of Some European Trends in Public Attitudes to Government

There is growing evidence that the most fundamental beliefs about the proper role and scope of government in the democratic nation states of Western Europe are changing, and that these changes may, in their turn, have a profound effect on the future shape of government. The nature and pace of these changes is still not well understood because systematically comparative data bases of a longitudinal nature, with one major exception discussed below, are largely lacking. Some of the most important developments in public opinion about the role of government in democratic societies which have emerged from the research literature may be summarized as follows:

There is a clear trend towards the strengthening of feeling among the public that citizens can have, if they desire so, an impact on the political process and on political outcomes. This increased sense of personal political efficacy is strongly related to the desire to have a larger say in political matters, beyond the act of voting itself. The inclination to get involved in acts of non-institutionalized political participation (such as demonstrations and new political groups campaigning on specific issues) is visible in all liberal democracies.

Although there are differences between countries, there is good reason to believe that through processes of social and technological change, as well as through increasing education and the penetration of mass media communications into all sectors of post-industrial societies, the traditional linkages between individuals as members of socio-political interest groups and political parties have been weakened. It is unclear whether this process of de-alignment will result in re-alignment between (new) social cleavages and (new) political parties, or will create instead large parts of the electorate which have no firm ties to any specific political party.

One major new cleavage might be the idea of postmaterialism, combining a heightened sense of personal efficacy and desire for increased opportunities for political participation with a distinct change in priorities. In particular, there might be a change in emphasis from issues of personal economic well-being to issues of a global societal nature—in the realms of war and peace, of control of new technological developments, of responsibility of present to future generations regarding the environment.

With respect to the role of government these changes in mass orientations are perplexing and paradoxical because they seem at one and the same time to imply expectations of a reduced role and of increased responsibilities of democratic governments.

At present there exists one data base starting in 1974, which permits empirical comparative and longitudinal analysis, at least, of some of the above claims: the Eurobarometer survey studies carried out twice every year in each of the EEC countries on behalf of the European Commission. In the following paragraphs some of the most interesting results of the Eurobarometer surveys pertinent to the overall research question of the future role of democratic government will be briefly discussed. It has to be kept in mind that, for many of the trend variables, the European average is not very informative, because the individual member states differ with respect to the values of the variables and/or their development within the time span covered by the Eurobarometer surveys.

With regard to overall life satisfaction (asked 1975–87), there is a negative trend in Belgium and Ireland, a slightly positive trend in Italy, Luxembourg, and Denmark and a clear positive trend in Portugal. In the other member states of the EEC this variable remained more or less stable. The overall level of satisfaction is relatively high. (On average, almost four-fifths of European citizens are very or fairly satisfied.) Nevertheless, clear differences can be found between the individual member states, Denmark (about 95 per cent satisfied) and Greece and Italy (about two-thirds satisfied) being the extremes.

It is well known from previous research that there exists a substantial gap between personal life satisfaction on the one hand and satisfaction with public affairs on the other hand. Eurobarometer survey results are well in line with this finding that people are more pessimistic about public than private matters. In most of the countries, satisfaction with the way democracy works is considerably lower than overall life satisfaction. Concerning the results for the individual countries (1976–87), there is a slightly negative trend in Greece and a positive trend in Italy and Denmark. In Belgium, Ireland, and the Netherlands a negative trend exists until the early 1980s and then a slightly positive trend emerges. In Portugal a clearly positive development is to be found, whereas in France, Germany, Spain, and the United Kingdom no long-range trend can be identified. On the European average, about half of the citizens are very or fairly satisfied with the way democracy works in their country. The lowest level of satisfaction with democracy is still to be found in Italy, and the highest in Luxembourg, Denmark, and Germany.

One of the most stable and important findings in electoral sociology is the differential assessment of one's own economic situation and the general economic situation of the nation, which is most generally evaluated as far worse than the individual situation. These questions have *not* been asked in the Eurobarometer series. What has been asked, however, is the perception of *changes* in one's own financial situation and the general economic situation.

On examining survey results from questions seeking on assessment of changes in the country's economic situation over the past twelve months, there is a clearly positive trend on the European average, starting from a low level in autumn 1982 (14 per cent a lot or a little better; 62 per cent a little or a lot worse) and steadily increasing until autumn 1986 (36 per cent a lot or a little better; 30 per cent a little or a lot worse). In autumn 1987 the figures decreased for the first time, possibly owing to the October stock market crash. The positive trend occurs more or less in all the individual member states except Denmark and Greece, where a clearly negative trend is found.

The assessment of the changes in the financial situation of individual households over the previous twelve months at the aggregate level (in the same years, 1982–7) follows a similar development of the previous variable in most of the countries (the clearest exception being Denmark), but with considerably lower variations. A comparison of the two economic variables shows that the assessment of changes in the financial situation of households is not systematically higher or lower than the assessment of changes in the country's economic situation.

With respect to the basic attitude towards society (1976–87), a clear majority (between 55 and 65 per cent) of European citizens claim that the respective society must be gradually improved by reforms. Since the beginning of the 1980s, this majority has increased on the European average. A positive trend can be found in two-thirds of the individual member states (the exceptions being France, Luxembourg, Ireland, and Portugal) but with considerable differences in strength. Greece and Italy show the clearest increase, followed by Denmark and Germany. With the exception of Germany until the beginning of the 1980s, the percentage of European citizens stating that the present society must be defended strongly against all subversive forces is considerably lower (between 25 and 33 per cent) and slightly decreasing on the European average. Concerning individual member states, however, we find a clearly increasing trend in France, and since the 1980s the figures generally have increased also in Belgium and Luxembourg. The clearest decrease is to be found in Greece, Germany, and, since the 1980s, Italy. The percentage of European citizens stating that the entire way the society is organized must be radically changed by revolutionary action has never exceeded 7–8 per cent on the European average and has decreased to 4–5 per cent in the 1980s. Starting from the highest level, the clearest decrease can be found in France and Italy. In all other member states, except Spain, the percentages slightly decreased or remained stable.

Finally, turning to one of the questions asked only once (in the autumn of 1985), we find a relative low level of overall trust in government. Only between 5 and 8 per cent of organized citizens in France, Germany, Britain, Italy, and Spain answered that they 'almost always' trust the government to do what is right, whereas between one-fifth and one-fourth answered 'almost never'.

At first sight, these survey results are puzzling if not actually paradoxical. A second look at the figures suggests an interpretation and possible explanation for these findings which, though tentative and approximate, may have considerable implications and ramifications for the shape and content of public affairs. It seems that Europeans understand their economic predicament, and have lowered their expectations and are looking for more satisfaction than before outside economic and occupational rewards. Although they are reasonably satisfied with the way democracy works and place some faith in their own political efficacy, their belief in the responsiveness of governments and in the capability of governments to improve general economic trends is extremely limited. Unemployment, for example, is seen as a major problem, but the growing feeling is that governments can do rather little to control it.

These trends are not uniform across all nations or social groups, of course, but a general picture does seem to emerge from the survey results. Europeans seem to have accommodated to change by expecting and demanding less from both the economy and government. The result may be a degree of disengagement from politics, and an emerging privatized political style. This, perhaps, helps to explain why growing economic difficulties in many nations have not resulted in growing demands for political change, but rather in an increased electoral volatility which accepts and works within the existing political system, and its main political parties.

The Proposed Scientific Programme

The purpose of the programme is, first, to identify the nature and extent of shifts in mass opinion about the proper role and scope of government in Western Europe over the past one or two decades; secondly, to disentangle national patterns from general trends and, within as well as between nations, to look for similarities and differences in the orientations of social-structural, ideological, and other subgroups of the population; and thirdly, on this basis to understand and explain the shifts in an attempt to try to foresee the likely course of future patterns and trends. To do so on a cross-national comparative basis is to go a long way towards an assessment of the likely constraints which public opinion will place upon the future options of contemporary Western governments.

The scientific programme will not spend any time or money on generating new survey data. This is because the main emphasis is on studying changes over time and therefore looking at developments extending from the past into the present. In the second place, rich seams of survey data on the topic exist already and the intention is to exploit these data fully by re-analysing them. Thirdly, we intend to give these data another life by systematically placing national surveys in cross-national context. Some of the survey material is already in the form of comparative cross-national surveys, including especially the Eurobarometer surveys already mentioned, which also have the advantage of permitting some time-series analyses. In spite of all their pitfalls, they are an invaluable source of longitudinal cross-national analysis, and they have the added advantage of having been processed and documented by the Belgian Academic Survey Data Archive (BASS). In addition, there are also other international studies (e.g. the Political Action project, the European Values Study, and the International Social Survey Programme) which are valuable but more limited in their longitudinal depth. Clearly, most work is national and cross-sectional in nature, but comparable work on the same key topics has been done in most countries, including surveys of mass attitudes towards expenditure cuts, economic privatization, faith in government, and satisfaction with economic trends and performance. Some of these surveys have been carried out as part of national opinion surveys, some as part of more specialized, and often more local, surveys of political opinions.

Although each nation has its own group of experts on survey material of this kind, there is at present no linkage on a European scale adequate to develop cross-national analysis. The time is ripe to bring European scholars together, so that they can move on to the next and all-important stage of systematic comparative work. A subsidiary aim of the programme, therefore, is to create long overdue research linkages between European scholars in survey research which could then stimulate further work of a national kind and more comparative research as well. Another benefit should be the refining and sharpening of survey instruments which will improve the quality of future work and act as a foundation for another decade of time-series studies. In particular, the Eurobarometer survey, already mentioned as being so useful, might be refined and improved.

It is important that the work should not only be of a cross-national comparative nature, but also inter-disciplinary. This term is used in preference to multi-disciplinary' because the latter often means little more than placing the work of different disciplinary experts side by side, whereas the former calls for a concerted effort to integrate the approaches of different disciplines. The programme is intended to be both cross-national and inter-disciplinary, covering all the major democratic nation states of Europe, and the different academic disciplines which could bring something to the subject, including political science, sociology, history and psychology.

Research Plan

Exploratory Workshop

This workshop was held at the European Science Foundation on 29 September–1 October 1988 and was attended by leading social scientists with research expertise in this field. A draft of this document was circulated beforehand to the workshop participants. Participants were asked to bring with them a short account of the work carried out in their own country and information on existing relevant material and data sets, plus a brief summary of their own work and interests in the field. In addition, a first appraisal of the amount of comparative longitudinal data available on the topic in the Eurobarometer studies and in other sources was also presented at the workshop. Workshop discussions produced agreement on the proposed framework for the scientific programme and the subgroup research topics for detailed study (see below).

The programme will focus upon the work of four linked subgroups which will examine the following key aspects of the general topic:

Attitudes towards Democratic Politics. Democracy is a political order which is based and thrives upon the free consent of the governed; in this regard it is a unique type of political system. Beliefs in the legitimacy of democracy on these grounds are a central element of citizen attitudes towards politics and society. Strangely enough, despite the practical and conceptual importance of this, empirical research has only more recently addressed it. Two general research findings are of great importance for the proposed programme. First, it has been found both useful and empirically tenable to differentiate between various objects (government authorities, political communities) and types of attitudes (specific and diffuse support as well as combinations of the two). These findings, however, are mainly drawn from analysis of a handful of countries (in particular, the United States and West Germany) and need to be broadened across as many democratic polities as possible. Secondly, we are now quite certain that the crisis of legitimacy claimed on theoretical grounds to have occurred in Western democracies in the late 1960s and early 1970s did not happen. An essential research question for this programme is whether there are more recent developments which may make the crisis of legitimacy take place in the 1990s.

Earlier in the proposal reference was made to a number of perplexing and sometimes contradictory developments in citizen attitudes towards politics. One strand of research findings points to a 'participatory revolution', which sees rising citizen demands for more say in political matters reflected in increased levels of uninstitutionalized political participation (i.e. activities such as political demonstrations or new social movements, for example the ecological movement). Growing pressure arising from such participatory activities is seen by many as a serious challenge to contemporary institutions of social and political mediation such as political parties and interest groups. These developments coincide with deep-rooted changes in the social structure related to higher educational attainment, the emergence of modern technologies and their impact upon the economy and mass communications, and the internationalization of the modern world through communication (to name but a few). With respect to political parties, the research question challenging political scientists is to what extent these changes alienate or disentangle citizens from historically established ties with parties (de-alignment), and whether these changes may eventually produce firm links between newly established groups and old or newly founded parties (re-alignment), or leave citizens increasingly uprooted in political matters (high political volatility).

These developments may well be aggravated by two additional trends documented in the political science literature. On the one hand, citizens feel more politically competent, demand more of politics, and are more inclined to engage in politics. On the other hand, popular beliefs in the ability and willingness of political authorities to react properly to political demands from citizens seem to be on the wane. Obviously, such developments hold the potential of combining in an explosive mixture challenging the existing boundaries of the democratic state.

It is against this background that sub-group 1 will set out to study empirically with available data from the broadest possible range of democratic nations whether the above-described claims and trends are valid, and how common they are across nations. Answers to these questions will mark a major advance on the present state of research. From the outset, the work of this subgroup will have to be channelled regularly into the work of the three other subgroups because it is absolutely central to their own research concerns and that of the programme as a whole.

The Internationalization of Government. One feature of the shift in attitudes which seems to be revealed by the Eurobarometer surveys is the fact that the public wishes a contraction of national government activity at precisely the same time that international government agencies are rapidly expanding their spheres of activity and authority. The European Community (EC) is most notable in this regard, so far as Western Europe is concerned, but the list includes NATO, GATT, the European Court of Human Rights, the IMF, OPEC, and the World Bank. How do these opposite and contradictory trends—that is, a wish to contract national government activity, but an apparent acceptance of a growth of international government activity—fit together? Particularly relevant here is an answer to the question of how public attitudes towards national governments as centres of legitimacy orientation square with the increasing international diffusion of political responsibility.

In spite of the emergence of increasingly powerful international institutions of government (or perhaps because of them), modern societies are also developing more local political units. For example, almost every Western European state is currently creating or strengthening a regional level of government, and many are experimenting with community government as well. Indeed, the EC often seems to prefer to bypass national governments and deal directly with subnational ones, thereby strengthening them in some respects. This simultaneous development of both international and local forms of government is part of a modern trend towards multi-layered government the world over, but it is especially strong and advanced in Western Europe, and particularly worthy of research attention.

As 1992 approaches, attitudes towards the EC will once again become highly important. As an ideological issue, the EC has cut across many existing national political alignments, and the important question concerns whether the impact of major steps towards further European integration will encourage a tendency for political attitudes to continue to realign around pro- and anti-market, nationalist, and internationalist forces. Will this further weaken traditional ideological coalitions, and encourage building a sort of transnational consciousness which is unique in the modern world? This in turn prompts questions about what sorts of people most actively oppose and promote the new EEC ideal. How important is the whole matter on the agendas of national political groups? The research subgroup will monitor these trends, and will try to understand how they fit with the attitude changes being studied by other subgroups in the research programme.

The Scope of Government. The proper boundaries of the political have always been subject to change, negotiation, and redefinition, and have often been the subject of fierce political battles. For the past one hundred and fifty years, however, the boundaries have generally expanded in Western societies as the state has taken on more responsibilities and sought to regulate or control more areas of social and economic life. Now, however, the tide of public opinion seems to be flowing in the opposite direction, with greater public support for 'rolling back the frontiers of the state', for reducing public spending, and for state disengagement.

Public opinion has not simply reversed itself, however. Rather, it has shifted its weight so that the balance of opinion now seems to be generally in favour of cutting back on public activity and spending in some areas of life, but continuing to support state involvement in others. In other words, it is not true that public opinion is now contractionist where it was once expansionist, but rather it is more contractionist than it was, while maintaining its expansionist attitudes about some issues and policy areas. Moreover, these shifts in attitudes seem to be more emphatic in some countries or regions than in others. Equally, within each nation some social groups seem to show the new trends and patterns more strongly than others, while some adhere fairly faithfully to the old beliefs.

There are relatively few cross-national comparative surveys, and the various national surveys have not yet been put together. Available material suggests that public opinion in most Western nations does not favour public expenditure cuts as a general principle, but rather picks and chooses among different services, favouring the protection of some, the cutting of others, and showing a degree of ambivalence about a third category. Nor does a tendency to favour something like private pension schemes necessarily mean unfavourable attitudes towards state schemes, but rather a willingness to let both co-exist side by side. Although the embattled parties of government and opposition try to present public opinion in simple, for-or-against terms, the real state of public opinion appears to be more complicated and more subtle than this.

The issue of cutting public expenditure is rather different from those of economic privatization and deregulation because subjects such as welfare, health, and education are ideologically and historically endowed with symbolic importance, and yet they are also matters in which many members of the public have an immediate and direct interest and experience. This raises the question of how attitudes on the two sets of issues relate to each other and, on the other side of the coin, what attitudes different social and economic groups take towards the two sets of issues.

For most people, however, these issues are remote, complex, and technical, and their impact is often uncertain. How do these people form their attitudes? Do they take their cues from general ideological orientations (socialist, liberal, conservative) or from the political parties? Since the issues are so technical and uncertain, and lack salience for a large proportion of the public, how much room for manœuvre does a government have to influence opinion, and is such influence, if any, long-lasting or superficial? Do individuals who form a clear and strong opinion on an issue which directly affects them generalize this opinion to other issues which are remote? Do they distinguish between different sorts of privatization and deregulation? For example, do they make one sort of judgement about pension schemes, but treat banking or broadcasting as quite different matters? And do they qualify their approval of the changes in such a way that they might change their opinions if things do not work out as expected, or do they regard them as permanent and irreversible features of public policy?

The main task of this subgroup within the programme will be to fit the new contractionist trend in public opinion into a broad gauge historical picture to get a better idea of what is new and different about the 1980s. It will also compare and contrast the trends and movement in public opinion in different nations, and try to uncover the causal dynamics which lie behind them. Lastly, it will also seek to understand how and why different social groups vary in their expansionist and contractionist attitudes and in what sorts of areas the contrasts and similarities are most marked.

The Impact of Values   One of the most stimulating and controversial debates in political science over the last two decades is the claim made by Ronald Inglehart and other scholars that Western advanced industrial societies are characterized by trends involving substantial changes in socio-political values with increased emphasis on non-material and decreased emphasis on material values and issues. Previous studies of these changes have identified the most important value dimensions as: authoritarian–liberal; religious–secular; and materialist–postmaterialist. The Eurobarometer data have contained information since their beginning on the materialist–postmaterialist dimension and seem more or less to support the Inglehart claim. As more analytically and empirically refined analyses from national surveys accumulate, it becomes apparent that the emergence of the 'new politics', as it was once called in the mid-1970s, may have a substantial, if not overwhelming, impact on the future conduct of political affairs in Western democracies.

The subgroup concerned with this topic will primarily address the question whether changes in the above value dimensions are resulting in new cleavages and a systematic linkage between social groups and new political parties, or whether it will be accommodated within the given party systems. For instance, the emergence of Green parties has not followed identical paths in the various democracies under scrutiny, but the strength of the linkages between parts of the postmaterialist generation and Green parties makes such a re-alignment a likely outcome.

This is also interesting because research shows a two-fold distinction based on the conventional left–right political dimension, and the materialist–postmaterialist dimension. The second tends to cut across the first so as to challenge the social-democratic and socialist parties. Consequently, they will either come under pressure to re-align themselves around emerging ideological groups or suffer loss of support and perhaps a tendency to splinter.

This topic is important not only because of eventual changes in Western party systems. It is known that left postmaterialists are also carriers of decisively pro-participatory political attitudes, up to the point of civil disobedience, and of challenges to the legitimacy of present-day democratic regimes. It is, therefore, particularly important for this subgroup to bring together as much empirical evidence from national studies as possible in order to test the generality of the above-claimed developments.

Other Aspects of the Programme. Over and above these subgroups, the Steering Committee for the programme would be concerned with pulling together the various international surveys; for although these are often limited treatments of the subject, they also serve as a most useful framework on which the more subtle, penetrating, and detailed national studies can be made. These two types of data sets can be used to complement each other. In each case a major task of the subgroups will be to identify and explain national variations in opinion, and within each nation to identify and explain variations among different social and economic groupings. The programme is sensitive to the great importance of these national and social variations, and wishes to treat nations as a natural laboratory for research.

While the scientific programme will essentially adopt a European focus it is hoped that its findings will address wider questions. Of the approximately 170 nation states existing in the world, only between 25 and 30 are liberal democracies. The research will seek to improve our understanding of the conditions under which democratic governments can survive, and what the emerging status of public opinion towards this type of government is, and how it changes over time.

In addition, the research should produce substantial methodological pay-offs from a unique kind of cross-national work that for the first time will make a systematic effort to utilize existing national and cross-national data sources. The research would also seek to make recommendations on the future design of survey questionnaires to ensure compatibility between questionnaires and continuity in terms of questions and topics and hence strengthen the basis for longitudinal research.

Organizational Structure. The programme envisages the involvement of a maximum of thirty-five scholars in the research who would be organized into the four linked sub-topic groups mentioned above. A Steering Committee would be established comprising the programme directors (Professor M. Kaase and Professor K. Newton) and the group leader from each of the four sub-topic groups. A research co-ordinator would be appointed on a part-time basis to work in liaison with the programme directors. It is planned that the research co-ordinator will be based in an academic institution that houses a major data archive, as his/her important task will be to compile and prepare necessary data sets and make these available to the working groups.

Each subgroup would hold two working sessions per year and all the programme participants would meet three times over the five-year period (1989, 1991, and 1993) at a scientific conference to integrate the results of the subgroups' work within the objectives of the research programme as a whole. Throughout the programme, particular attention would be given to involve young post-doctoral scholars (and pre-doctoral where merited) in the work of the subgroups where their research interests were identified.

REFERENCES

Adorno, T. W., Frenkel-Brunswick, E., Levinson, D., and Sanford, R. (1950). *The Authoritarian Personality*. New York: Harper.

Aldrich, J. H., *et al.* (1989). 'Foreign Affairs and Issue Voting: Do Presidential Candidates "Waltz Before a Blind Audience?"' *American Political Science Review* 83: 123–41.

Alford, R. R. (1964). *Party and Society*. London: John Murray.

Allerbeck K. R. (1976). *Demokratisierung und sozialer Wandel in der Bundesrepublik Deutschland. Sekundäranalyse von Umfragedaten 1953–1974*. Opladen: Westdeutscher Verlag.

Almond, G. A. (1950). *The American People and Foreign Policy*. New York: Praeger.

—— and Verba, S. (1963). *The Civic Culture: Political Attitudes and Democracy in Five Nations*. Princeton, NJ: Princeton University Press.

Alt, J. E. (1983). 'The Evolution of Tax Structures'. *Public Choice* 41: 181–222.

Anderson, P. (1992). 'The Ends of History'. In *Zone of Engagement*. London: Verso.

Avineri, S., and de-Shalit, A. (eds.) (1992). *Communitarianism and Liberalism*. Oxford: Oxford University Press.

Baker, K. L., Dalton, R. J., and Hildebrandt, K. (1981). *Germany Transformed: Political Culture and the New Politics*. Cambridge, Mass.: Harvard University Press.

Barber, B. R. (1993). 'Reductionist Political Science and Democracy'. In *Reconsidering the Democratic Public*, ed. G. E. Marcus and R. L. Hanson. State College, Pa.: Pennsylvania State University Press.

Barnes, S. H., Kaase, M., *et al.* (1979). *Political Action: Mass Participation in Five Western Democracies*. Beverly Hills, Calif.: Sage.

Bartolini, S., and Mair, P. (1990). *Identity, Competition and Electoral Availability: The Stabilization of European Electorates 1885–1985*. Cambridge: Cambridge University Press.

Beck, U. (1986). *Die Risikogesellschaft*. Frankfurt am Main: Suhrkamp.

Beer, S. H. (1982). *Britain against Itself: The Political Contradictions of Collectivism*. London: Faber and Faber.

Beetham, D. (1991). *The Legitimation of Power*. Basingstoke: Macmillan.

Bell, C., and Newby, H. (1971). *Community Studies*. London: Allen and Unwin.

Bell, D. (1960). *The End of Ideology*. Glencoe, Ill.: Free Press.

Bell, D. (1975). 'The Revolution of Rising Entitlements'. *Fortune*, April: 98–103.

—— (1976a). 'The End of American Exceptionalism'. In *The American Commonwealth,* ed. N. Glazer and I. Kristol. New York: Basic Books.

—— (1976b). *The Cultural Contradictions of Capitalism*. New York: Basic Books.

Bell, D. (1993). *Communitarianism and its Critics*. Oxford: Clarendon.

Berelson, B. R. (1970). 'Survival through Apathy'. In *Frontiers of Democratic Theory*, ed. H. S. Kariel. New York: Random House.

Berg, K., and Kiefer, M.-L. (eds.) (1992). *Massenkommunikation*, iv. *Eine Langzeitstudie zur Mediennutzung und Medienbewertung 1964–1990*. Baden-Baden: Nomos Verlagsgesellschaft.

Berg-Schlosser, D. (1993). 'Das Scheitern der Weimarer Republik–Bedingungen der Demokratie im europäischen Vergleich'. Mimeo, Marburg.

—— and De Muir, G. (1994). 'Conditions of Democracy in Interwar Europe: A Boolean Test of Major Hypotheses'. *Comparative Politics 26*: 253–79.

Birch, A. (1984). 'Overload, Ungovernability and Delegitimation: The Theories and the British Case'. *British Journal of Political Science* 14: 135–60.

Blumenthal, M. D., Kahn, R. L., Andrews, F. M., and Head, K. B. (1972). *Justifying Violence: Attitudes of American Men*. Ann Arbor, Mich.: Institute for Social Research.

Böckenförde, E.-W. (1991). *Staat, Verfassung, Demokratie: Studien zur Verfassungstheorie und zum Verfassungrecht*. Suhrkamp Taschenbuch Wissenschaft no. 953. Frankfurt am Main: Suhrkamp.

Brittan, S. (1975). 'The Economic Contradictions of Democracy'. *British Journal of Political Science* 5: 129–59.

—— (1989)'"The Economic Contradictions of Capitalism" Revisited'. *Political Quarterly* 60: 190–208.

Budge, I. (1981). 'Review of "Political Action"'. *American Political Science Review* 75: 221–2.

—— (1993). 'Direct Democracy: Setting Appropriate Terms of Debate'. In *Prospects for Democracy*, ed. D. Held. Cambridge: Polity Press.

—— Robertson, D., and Hearl, D. (1987). *Ideology, Strategy and Party Change: Spatial Analyses of Post-war Election Programmes in 19 Democracies*. Cambridge: Cambridge University Press.

Butler, D., and Stokes, D. (1969). *Political Change in Britain*. Basingstoke: Macmillan.

—— (1971). *Political Change in Britain: Forces Shaping Electoral Choice*. Harmondsworth, Middx: Penguin.

Castles, F. G., and Wildenmann, R. (1986). *Vision and Realities of Party Government*. I. *Future of Government*, ed. R. Wildenmann. Berlin and New York: de Gruyter.

Commission of the European Communities (1973–). *Eurobarometer: Public*

Opinion in the European Community. Brussels: Commission of the European Communities.

Commission of the European Communities (1993*a*). *Eurobarometer: Public Opinion in the European Community*, No. 39. Brussels: Commission of the European Communities.

——— (1993*b*). *Eurobarometer: Trends 1974–1992*. Brussels: Commission of the European Communities.

Converse, P. E. (1964). 'The Nature of Belief Systems in Mass Publics'. In *Ideology and Discontent*, ed. D. Apter. New York: Free Press.

——— (1970). 'Attitudes and Non-Attitudes: Continuation of a Dialogue'. In *The Quantative Analysis of Social Problems*, ed. E. R. Tufte. Reading. Mass.: Addison-Wesley.

Coughlin, R. M. (1980). *Ideology, Public Opinion and Welfare Policy*. Berkeley, Calif.: Institute of International Studies, University of California.

Crewe, I. (1988). 'Has the Electorate Become Thatcherite?' In *Thatcherism*, ed. R. Skidelsky. Oxford: Basil Blackwell.

Crook, S., Pakulski, J., and Waters, J. (1992). *Postmodernization: Change in Advanced Industrial Society*. London: Sage.

Crozier, M. J., Huntington, S. P., and Watanuki, J. (1975). *The Crisis of Democracy: Report on the Governability of Democracies to the Trilateral Commission*. New York: New York University Press.

Dahl, R. A. (1989). *Democracy and its Critics*. New Haven, Conn., and London: Yale Univeristy Press.

Dalton, R. J. (1988). *Citizen Politics in Western Democracies: Public Opinion and Political Parties in the United States, Britain, West Germany and France*. Chatham, NJ: Chatham House.

——— and Eichenberg, R. C. (1990). 'Europeans and the European Community: The Dynamics of Public Support for European Integration'. Paper presented to the Annual Meeting of the American Political Science Association, San Francisco.

——— (1991) 'Economic Evaluations and Citizen Support for European Integration'. Paper presented to the Annual Meeting of the American Political Science Association, Washington, DC.

——— and Küchler, M. (eds.) (1990). *Challenging the Political Order: New Social and Political Movements in Western Democracies*. Cambridge: Polity Press.

——— and Rohrschneider, R. (1990). 'Wählerwandel und die Abschwächung der Parteineigung von 1972 bis 1987'. In *Wahlen und Wähler: Analysen aus Anlaß der Bundestagswahl 1987*, ed. M. Kaase and H.-D. Klingemann. Opladen: Westdeutscher Verlag.

Deutsch, K. W. (1952). *Nationalism and Social Communication*. Cambridge, Mass.: MIT Press.

Deutsch, K. W. (1968). *Analysis of International Relations*. Englewood Cliffs, NJ: Prentice-Hall.

—— (1972). 'Attaining and Maintaining Integration'. In *European Integration*, ed. M. Hidges, Harmondsworth, Middx: Penguin.

—— et al. (1957). *Political Community and the North Atlantic Area: International Organization in the Light of Historical Experience*. Princeton, NJ: Princeton University Press.

Diamond, L. (1992). 'Economic Development and Democracy Reconsidered'. In *Re-examining Democracy: Essays in Honor of S. M. Lipset*, ed. G. Marks, and L. Diamond. Newbury Park, Calif.: Sage.

Dienel, P. C. (1991). *Die Planungszelle: Der Bürger plant seine Umwelt: Eine Alternative zur Establishment-Demokratie*, 2nd edn. Opladen: Westdeutscher Verlag.

Diewald, M. (1991). *Soziale Beziehungen: Verluste oder Liberalisierung? Soziale Unterstützung in informellen Netzwerken*. Berlin: Rainer Bohn Verlag.

Dittrich, K., and Johansen, L. N. (1983). 'Voting Turnout in Europe, 1945–1978: Myths and Realities'. In *Western European Party Systems: Continuity and Change*, ed. H. Daalder and P. Mair. London: Sage.

Dogan, M. (1994). 'The Decline of Nationalisms within Western Europe'. *Comparative Politics* 26: 281–305.

Douglas, J. D. (1989). *The Myth of the Welfare State*. New Brunswick, NJ.: Transaction Press.

Downs, A. (1957). *An Economic Theory of Democracy*. New York: Harper.

Dubiel, H. (1992). 'Konsens oder Konflikt? Die normative Integration des demokratischen Staates.' In *Staat und Demokratie in Europa*, xviii. *Wissenschaftlicher Kongreß der Deutschen Vereinigung für Politische Wissenschaft*, ed. B. Kohler-Koch. Opladen: Leske and Budrich.

Easton, D. (1965). *A Systems Analysis of Political Life*. New York: John Wiley.

—— (1975). 'A Re-Assessment of the Concept of Political Support'. *British Journal of Political Science* 5: 435–57.

Eichenberger, K. (1977). 'Der geforderte Staat: Zur Problematik der Staatsaufgaben'. In *Regierbarkeit: Studien zu ihrer Problematisierung*, ed. I. Band, W. Hennis, P. G. Kielmansegg, and U. Matz. Stuttgart: Ernst Klett.

Etzioni, A. (1968). *The Active Society: A Theory of Societal and Political Processes*. London: Macmillan Collier.

Everts, P., and Faber, A. (1990). 'Public Opinion, Foreign Policy and Democracy'. Paper prepared for the ECPR-Joint Sessions, Bochum.

Feld, W. J., and Wildgen, J. K. (1976). *Domestic Political Realities and European Unification: A Study of Mass Publics and Elites in the European Community Countries*. Boulder, Col.: Westview Press.

Feldman, S. (1988). 'Structure and Consistency in Public Opinion: The Role of Core Beliefs and Values'. *American Journal of Political Science* 32: 416–40.

Fest, J. (1993). *Die schwierige Freiheit. Über die offene Flanke der offenen Gesellschaft*. Berlin: Siedler Verlag.

Fleishman, J. A. (1988). 'Attitude Organisation in the General Public: Evidence for a Bi-dimensional Structure'. *Social Forces* 67: 159–84.

Flora, P. ed. (1988). 'Introduction'. In *Growth to Limits: The Western European Welfare States since World War II*, ii. Berlin: de Gruyter.

Free, L. A., and Cantril, H. (1969). *The Political Beliefs of Americans: A Study of Public Opinion*. New Brunswick, NJ: Rutgers University Press.

Fuchs, D. (1989). *Die Unterstützung des politischen Systems der Bundesrepublik Deutschland*. Opladen: Westdeutscher Verlag.

────── (1993). 'Trends of Political Support in the Federal Republic of Germany'. In *Political Culture in Germany*, ed. D. Berg-Schlosser and R. Rytlewski. London: Macmillan.

────── Guidorossi, G., and Svensson, P. (1992). 'Support for the Democratic System'. Paper prepared for presentation at the meeting of the ESF-project 'Beliefs in Government', Oxford, November.

────── and Klingemann, H.-D. (1989). 'The Left-Right-Schema'. In *Continuities in Political Action: A Longitudinal Study of Political Orientations in Three Western Democracies*, ed. M. K. Jennings, J. W. van Deth, *et al.* Berlin: de Gruyter.

────── and Rucht, D. (1994). 'Support for New Social Movements in Five Western European Countries'. In *Social Change and Political Transformation*, ed. C. Rootes and H. Davis. London: UCL Press.

Fukuyama, F. (1989). 'The End of History?' *The National Interest* 16: 1–14.

────── (1992) *The End of History and the Last Man*. New York: Free Press.

Gans, H. J. (1967). *The Levittowners*: New York: Vintage Books.

George, S. (1990). *An Awkward Partner: Britain in the European Community*. Oxford: Oxford University Press.

Glatzer, W., and Zapf, W. (1984). *Lebensqualität in der Bundesrepublik Deutschland. Objektive Lebensbedingungen und Subjektives Wohlbefinden*. Frankfurt and New York: Campus.

Göhler, G. (1992). 'Konflikt und Integration: Koreferat zu Helmut Dubiel'. In *Staat und Demokratie in Europa*, xviii. *Wissenschaftlicher Kongreß der Deutschen Vereinigung für Politische Wissenschaft*, ed. B. Kohler-Koch. Opladen: Leske and Budrich.

Goodin, R. (1988). *Reasons for Welfare*. Princeton, NJ: Princeton University Press.

────── (1992). *Green Political Theory*. Cambridge: Polity Press.

Gould, F. (1983). 'The Development of Public Expenditures in Western Industrialised Countries: A Comparative Analysis'. *Public Finance* 39: 38–69.

Graber, D. A. (1994). 'Why Voters Fail Information Tests: Can the Hurdles be Overcome?' *Political Communication* 11: 331–46.

Habermas, J. (1973). *Legitimationsprobleme in Spätkapitalismus*. Frankfurt am Main: Shurkamp.

—— (1975). *Legitimation Crisis*. Boston: Beacon Press.

Hadenius, A. (1985). 'Citizens Strike a Balance: Discontent with Taxes, Content with Spending'. *Journal of Public Policy* 5: 349–63.

—— (1986). *A Crisis of the Welfare State*. Stockholm: Almqvist and Wicksell.

Hamilton, R. F., and Wright, J. D. (1986). *The State of the Masses*. Chicago: Aldine.

Handley, D. H. (1981). 'Public Opinion and European Integration: The Crisis of the 1970s'. *European Journal of Political Research* 9: 335–64.

Harvey, D. (1989). *The Condition of Postmodernity*. Oxford: Basil Blackwell.

Helliwell, J. F. (1994). 'Empirical Linkages between Democracy and Economic Growth'. *British Journal of Political Science* 24: 225–48.

Hennis, W., Kielmansegg, P. G., and Matz, U. (eds.) (1977). *Regierbarkeit*, i. Stuttgart: Kohlhammer.

——,——,—— (eds.) (1979). *Regierbarkeit*, ii. Stuttgart: Kohlhammer.

Highley, J., and Moore, G. (1981). 'Elite Integration in the United States and Australia'. *American Political Science Review* 75: 581–97.

Hildebrandt, K., and Dalton, R. J. (1978). 'The New Politics: Political Change or Sunshine Politics'. In *Elections and Parties: Socio-Political Change and Participation in the West German Federal Election of 1976*, ed. M. Kaase and K. von Beyme. Beverly Hills, Calif.: Sage.

Hirschman, A. O. (1982). *Shifting Involvements: Private Interest and Public Action*. Princeton NJ: Princeton University Press.

—— (1991). *The Rhetoric of Reaction: Perversity, Futility, Jeopardy*. Cambridge, Mass.: Belknap Press.

Hoffman, S. (1966) 'Obstinate or Obsolete? The Fate of the Nation-State and the Case of Western Europe'. *Daedalus* 95: 862–915.

Hofrichter, J., and Klein, M. (1993). *The European Parliament in the Eyes of EC Citizens*. Mannheim: University of Mannheim.

Huntington, S. P. (1974). 'Post Industrial Politics: How Benign Will it Be?' *Comparative Politics* 6: 147–77.

—— (1976). 'The Democratic Distemper'. In *The American Commonwealth*, ed. N. Gazer and I. Kristol. New York: Basic Books.

—— (1991). *The Third Wave: Democratisation in the Late Twentieth Century*, Norman, Okla.: University of Oklahoma Press.

—— (1993). 'The Clash of Civilizations? The Next Pattern of Conflict'. *Foreign Affairs* 72: 22–49.

Inglehart, R. (1971). 'The Silent Revolution in Europe: Intergenerational Change in Post-Industrial Societies'. *American Political Science Review* 65: 991–1017.

Inglehart, R. (1977*a*). 'Long Term Trends in Mass Support for European Unification'. *Government and Opposition* 12: 150–77.

—— (1977*b*). *The Silent Revolution: Changing Values and Political Styles among Western Publics*. Princeton, NJ: Princeton University Press.

—— (1988). 'The Rennaissance of Political Culture'. *American Political Science Review* 82: 1203–30.

—— (1990). *Culture Shift in Advanced Industrial Societies*: Princeton, NJ: Princeton University Press.

—— (1991). 'Trust between Nations: Primordial Ties, Societal Learning and Economic Development'. In *Eurobarometer: The Dynamics of European Public Opinion: Essays in Honour of Jacques-René Rabier*, ed. K. Reif and R. Inglehart. London: Macmillan.

—— and Abramson, P. A. (1994). 'Economic Security and Value Change'. *American Political Science Review* 88: 336–54.

—— and Klingemann, H.-D. (1979). 'Ideological Conceptualization and Value Priorities'. In S. H. Barnes, M. Kaase, *et al.*, *Political Action: Mass Participation in Five Western Democracies*. Beverly Hills, Calif.: Sage.

—— and Rabier, J.-R. (1978). 'Economic Uncertainty and European Solidarity: Public Opinion Trends'. *Annals of the American Association of Political and Social Science* 440: 66–97.

—— and Reif, K. (1991). 'Analysing Trends in West European Opinion: The Role of the Eurobarometer Surveys'. In *Eurobarometer: The Dynamics of European Public Opinion: Essays in Honour of Jacques-René Rabier*, ed. K. Reif and R. Inglehart. London: Macmillan.

International Social Survey Programme (1987). *Role of Government, 1985: Codebook ZA*, No. 1490. Cologne: Zentralarchiv für Empirische Sozialforschung, Universität zu Köln.

Janssen, J. H. (1991). 'Postmaterialism, Cognitive Mobilization and Public Support for European Integration'. *British Journal of Political Science* 21: 443–68.

Jennings, M. K., van Deth, J. W., *et al.* (1990). *Continuities in Political Action: A Longitudinal Study of Political Orientations in Three Western Democracies*. Berlin and New York: de Gruyter.

Kaase, M. (1982). 'Partizipatorische Revolution: Ende der Parteien?' In *Bürger und Parteien: Ansichten und Analysen einer schwierigen Beziehung*, ed. J. Raschke. Opladen: Westdeutscher Verlag.

—— (1992). 'Direct Political Participation in the Late Eighties in the EC Countries'. In *From Voters to Participants*, ed. P. Gundelach and K. Siune. Aarhus: Politica.

—— (1994). 'Is There Personalization in Politics? Candidates and Voting Behavior in Germany'. *International Political Science Review* 15: 223–42.

—— and Barnes, S. H. (1979). 'Conclusion: The Future of Political Protest in Western Democracies'. In S. H. Barnes, M. Kaase, *et al.*, *Political Action:*

Mass Participation in Five Western Democracies. Beverly Hills, Calif.: Sage.

―――― and Klingemann, H.-D. (1982) 'Social Structure, Value Orientations, and the Party System: The Problem of Interest Accommodation in Western Democracies'. *European Journal of Political Research* 10: 367–86.

―――― and Neidhardt, F. (1990). 'Politische Gewalt und Repression: Ergebnisse von Bevölkerungsumfragen'. In *Analysen und Vorschläge der Unabhängigen Regierungskommission zur Verhinderung und Bekämpfung von Gewalt (Gewaltkommission)*, iv. *Ursachen, Prävention und Kontrolle von Gewalt*, ed. H.-D. Schwind, J. Baumann, *et al.* Berlin: Duncker and Humblot.

Katz, D., Gutek, B. A., Kahn, R. L., and Barton, E. (1975). *Bureaucratic Encounters: A Pilot Study in the Evaluation of Government Services*. Ann Arbor, Mich.: Institute for Social Research.

Katz, R. S. (1987). *Party Governments: European and American Experiences*, ii. *Future of Government*, ed. R. Wildenmann. Berlin: de Gruyter.

Key, V. O. (1966). *The Responsible Electorate*. Cambridge, Mass.: Belknap Press.

Kielmansegg, P. G. (1988). *Das Experiment der Freiheit, Zur gegenwärtigen Lage des demokratischen Verfassungsstaats*. Stuttgart: Klett-Cotta.

Kiewiet, R. D., and Rivers, D. (1985). 'A Retrospective on Retrospective Voting'. In *Economic Conditions and Electoral Outcomes: The United States and Western Europe*, ed. H. Eulau and M. S. Lewis-Beck. New York: Agathon Press.

King, A. (1975). '"Overload": Problems of Governing in the 1970s'. *Political Studies* 23: 284–96.

Klages, H. (1988). *Wertedynamik: Über die Wandelbarkeit des Selbstverständlichen*. Zürich: Edition Interfrom.

―――― and Kmieciak, P. (eds.) (1979). *Wertwandel und gesellschaftlicher Wandel*. Frankfurt and New York: Campus.

Klingemann, H.-D. (1979). 'The Background of Ideological Conceptualization'. In S. H . Barnes, M. Kaase, *et al.*, *Political Action: Mass Participation in Five Western Democracies*. Beverly Hills, Calif.: Sage.

―――― (1986). 'Umweltprolematik in den Wahlprogrammen der etablierten politischen Parteien in der Bundesrepublik Deutschland'. In *Umwelt, Wirtschaft, Gesellschaft: Wege zu einem neuen Grundverständnis*, ed. R. Wildenmann. Stuttgart: Staatsministerium Baden-Württemberg.

―――― Hofferbert, R. I., and Budge, I. (1994). *Parties, Policies and Democracy*. Boulder, Colo.: Westview.

―――― and Volkens, A. (1995). 'The Structure of Party Systems in the OECD Countries'. In *Societal Problems, Political Structures, and Political Performance: Towards a Typology of Democratic Political Systems*, ed. H.-D. Klingemann. In preparation.

Klosko, G. (1993). 'Rawls' "Political" Philosophy and American Democracy'. *American Political Science Review* 87: 348–59.

Kornhauser, W. (1960). *The Politics of Mass Society*. London: Routledge & Kegan Paul.

Kriesi, H. (1993). *Political Mobilization and Social Change: The Dutch Case in Comparative Perspective*. Aldershot: Avebury.

Kuklinski, J. H. *et al.* (1991). 'The Cognitive and Affective Bases of Political Tolerance Judgements'. *American Journal of Political Science* 35: 1–27.

—— (1993). 'The New American Dilemma: Racism and Racial Resentment'. Mimeo.

Lane, J.–E., McKay, D., and Newton, K. (1991). *Political Data Handbook: OECD Countries*. Oxford: Oxford University Press.

Lane, R. (1962). *Political Ideology*. New York: Free Press.

Lash, S., and Urry, J. (1987). *The End of Organized Capitalism*. Cambridge: Polity Press.

Laver, M. J., and Budge, I. (1993). *Party Policy and Government Coalitions*. London: Macmillan.

Lewin, L. (1991). *Self Interest and Public Interest in Western Politics*. Oxford: Oxford University Press.

Lieberam, E. (1977). *Krise der Regierbarkeit: ein neues Thema bürgerlicher Staatsideologie*. Frankfurt am Main: Verlag marxistische Blätter.

Lijphart, A. (1984). *Democracies: Patterns of Majoritarian and Consensus Government in Twenty-One Countries*. New Haven, Conn.: Yale University Press.

—— (1991). 'Constitutional Choices for New Democracies'. *Journal of Democracy* 2: 72–84.

—— (1994). 'Democracies: Forms, Performance and Constitutional Engineering'. *European Journal of Political Research* 25: 1–17.

Lindberg, L. N., and Scheingold, S. A. (1970). *Europe's Would-Be Polity: Patterns of Change*. Englewood Cliffs, NJ.: Prentice Hall.

Linz, J. J., and Stepan, A. (eds.) (1978). *The Breakdown of Democratic Regimes: Latin America*. Baltimore: Johns Hopkins University Press.

Lippmann, W. (1922). *Public Opinion*. New York: Free Press.

Lipset, S. M. (1960). *Political Man: The Social Bases of Politics*. New York: Doubleday.

—— (1963). *Political Man: The Social Bases of Politics*. London: Heinemann.

—— (1994). 'The Social Requisites of Democracy Revisited'. 1993 Presidential address to the Meeting of the American Sociological Association. *American Sociological Review* 59: 1–22.

—— and Rokkan, S. (1967). 'Cleavage Structures, Party Systems and Voter Alignments: An Introduction'. In *Party Systems and Voter Alignments:*

Cross-National Perspectives, ed. S. M. Lipset and S. Rokkan. London: Macmillan.

Lipset, S. M., and Schneider, W. (1987). *The Confidence Gap: Business, Labor and Government in the Public Mind*. Baltimore: Johns Hopkins University Press.

Luhmann, N. (1969). *Legitimation durch Verfahren*. Neuwied and Berlin: Luchterhand.

—— (1981). *Politische Theorie im Wohlfahrtsstaat*. Munich: G. Olzog Verlag.

—— (1986). *Ökologische Kommunikation: Kann die moderne Gesellschaft sich auf ökologische Gefährdungen einstellen?* Opladen: Westdeutscher Verlag.

Maag, G. (1991). *Gesellschaftliche Werte: Strukturen, Stabilität und Funktion*. Opladen: Westdeutscher Verlag.

Maguire, M. (1983). '"Is There Still Persistence?" Electoral Change in Western Europe, 1948–1979'. In *Western European Party Systems: Continuity and Change*, ed. H. Daalder and P. Mair. London: Sage.

Maier, C. (1992). 'Democracy since the French Revolution'. In *Democracy*, ed. J. Dunn. Oxford: Oxford University Press.

Margolis, M. (1979). *Viable Democracy*. London: Macmillan.

Mark, G., and Diamond, L. (eds.) (1992). *Re-examining Democracy*: *Essays in Honor of S. M. Lipset*. Newbury Park, Calif.: Sage.

Marsh, A. (1975). '"The Silent Revolution": Value Priorities and the Quality of Life in Britain'. *American Political Science Review* 69: 21–30.

Marshall, T. H. (1963). 'Citizenship and Social Class'. In *Sociology at the Crossroads*. London: Heinemann.

McClosky, H. (1964). 'Consensus and Ideology in American Politics'. *American Political Science Review* 58: 361–82.

McKay, D. (1979). 'The United States in Crisis: A Review of the American Political Literature'. *Government and Opposition* 14: 373–85.

Melucci, A. (1980). 'The New Social Movements: A Theoretical Approach'. *Social Science Information* 19: 199–226.

Merkl, P. (1988). 'The Challenges and the Party Systems'. In *When Parties Fail: Emerging Alternative Organisations*, ed. K. Lawson and P. Merkl. Princeton, NJ: Princeton University Press.

Merritt, R. L., and Puchala, D. A. (1968). *Western European Perspectives on International Affairs: Public Opinion Studies and Evaluations*. New York: Praeger.

Meulemann, H. (1985). 'Wertewandel in der Bundesrepublik zwischen 1950 und 1980: Versuch einer zusammenfassenden Deutung vorliegender Zeitreihen'. In *Wirtschaftlicher Wandel, religiöser Wandel und Wertewandel: Folgen für das politische Verhalten in der Bundesrepublik Deutschland*, ed. D. Oberndörfer, H. Rattinger, and K. Schmitt. Berlin: Duncker and Humblot.

Miegel, M., and Wahl, S. (1993). *Das Ende des Individualismus: Die Kultur des Westens zerstört sich selbst*. Munich: Verlag Bonn Aktuell.

Milbrath, L. W. (1965). *Political Participation*. Chicago: Rand McNally.

Miller, W. E., and Levitin, T. E. (1976). *Leadership and Change: Presidential Elections from 1952 to 1976*. Cambridge, Mass.: Winthrop.

Milward, A. S. (1992). *The European Rescue of the Nation State*. London: Routledge.

Muller, E. N. (1979). *Aggressive Political Participation*. Princeton, NJ: Princeton University Press.

—— Jukam, T. O., and Seligson, M. A. (1982). 'Diffuse Support and Anti-system Political Behavior: A Comparative Analysis'. *American Journal of Political Science* 26: 240–63.

Müller-Rommel, F. (1993). *Grüne Parteien in Westeuropa: Entwicklungsphasen und Erfolgsbedingungen*. Opladen: Westdeutscher Verlag.

Murray, R. (1989). 'Benetton Britain'. In *New Times: the Changing Face of Politics in the 1990s*, ed. S. Hall and M. Jacques. London: Lawrence and Wishart.

Neidhardt, F. (1985). 'Einige Ideen zu einer allgemeinen Theorie sozialer Bewegungen'. In *Sozialstruktur im Umbruch: Karl Martin Bolte zum 60. Geburtstag*, ed. S. Hradil. Opladen: Leske and Budrich.

—— and Rucht, D. (1993). 'Auf dem Weg in die "Bewegungsgesellschaft"?' *Soziale Welt* 44: 305–26.

Neuman, R. W. (1986). *The Paradox of Politics: Knowledge and Opinion in the American Electorate*. Cambridge, Mass.: Harvard University Press.

Newton, K. (1969). *The Sociology of British Communism*. London: Allen Lane the Penguin Press.

—— (1993). 'Economic Voting in the 1992 Election'. In *British Elections and Parties Yearbook*, ed. D. Denver *et al.* Brighton: Harvester Wheatsheaf.

Nielsen, H. J. (1976). 'The Uncivic Culture: Attitudes towards the Political System in Denmark and the Vote for the Progress Party'. *Scandinavian Political Studies* 11: 147–56.

Noelle-Neumann, E. (1988). 'Das Fernsehen und die Zukunft der Lesekultur'. In *Die verstellte Welt: Beiträge zur Medienökologie*, ed. W. D. Fröhlich, R. Zitzlsperger, and B. Franzmann. Frankfurt am Main: Fischer Taschenbuch Verlag.

—— and Köcher, R. (1993). *Allensbacher Jahrbuch der Demoskopie 1984–1992*, ix, ed. E. Noelle-Neumann and R. Köcher. Munich, New York, London, and Paris: K. G. Saur; Allensbach am Bodensee: Verlag für Demoskopie.

Nussbaum, M. C. (1993). 'Menschliches Tun und soziale Gerechtigkeit: Zur Verteidigung des aristotelischen Essentialismus'. In *Gemeinschaft und*

Gerechtigkeit, ed. M. Brumlik and H. Brunkhorst. Frankfurt am Main: Fischer Taschenbuchverlag.

O'Connor, J. (1973). *The Fiscal Crisis of the State*. New York: St Martin's Press.

Offe, C. (1972). *Struturprobleme des kapitalistischen Staates*. Frankfurt am Main: Suhrkamp.

―――― (1979) '"Unregierbarkeit": Zur Renaissance konservativer Krisenstrategien'. In *Stichworte zur geistigen Situation der Zeit'*, i, ed. J. Habermas. Frankfurt am Main: Suhrkamp.

―――― (1984). *Contradictions of the Welfare State*, ed. J. Keane. London: Hutchinson.

―――― (1985). 'New Social Movements: Challenging the Boundaries of Institutional Politics?' *Social Research* 52: 817–68.

―――― (1993). 'Die Integration nachkommunistischer Gesellschaften: Die ehemalige DDR im Vergleich zu ihren osteuropäischen Nachbarn'. In *Lebensverhältnisse und soziale Konflikte im neuen Europa: Verhandlungen des 26. Deutschen Soziologentages in Düsseldorf 1992*, ed. B. Schäfers. Frankfurt and New York: Campus.

Ohmae, K. (1989). 'Managing in a Borderless World'. *Harvard Business Review* 3: 152–61.

Page, B. I., and Shapiro, R. I. (1993). 'The Rational Public and Democracy'. In *Reconsidering the Democratic Republics*, ed. G. E. Marcus and R. L. Hanson. State College, Pa.: Pennsylvania State University Press.

Parekh, B. (1993). 'The Cultural Particularity of Liberal Democracy'. In *Prospects for Democracy: North, South, East and West*, ed. D. Held. Cambridge: Polity Press.

Parkin, F. (1968). *Middle Class Radicalism*. New York: Praeger.

Parry, G., Moyser, G., and Day, N. (1992). *Political Participation and Democracy in Britain*. Cambridge: Cambridge University Press.

Pateman, C. (1970). *Participation and Democratic Theory*. Cambridge: Cambridge University Press.

Peacock, A., and Wiseman, J. (1967). *The Growth of Public Expenditure in the United Kingdom*. London: Allen and Unwin.

Pechman, J. A. (1988). *World Tax Reform: A Progress Report*. Washington, DC: Brookings Institution.

Pedersen, M. N. (1983). 'Changing Patterns of Electoral Volatility in European Party Systems 1948–1977: Explorations in Explanation'. In *Western European Party Systems: Continuity and Change*, ed. H. Daalder and P. Mair. London: Sage.

Peltzman, S. (1980). 'The Growth of Government'. *Journal of Law and Economics* 23: 285–87.

Peters, B. (1991*a*). *The Politics of Taxation*. Oxford: Basil Blackwell.

———— (1991*b*). *European Politics Reconsidered*. New York: Holmes and Meir.

Pierce, R., and Sullivan, J. L. (1980) 'An Overview of the American Electorate', in *The Electorate Reconsidered*, ed. J. C. Pierce and J. L. Sullivan. Berkley, Calif.: Sage.

Poguntke, T. (1994). 'Explorations into a Minefield: Anti-Party Sentiment, Conceptual Thoughts and Empirical Evidence'. Paper prepared for the ECPR Joint Sessions. Madrid, Mimeo.

Popkin, S. (1991). *The Reasoning Voter*. Chicago: University of Chicago Press.

Powell, G. Bingham, Jr. (1982). *Contemporary Democracies: Participation, Stability and Violence*. Cambridge, Mass.: Harvard University Press.

———— (1989). 'Constitutional Design and Citizen Electoral Control'. *Journal of Theoretical Politics* 1: 107–30.

Prezeworski, A., and Teune, H. (1970). *The Logic of Comparative Social Inquiry*. New York: John Wiley.

Prothro, J. W., and Grigg, C. M. (1960). 'Fundamental Principles of Democracy: Bases of Agreement and Disagreement'. *Journal of Politics* 22: 276–94.

Pruitt, D. G. (1965). 'Definition of the Situation as a Determinant of International Action'. In *International Behaviour: A Social-Psychological Analysis*, ed. H. C. Kelman. New York: Holt, Rinehart and Winston.

Putnam, R. D. (1993). *Making Democracy Work: Civic Traditions in Modern Italy*. Princeton, NJ: Princeton University Press.

Rawls, J. (1971). *A Theory of Justice*. Cambridge, Mass.: Harvard University Press.

———— (1985). 'Justice as Fairness: Political not Metaphysical'. *Philosophy and Public Affairs* 14: 223–51.

Rokeach, M. (1960). *The Open and the Closed Mind: Investigations into the Nature of Belief Systems and Personality Systems*. New York: Basic Books.

———— (1973). *The Nature of Human Values*. New York: Free Press.

Rorty, R. (1990). *Contingency, Irony, and Solidarity*. Cambridge: Cambridge University Press.

———— (1991). 'The Priority of Democracy to Philosophy'. In *Philosophical Papers*, 1, *Objectivity, Relativism, and Truth*. Cambridge: Cambridge University Press.

Rose, R. ed. (1980). *Challenge to Governance*. Beverly Hills, Calif.: Sage.

———— and Peters, G. (1978). *Can Government Go Bankrupt?* New York: Basic Books.

Rosenau, J. N. (1961). *Public Opinion and Foreign Policy: An Operational Formulation*. New York: Random House.

Rosenau, P. M. (1992). *Post-Modernism and the Social Sciences*. Princeton, NJ: Princeton University Press.

Rucht, D. (1994). *Modernisierung und neue soziale Bewegungen*. Frankfurt and New York: Campus.

Rueschemeyer, D., Stephens, E., and Stephens, J. D. (1992). *Capitalist Development and Democracy*. Chicago: University of Chicago Press.

Sartori, G. (1987). *The Theory of Democracy Revisited*, i. *The Contemporary Debate*; ii, *The Classical Issues*. Chatham, NJ: Chatham.

Scharpf, F. W. (1985). 'Die Politikverflechtungs-Falle: Europäische Integration und deutscher Föderalismus im Vergleich'. *Politische Vierteljahresschrift* 26: 323–56.

—— (1992). 'Die Handlungsfähigkeit des Staates am Ende des Zwanzigsten Jahrhunderts'. In *Staat und Demokratie in Europa*, xviii. *Wissenschaftlicher Kongreß der Deutschen Vereinigung für Politische Wissenschaft*, ed. B. Kohler-Koch. Opladen: Leske and Budrich.

—— Reissert, B., and Schnabel, F. (1976). *Politikverflechtung: Theorie und Empirie des kooperativen Föderalismus in der Bundesrepublik*. Kronberg: Scriptor.

Scheuch, E. K. (1990). 'The Development of Comparative Research: Towards Causal Explanations'. In *Theory and Practice in International Social Research*, ed. E. Øyen. London: Sage.

—— (1993). 'Vereine als Teil der Privatgesellschaft'. In *Vereine in Deutschland*, ed. H. Best. Bonn: Informationszentrum Sozialwissenschaften.

Schumpeter, J. A. (1942). *Capitalism, Socialism and Democracy*. New York: Harper and Row.

Scott, A. (1990). *Ideology and New Social Movements*. London: Unwin Hyman.

Sears, D., and Citrin, J. (1985). *Tax Revolt: Something for Nothing in California*. London and Cambridge, Mass.: Harvard University Press.

Sharpe, L. J. (1988). 'The Growth and Decentralisation of the Modern Democratic State'. *European Journal of Political Research* 16: 365–80.

—— (1989). 'Fragmentation and Territoriality in the European State System'. *International Political Science Review* 10: 223–38.

—— and Newton, K. (1983). *Does Politics Matter?* Oxford: Oxford University Press.

Simmel, G. (1955). *Conflict and the Web of Group Affiliation*. London: Collier Macmillan.

Sniderman, P. M. (1981). *A Question of Loyalty*. Berkeley, Calif.: University of California Press.

Stimson, S. C. and Milgate, M. (1993). 'Utility, Property and Political Participation: J. Mill on Democratic Reform'. *American Political Science Review* 87: 901–11.

Streeck, W. (1987). 'Vielfalt und Interdependenz: Überlegungen zur Rolle von intermediären Organisationen in sich ändernden Umwelten'. *Kölner Zeitschrift für Soziologie und Sozialpsychologie* 39: 471–95.

Tarrow, S. (1994). *Power in Movement: Social Movements, Collective Action and Politics*. Cambridge: Cambridge University Press.

Tichenor, P. J., Donohue, G. A., and Olien, C. A. (1970). 'Mass Media Flow and Differential Growth in Knowledge'. *Public Opinion Quarterly* 34: 159–70.

Touraine, A. (1981). *The Voice and the Eye: An Analysis of Social Movements*. Cambridge: Cambridge University Press.

Uehlinger, H.-M. (1988). *Politische Partizipation in der Bundesrepublik*. Opladen: Westdeutscher Verlag.

Vanhanen, T. (1990). *The Process of Democratization: A Comparative Study of 147 States*. New York: Crane Russak.

Verba, S., and Nie, N. H. (1972). *Participation in America*. New York: Harper and Row.

——, —— and Kim, J. (1978). *Participation and Political Equality*. Cambridge: Cambridge University Press.

—— *et al.* (1993). 'Citizen Activity: Who Participates? What Do They Say?' *American Political Science Review* 87: 303–18.

Waisman, C. H. (1992). 'Capitalism, the Market, and Democracy'. In *Re-examining Democracy: Essays in Honor of S. M. Lipset*, ed. G. Marks and L. Diamond. Newbury Park, Calif.: Sage.

Wallace, W. (1994). 'Rescue or Retreat? The Nation State in Western Europe, 1945–93'. *Political Studies* 42: 52–76.

Walzer, M. (1992). *Zivile Gesellschaft und Amerikanische Demokratie*. Berlin: Rotbuch-Verlag.

Weil, F. D. (1989). 'The Sources and Structure of Legitimation in Western Democracies: A Consolidated Model Tested with Time-Series Data in Six Countries since World War II'. *American Sociological Review* 54: 682–706.

Weir, S., and Hall, W. (eds.) (1994) *Ego Trip*. London: Charter 88 Trust.

Westle, B. (1989). *Politische Legitimität: Theorien, Konzepte, empirische Befunde*. Baden-Baden: Nomos.

Wilensky, H. L. (1975). *The Welfare State and Inequality: Structural and Ideological Roots of Public Expenditures*. Berkeley, Calif.: University of California Press.

Wilmott, P., and Young, M. (1960). *Family and Class in a London Suburb*. London: Routledge and Kegan Paul.

Zeus (1990). *Structure in European Attitudes*. Report prepared on behalf of the Cellule de Prospective of the Commission of the European Communities. Mannheim: Zeus/University of Mannheim.

Ziegler, A. H. (1987). 'The Structure of Western European Attitudes towards Atlantic Cooperation: Implications for the Western Alliance'. *British Journal of Political Science* 17: 457–77.

Zilleßen, H., Dienel, P. C., and Strubelt, W. (eds). (1993). *Die Modernisierung der Demokratie: Internationale Ansätze*. Opladen: Westdeutscher Verlag.

AUTHOR INDEX

Abramson, P. A. 34, 144, 149
Adorno, T. W. 9
Aldrich, J. H. 113
Alford, R. R. 27
Allerbeck 11, 42
Almond, G. A. 3, 9, 105, 122
Alt, J. E. 76
Anderson, P. 126

Baker, K. L. 42, 77, 144
Barber, B. R. 79
Barnes, S. H. 3, 41, 43, 51, 145, 161
Bartolini, S. 44, 139, 140
Beck, U. 53, 154, 155
Beer, S. H. 29
Beetham, D. 23
Bell, C. 155
Bell, D. 25, 27, 31, 32, 33, 34, 158
Berg, K. 141
Berg-Schlosser, D. 150
Birch, A. 11, 23, 24
Blumenthal, M. D. 146
Böckenförde, E. W. 129
Brittan, S. 24, 26, 72, 89
Budge, I. 7, 63, 78, 129, 133, 136, 144, 148
Butler, D. 79, 137

Cantril, H. 86
Castles, F. G. 130
Citrin, J. 86
Commission of the European Communities 127, 147, 149
Converse, P. E. 79, 139
Coughlin, R. M. 95
Crewe, I. 77, 90
Crook, S. 29, 155
Crozier, M. J. 17, 25, 72, 140

Dahl, R. A. 127, 128

Dalton, R. J. 42, 44, 77, 79, 115, 140, 141, 144, 145
Day, N. 32, 52, 145, 146
Deutsch, K. W. 13, 112, 119
Diamond, L. 164
Dienel, P. C. 129, 162
Diewald, M. 156
Dittrich, K. 143
Dogan, M. 97
Donohue, G. A. 142
Douglas, J. D. 67
Downs, A. 139
Dubiel, H. 159

Easton, D. 9, 114, 131, 160
Eichenberg, R. C. 115
Eichenberger, K. 73
Etzioni, A. 158
Everts, P. 108

Faber, A. 108
Feldman, S. 79
Fleishman, J. A. 79
Flora, P. 134
Free, L.A. 86
Fuchs, D. 57, 58, 60, 131, 133, 151, 168
Fukuyama, F. 32, 33, 37, 126, 163

Gans, H. J. 155
George, S. 111
Goehler, G. 159
Goodin, R. 65, 77
Gould, F. 65
Graber, D. A. 79, 107
Grigg, C. M. 9

Habermas, J. 23, 74
Hadenius, A. 76
Hall, S. 160
Hamilton, R. F. 15
Handley, D. H. 115

Harvey, D. 28
Hearl, D. 78, 148
Helliwell, J. F. 164
Hildebrandt, K. 42, 144
Hirschman, A. O. 44, 161
Hofferbert, R. I. 7, 63, 133, 136, 148
Hoffman, S. 97, 116
Hofrichter, J. 105
Huntington, S. P. 5, 16, 17, 25, 27, 72, 126, 127, 133, 140, 150, 163

Inglehart, R. 3, 6, 12, 34, 35, 39, 42, 44, 50, 77, 90, 102, 104, 106, 108, 112, 115, 119, 142, 144, 149, 155, 166

Janssen, J. H. 112
Johansen, L. N. 143
Jukam, T. O. 168

Kaase, M. 3, 41, 43, 48, 49, 50, 51, 52, 144, 145, 146, 147, 161
Katz, D. 147
Katz, R. S. 130
Key, V. O. 85, 143
Kiefer, M.-L. 141
Kielmansegg, P. G. 151
Kim, J. 3, 48, 145, 146
King, A. 11, 24
Klages, H. 42, 144, 167
Klein, M. 105
Klingemann, H.-D. 7, 43, 48, 50, 63, 133, 136, 148
Klosko, G. 133, 154, 160
Kmieciak, P. 42
Koecher, R. 141
Kornhauser, W. 18, 19, 20, 24, 53, 155
Kriesi, H. 11, 59
Kuechler, M. 145
Kuklinski, J. H. 154

Lane, J.-E. 139
Lane, R. 9, 79
Lash, S. 28
Laver, M. J. 148
Levitin, T. E. 42
Lewin, L. 85
Lieberam, E. 11

Lijphart, A. 7, 127, 132, 136, 139, 163
Lindberg, L. N. 112, 122
Linz, J. 5
Lipset, S. M. 31, 32, 33, 34, 139, 140, 164
Luhmann, N. 132, 133, 132, 153, 160

Maag, G. 144
McClosky, H. 9
McKay, D. 25, 139
Maguire, M. 44
Maier, C. 24
Mair, P. 44, 139, 140
Margolis, M. 79
Marsh, A. 167
Marshall, T. H. 128
Melucci, A. 27
Merkl, P. 27
Meulemann, H. 11, 42
Miegel, M. 48, 157, 166
Milbrath, L. W. 145
Milgate, M. 128
Miller, W. E. 42
Milward, A. S. 97, 115
Moyser, G. 145, 146
Muller, E. 168
Muller, E. N. 145
Murray, R. 28

Neidhardt, F. 49, 52, 58, 146
Newby, H. 155
Newton, K. 75, 136, 139, 155
Nie, N. H. 3, 48, 52, 145, 146
Nielsen, H. J. 94
Noelle-Neumann, E. 44, 141, 142
Nussbaum, M. C. 160

Offe, C. 22, 23, 26, 67, 74, 77, 134, 150
Ohmae, K. 97
Olien, C. A. 142

Page, B. I. 85
Pakulski, J. 29, 155
Parekh, B. 163
Parkin, F. 26
Parry, G. 52, 145, 146
Pateman, C. 139, 159

Peacock, A. 65
Pechman, J. A. 67, 94
Pederson, M. N. 44
Peters, B. 24, 67, 86
Pierce, R. 79
Poguntke, T. 53, 169
Popkin, S. 79, 121, 122, 143
Powell, G. B., Jr. 127, 132
Prothro, J. W. 9
Pruitt, D. G. 119
Puchala, D. A. 99, 103, 105, 106, 107
Putnam, R. D. 136

Rabier, J.-R. 115
Rawls, J. 133, 154, 158, 162, 165
Reif, K. 102
Rivers, D. 135
Robertson, D. 148
Rohrschneider, R. 140
Rokeach, M. 9, 79
Rokkan, S. 9, 139
Rorty, R. 162
Rose, R. 24, 134
Rosenau, P. M. 112, 129, 165
Rucht, D. 57, 58, 59
Rueschemeyer, D. 130, 165

Sartori, G. 129, 139, 159, 161
Scharpf, F. W. 131
Scheingold, S. A. 112, 122
Scheuch, E. K. 3, 155
Schneider, W. 140
Schumpeter, J. A. 139
Sears, D. 86
Seligson, M. A. 168
Shapiro, R. I. 85
Sharpe, L. J. 97, 136
Simmel, G. 19
Sniderman, P. M. 10, 151
Stepan, A. 5

Stephens, E. 130, 165
Stimson, S. C. 128
Stokes, D. 79, 137
Streeck, W. 57, 156
Strubelt, W. 162
Sullivan, J. L. 79
Svensson, P. 29, 168

Tarrow, S. 27, 58
Teune, H. 7
Tichenor. P. J. 142
Touraine, A. 26

Uehlinger, H.-M. 49, 52, 145
Urry, J. 28

Vanhanen, T. 127, 130, 164
Verba, S. 3, 9, 48, 52, 145, 146, 161
Volkens, A. 148

Wahl, S. 48, 157, 166
Wallace, W. 97
Walzer, M. 159, 165
Watanuki, J. 17, 25, 72, 140
Waters, J. 29, 155
Weil, F. D. 168
Westle, B. 60, 131, 151, 168
Wildenmann, R. 130
Wilensky, H. L. 68, 69, 89
Wilmott, P. 155
Wiseman, J. 65
Wright, J. D. 15

Young, M. 155

ZEUS 114
Ziegler, A. H. 98, 108
Zilleflen, H. 162

SUBJECT INDEX

accountability of government 134, 136, 160

action, political 6, 23, 27, 38, 50, 52, 119, 143, 145, 146

action groups 22, 23
  see also direct political action; new social movements

activism, political 52, 170

administration 32

advanced capitalist state,
  see capitalism

affective dimension 10

affluence 17, 18, 32, 90

age 13, 48, 70, 82, 92, 157, 166
  see also older cohorts; young

agenda, political:
  and activists and citizens 146
  changes in 91, 96
  in the future 172
  and internationalisation 134
  and left–right dimension 133
  and political competition 171
  and valance politics 137
  see also materialism; new political agenda; old political agenda; postmaterialism

aggregate public opinion 98, 104

alienation:
  and end of history 33–4
  and end of ideology 32
  and European politics 88, 92
  and legitimation crisis 23
  and mass media 30, 53
  and modern society 20, 37–8
  and overload 25
  see also anomie; cynicism; distrust of government

allegiance, political 60, 72, 135, 148, 151

American politics 15, 25, 32, 95, 109, 138

animal rights 39

anomie 33, 34, 37

anti-party 27, 38, 169

anti-politics 38, 169

apathy 16, 51, 152

arts 80

attitudes, political:
  changes in 6, 40, 63, 148–9, 166
  towards democracy 20, 36–9
  of élites and masses 9
  towards international government 13, 14, 97–9, 105, 114–15, 121–4
  towards political regimes 60, 168
  towards role of government 12
  structure of 79–88, 108–12
  and unconventional behavior 50, 144–5
  and voting studies 11
  towards the welfare state 71, 72, 75–6, 78, 91–6
  west European patterns 88–9
  see also agenda, political; materialism; opinion clusters; postmaterialism

Austria 14, 41, 51, 91, 113, 170

authoritarian personality 9

authoritarian regimes 5, 126–7, 139, 143, 145, 171
  see also dictatorship; totalitarianism

authoritarianism and the end of history 32, 163

authorities, regime and community 9, 60, 132, 148, 160, 168

authority, political:
  delegitimation of 25
  of the state 24, 26, 134, 150
  traditional and rational-legal 153–4, 163

basic values 114

behaviour, political 6, 43, 49, 50, 63, 144, 145

Belgium 51, 61, 102, 116–17

belief system 133

beliefs in government 3, 10, 92
benefits 29, 76, 77, 95, 100, 109, 135
  see also welfare state
big government 12, 65, 90, 98, 122
binary *or* bipolar codes 132–4, 160
borderless world 97
boycotts 27, 39, 50
  see also direct political action; protest
    parties; unconventional political
    behaviour
Britain 44, 51, 53, 58, 61, 63, 66, 80, 90,
    99, 102–3, 105–6, 111, 116–17, 123,
    128, 149, 156, 160
bubble-up model 7, 112–13
  see also cascade model
bureaucracy 20, 32, 131
business 32, 74, 94, 124

Canada 66
capital accumulation 21–2
capitalism 16, 22–3, 28, 31, 77, 89, 148
capitalist state 23
cascade model 112-13
  see also bubble-up model
central and eastern Europe 5, 13, 126,
    151, 163, 171
central and southern Europe 53
centralization 14, 20
  see also decentralization
charities 19
  see also voluntary associations
Christian Democracy 7, 88
church attendance 7
citizens 5, 7
  citizen associations and action
    groups 19, 22, 50, 63; *see also*
    voluntary associations
  and attitudes and values 8, 40, 42
  and democracy 8–10, 18, 20, 23, 32,
    127
  and élites 19
  and international government 13, 97–
    125
  and parties 53
  and postmodernism 29–30
  and rational choice 76
  satisfaction 8

  and the scope of government 65–6, 72,
    75
  and sociotropic and pocket book
    attitudes 86–8
  sophistication 82–5
  and the state 11, 22–3, 25, 29, 52–3, 62
Citizens and the State 2, 10, 12, 60, 75,
    89, 92, 94, 146
citizenship 31, 124, 128, 168
  European citizenship 98, 117–19
civic culture 29, 169
civil disobedience 27, 49, 145–6
  see also direct political action;
    unconventional political behaviour
civil service 61
civil society 151, 158
class 13, 36, 68, 71, 92, 157
  and the end of ideology 31
  and the left–right dimension 133
  and legitimacy crisis 22
  and mass society 20
  and the middle mass 68–9
  and new social movements 27
  and overloaded government 71
  and political activism 161, 170
  and political attitudes 92, 115
  and postmaterialism 34
  and postmodernism 29, 89
  and the scope of government 71
  and voting 43, 48
class cleavage 34, 133
class struggle 27
cleavage model 43
cleavage voting 43, 48
cleavages, political 19, 26, 139
cleavages, social 26
coalition government 132
coalitions 29, 90, 149, 168–9
cognitive mobilization 35, 44, 108, 142–3
cohort analysis 6, 167
collapse of communism 16, 152, 158
collectivism 29, 155
Cologne Zentralarchiv für Empirische
    Sozialforschung (ZA) 4
commercial polling agencies 10
Commission of the European
    Communities 127, 147, 149

communication, political:
  and bipolar codes 132
  government control of 81, 88, 92
  and international data transference 136
  and mass theory 19–20
  and postmaterialism 35
  see also mass media
communications 14, 21, 118
communism 16, 19, 21, 62, 78, 126
communitarianism 149, 157–8, 171
  see also liberalism
community, political:
  and authorities and regime 9, 132
  and democracy 32, 128, 158, 162–3
  and legitimation crisis 23
  and mass theory 19–20, 155
  and postmaterialism 35, 39
  and postmodernism 30, 156
  and 1939–45 sense of 65
  and political participation 146
community associations, *see* voluntary
  associations
competence, political 37
  see also efficacy, political
competing élites 20, 139
competition:
  between nations 16, 97, 118, 163–4,
    171
  market 135, 149
  pluralist 60, 128, 132; *see also*
    pluralist democracy
compromise 25, 27, 31, 38
confidence in government 25
  see also competence, political; trust,
    political
confidence in institutions 61, 93–4, 141
consensus:
  and democracy 154, 159, 163
  and end of history 32
  and end of ideology 31, 38
  and European integration 14, 23; *see*
    also permissive consensus
constitution 130, 138, 170
constitutional structure 14
consultation, political 23
consumer protection 80, 110
consumerism 29–30, 33, 34

see also postmodernism
contradictions, political 21
conventional political behaviour 27, 37,
  43, 49–50
core beliefs 79
corporate actors 50, 127
corporate tax 94
corporatism 7
Council of European Social Science Data
  Archives (CESSDA) 4
Council of Ministers 13, 105
country size 7
courts 131, 169
crime 30, 157
crises, political 18–30, 36–8
  see also crises of welfare state;
    democracy, democratic crisis;
    legitimacy crisis
crisis of legitimacy, *see* legitimacy crisis
crisis of the welfare state, *see* welfare
  state, crisis of
cultural diversity 124
cultural minorities 27
cultural policy 111
culture:
  European culture 124, 163
  political 9, 13, 29, 35, 164, 169
  and public policy 80, 82, 93, 135
culture shift 18
  see also postmaterialism; silent
    revolution
circles of opinion 90
cynicism 30, 38
  see also alienation; distrust of
    government

data archives 3
data indifference 15
data protection 111
dealignment 17, 140, 155, 169
decentralization 14, 171
  see also centralization
defence 73, 78, 80–1, 91, 96, 108–9, 111
demands, political:
  and changing state structures 148
  and legitimacy crisis 21–4
  and mass theory 20

and new political agendas 150
and new social movements 26–7
and overload 24–6, 37
for political rights 171
and the welfare state 68–75
see also inputs
democracy 5, 6, 8, 10, 11, 14, 15, 152,
    158
and accountability 100
conditions of 127–9, 130, 139
democratic change 18, 30–9
and democratic citizens 138–146, 147
democratic crisis 16–30, 36–9, 150–1
democratic deficit 13, 107, 117, 121,
    134, 170
democratic distemper 25
democratic politics 2, 18, 20, 33, 31,
    43, 60, 132, 163
democratic regimes 134
and economics 164–5
and end of history 103
future of 170–2
and individualism 162
and legitimacy 167–70
and postmodernism and
    postmaterialism 165–7
and rules of game 8, 132–3, 153–5,
    157, 159–60
and satisfaction with 8, 41, 60–3, 117,
    127, 168
and support for the European
    Union 115–17, 124
and three waves of
    democratization 126
and two changes of government 127
see also direct democracy; pluralist
    democracy; polyarchy
demonstrations 23, 39, 50
see also direct political action; protest
    politics; unconventional political
    behaviour
Denmark 3, 14, 61, 66, 73, 90, 94, 102,
    113, 116, 117, 119, 123, 156
depoliticization 16
Deutschmark and European currency 14
deviant cases 11
dictatorship 17

see also authoritarian dictatorship;
    totalitarianism
diffuse support 114
direct democracy 29, 129
direct political action 23, 27, 38, 146
see also civil disobedience;
    unconventional political behaviour
discussion, political 44
disillusionment with politics 25, 33–4,
    37–8, 67, 74–5
see also dissatisfaction with politics
dissatisfaction with politic 25, 37, 61, 72,
    93, 148, 158, 169
see also dissillusionment with politics
distrust of government 25, 29–30, 37–8,
    119
distrust of people 119–21, 124
see also trust, personal; trust, political
dogmatism, political 9
dominance model 77
doorstep opinions 79, 121

East Germany 117
eastern Europe 5, 13, 126, 151, 163, 171
ecology 58
see also environment; environmental
    pollution; environmental protection
economic:
benefits 100
change and mass society 19, 155
change and political attitudes 41, 71,
    74, 76, 89, 92, 114–15, 123
change as a source of social and
    political change 36–7, 40, 63
contradictions 21–2, 26, 89
development 7, 11, 73, 91, 134, 156,
    164
élites 135
equality 71, 76, 78, 82, 86, 90, 95, 164,
    167
growth 12, 34, 65–7, 77, 115, 134–5,
    149, 163, 165, 172
individualism and self-interest 68, 112,
    114–15
integration 14, 115
interests 24, 88
intervention 31, 73, 81, 85, 88, 91

management 65, 91
performance 62, 149, 165
record of government 136
rights 128
security 80, 167
and social change 36
stability 34
Economic and Social Research Council 1
economically developed countries 51, 72
economics:
 and democracy 164–5
 and postmaterialism 144, 166
economy 28, 42, 96
education:
 and cognitive mobilisation 142
 and democracy 128, 154, 157
 and political attitudes 41, 44, 68, 70–1,
  76, 92, 106, 108, 146
 and political change 36, 120
 and postmaterialsm 11, 35, 42, 67, 77
 and public policy on 21, 66, 80–1, 95,
  110
educational organisations 19
efficacy, political 37, 63
 see also competence, political
egalitarianism 44
 see also economic equality; equality
election campaigning 43
elections 113, 143, 145, 150, 168
 see also voting
electoral participation 137
 see also voting
electoral volatility 29, 37
élites, political:
 and attitudes 9, 11
 and democracy 127, 131, 139, 143,
  158, 162
 dissatisfaction with 169
 élite directed polities 7, 35, 50
 élite divided polities 7, 35, 50, 112–14,
  122–3
 élite manipulation 39
 élite opinion 98, 112–13
 and mass theory 19–20, 53
 and postmodernism 29
employment 75, 92, 115, 135, 166
end of history 18, 32–5, 37, 126, 163

end of ideology 18, 32–5, 38, 57
energy supplies 110
entertainment 30
entrepreneurs, political 50
environment 27, 42, 73, 82, 91, 93, 128,
 134, 140, 148, 156
environmental pollution 149
environmental protection 35, 77, 78, 80,
 81, 91, 110, 111, 114
 see also ecology
equality:
 attitudes towards 71, 78, 88, 90, 92, 95,
  167
 and democracy 162, 164
 and end of history 33
 and freedom 75, 151, 153
 and German Länder 131
 of opportunity 82, 86
 and participation 161, 170
 and postmaterialism 35, 39
 and rational choice 76
 see also economic equality
estrangement 16
ethnic groups 27
Eurobarometer 4, 12, 78, 80, 81, 99, 100,
 102, 104, 105, 106, 109, 110, 114,
 115, 119, 120, 144, 147, 166, 168
European citizenship 98, 118, 124
European Commission 12, 99
European Community 78, 80, 99, 100,
 102, 104, 111, 114–15, 119, 123
 see also European unification;
  European Union
European Consortium for Political
 Research 1
European Court 13, 138
European identity 112, 118
European integration 13, 14, 102, 111,
 115, 124, 138
European Parliament 13, 102, 105, 107,
 121, 134
European Science Foundation 1
European unification 100, 103, 108, 109,
 111, 113, 121, 123
European Union (EC) 4–5, 13, 14, 100,
 102–11, 113–19, 121–4, 127, 145,
 147, 149, 167, 170

European Values Survey 3
Europeanism 98, 115, 124
Exchange Rate Mechanism 102, 107
exhaustion of political ideas 31
expressive participation 51
external efficacy 63
extremism, political 19, 21, 31, 37

fairness 22, 23, 76
fairness of political issues 80, 109
farmers and fishermen 115
fascism 21, 32
federal systems 131, 160, 170
Finland 14, 66, 90, 113
fiscal crisis of the state 21–2, 24–5, 68–71, 95
Fordism 28
foreign aid 39, 78, 110, 111, 134
foreign policy 99, 103–5, 111, 122
fractionalization of parties 168
France 14, 19, 36, 41, 44, 58, 61, 62, 99, 102, 103, 105, 106, 113, 116, 117
franchise 161
freedom:
  and democracy 159, 163
  economic 22
  and end of history 33
  and equality 75, 151, 153, 164
  and postmaterialism 35, 39, 77, 165
  and postmodernism 29, 165
  of the press 92
  of speech 35
  and state power 31
  see also equality; liberalism; liberty
frequency of political discussion 44

GDP 66
gender 13, 39, 41, 92, 95
generation 6, 35, 40, 42, 71, 96, 148, 166, 172
  see also age; cohort analysis
generational replacement 63
geographical mobility 68
German reunification 111
Germany 3, 5, 11, 19, 41–2, 44, 51, 58, 61, 63, 66, 73, 80, 90, 99, 102–3,

105–6, 111, 117, 127, 131–2, 140–2, 144, 147, 149, 156, 170
Glistrup Party 94
global village 97
globalization of politics 14, 149
government:
  beliefs in 8–10
  and citizens 129–38, 146–9
  and democratic crisis 17–30, 150–71
  instability 62
  international 13–14, 97–125
  legitimacy of 21–4, 60–3, 167–70
  management of the economy 73, 90
  and new social movements 26–30
  overload 11, 24–6, 32, 71, 77
  policies and output 7–8, 136
  programmes 66–7, 69–71, 73–4, 77–8, 136
  regulation 96
  role of 12
  scope of 68–96
  services 65, 67, 81, 92, 95
  spending 65–6, 73, 86–90, 95–6
  see also democracy; regime, political; state
Great Britain 44, 51, 53, 61, 90, 99, 105, 106, 111
Great Depression 65
Greece 62, 73, 102, 115, 117
green politics 39, 48
  see also ecology; new social movements
group membership 6, 156
groups:
  as channels of communication 7
  and classes 139
  and democracy 129
  and ideological fragmentation 73
  income groups and taxes 76–7, 94
  intermediary groups 156
  and legal and illegal action 146, 157
  and legitimacy crisis 22
  local citizen groups 63
  and mass theory 19–20
  and new social movements 27, 57
  and overload 24–5, 71, 73
  and political attitudes 79–80

and political information 142
and political parties 169
and postmodnerism 165
see also interest groups; pressure
    groups
gut rationality 121–2

health 21, 66, 70, 80, 81, 95, 111, 152
hedonism 16, 157
hereditary monarchy 32
hierarchy 23, 35, 68
higher education 42, 44
historical analysis 3, 129, 162, 164
see also end of history
Hitler 21
holocaust 5, 127
homogeneity, political 124
see also pluralism
housing 21, 80, 95, 156

identification, political 116, 124, 152,
    155
see also identification with political
    parties
identity:
    and end of history 33–4
    European 112, 118, 124
    and mass theory 19
    national 116, 124
    see also identification, political;
        identification with political parties
ideology:
    and Christian democracy 88
    and democracy 128, 158, 160, 162–3
    and east–west confrontation 8, 16, 151,
        158
    and end of history 32–4
    ideological meltdown 78
    ideological passions 31
    ideological polarization 53
    and new social movements 60
    political 9
    and political parties 140
    and postmaterialism 34–5
    success ideology 68, 71
    see also end of ideology

ignorance, political 98, 105, 106, 111,
    112, 119, 121, 159
illegal political participation 52
IMF 97
income 41, 71, 84, 92, 115, 149
    differences 70, 80, 82
    groups 76, 94
    indirect taxes 94
    maintenance 21
    tax 94
    see also tax; wealth
incremental change 27
individual resources 48, 63
individual rights 126, 151, 159, 162
individual stability 44
individualism:
    and end of history 33–4
    and mass of political attitudes 79
    and postmaterialism 34, 165–6
    and postmodernism 29–30, 165–6
    and the welfare state 67–71
    in the West 16, 156, 162
    see also economic individualism and
        self-interest
individualization 155, 157, 158
industrial societies 20, 133
industrialization 42
industry 20, 28, 70, 85, 95
inequality 82, 146, 151, 158
inflation 34, 66, 75, 80, 95
information:
    and electoral participation 137, 139
    gap 142
    about international politics 104–8, 121
    low information rationality 122, 142
    and modes of research 4, 7–10
    political and postmodernism 30
    technology 28, 162
innovation 12, 141, 162
inputs 9, 130
    see also demands, political
institutional properties of political
    systems 41
institutionalization 151, 168
institutions:
    and communications 7

and democracy 129–33, 137, 147,
    151–4, 158–60, 164
and end of history 33
and European Court 140
identification with 10
information about public
    institutions 107
and legitimacy 167–8
and macro analysis 6, 127
and overload theory 25
and political parties 148
and postmodernism 29, 165
trust in public institutions 38, 61–3, 94,
    141
integration theory 113
Integrationists 104–5
intellectuals 15, 31, 32
intelligentsia 15
interest groups 11, 23, 29, 35, 43, 48, 78,
    154, 161, 171
    see also pressure groups
interest representation 41, 57
interests:
    and legitimacy crisis 22
    and liberal ideology 160
    in mass society 19
    national 80
    and overload 24–6, 71, 73
    personal 16, 23, 85, 170
    political interest 13, 18, 35, 39, 44,
        106, 141
    and rational choice 89
    and representation 128
    social 24
    and sociotropic versus pocket–book
        motives 85–8
intermediary organizations 19, 48, 53,
    57, 156
    see also citizen associations; voluntary
        associations
intermediate level of government 5
international:
    attitudes 39, 98, 99
    communications 14
    control 103
    government 13, 64, 97, 118, 160
    organizations 14, 171

politics 98, 104, 121
regimes 14
International Social Survey Programme 3
internationalism 14, 35, 102, 104, 117,
    124
internationalization 2, 13, 134, 170
involvement, political 22, 29, 43, 57,
    134, 161, 169
    see also interest, political;
        participation, political
isolationists 104–5
issue preferences 144
issue publics 73, 79, 80
issues, political 20, 31, 123
Italy 28, 41, 58, 61, 62, 73, 80, 91, 99,
    102, 103, 105, 106, 117, 127, 128

Japan 66, 132
job security 165
judgements, political 107
judiciary 8, 130, 131, 138
justice 23, 76, 114, 151, 163

labour 28, 68, 71, 79, 142, 143
law and order 73, 80, 82, 93, 108
laws 65, 137, 164
Le Pen 19
leaders 11, 25, 112, 113, 165
    see also élites, political
leadership 25, 148, 169
left academies and intellectuals 151
left ideology 31
left parties:
    and cleavage politics 43
    and legal and illegal political
        action 146
    and legitimacy crisis 143
    and new social movements 41, 171
    and postmaterialism 35, 44, 140
    and scope of government 90–3
    see also communism; socialism
left–right cycles of opinion 90
left-right parties 27, 34, 43, 88, 133, 139,
    159
legal:
    political participation 49–50, 52, 145–6
    rights 128

state (Rechtsstaat) 5, 159
  system 61
legislative 8, 130, 138, 160
legislators 143
legitimacy:
  crisis 11, 17, 21–4, 26, 37, 74–5, 77,
    89, 135, 143, 148, 168
  of democratic order 10, 60–3, 129,
    131, 148–9
  and the modern state 167–71
  and the nation state 134
  and secularization 154
leisure clubs 19
liberal:
  liberal–conservative dimension 133
  liberal democracies 16, 18, 34, 126,
    152, 162–3, 165
  liberal–socialist conditions 149
  liberal theories 11, 36, 86, 88, 154,
    158–60, 162
  liberal democratic consensus 32, 38
liberalism:
  and communitarianism 121
  and end of ideology 33
  and overload 26
  and pluralism 5
  and postmodernism 29, 166
  and welfare state backlash 70
libertarianism 44
liberty 33
  see also freedom
life styles 13, 30, 69, 156, 159, 161
linkage politics 37
local authorities 135
localism 29
lower middle class 68
Luxembourg 61, 102, 104, 116, 117

Maastricht Treaty 13, 107
McCarthyism 19
majoritarian democracy 7, 132, 163
marginal groups 25
market competition 135
market economy 164
markets 149
Marxist theories 11
mass comunication 20

mass media 6, 30, 42, 104, 118, 136,
    142–3, 147, 165, 172
mass parties 27
mass political attitudes:
  towards democracy 5, 36, 63
  and élite attitudes 9
  and input into government 94–5
  towards international government 14,
    97–107, 121–5
  towards the scope of government 64–
    78, 95–6
  short-term fluctuations in 6
  sociotropic and pocket book nature
    of 85–8, 114–15
  structure of 78–85, 107–12
mass publics 50, 133, 137
mass theory 17–21, 26, 36–8, 53
material goals 77
materialism 12–13, 33–4, 43–4, 77, 80,
    92, 108, 144, 106
  see also postmaterialism
media, *see* mass media
membership:
  of the EU 100–2, 109, 115, 117
  of groups 6, 38, 53, 57–60, 156
  of NATO 103–5
  of new social movements 58–9
  of parties 37, 53, 57–60, 169
micro level 5, 153
middle mass 67–8, 70–1, 89
military 78, 80–2, 104, 108–9, 122
Mill, James 128
Mill, J. S. 139
mobilization 35, 39, 44, 50, 52, 63, 108,
    142, 143, 145
moderation, political 27, 31–2, 38
modernism 28
modernization 158, 164
moral order 23
most similar systems design 7
movement society 58–9
multiparty government 132
multiple identities 118

nation building 118
nation states 7, 97, 118

national:
  boundaries 128
  defence 80, 82, 91, 108–9, 111
  democracy 117, 124
  differences 41, 56, 166
  identities 116
  interest 30, 112, 123
  pride 98, 116, 118, 124
  research 1, 9, 40
  solidarity 65
  voting studies 11–12
  wealth 90
  see also GDP
National Front 19
nationalism 14, 25, 98, 114, 115, 124
nationalization 91
NATO 14, 97, 103, 104, 105, 106, 107, 108, 109, 111, 122
natural monopolies 85
Nazism 21
Netherlands 41, 51, 58, 61, 90, 102, 116, 117, 156
networks 58, 156, 159
new left 140
new political agenda 12, 34–6, 62, 72–81, 95–6, 150, 165–7
  see also agenda, political; green parties; old political agenda; postmaterialism; postmodernism
new politics 18, 29, 30, 42
new social movements:
  and democratic crisis 17, 22–8, 34, 38
  as intermediary links 57–60
  and parties and pressure groups 11, 22, 41, 58, 96, 171
  and political action 63, 145
  and postmaterialism and postmodernism 35, 39, 77, 155
  and *The Impact of Values* 14
  see also action groups; green politics; movement society; peace movement; pressure groups; protest politics; women's movements
newspapers 92, 141
  see also mass media
niche marketing 28
non-attitudes 79

Northern Ireland 61
Norway 3, 14, 53, 66, 90, 113

OECD 11, 40, 66, 67, 127, 135, 137, 150, 151, 157, 163, 164, 165, 168
old interest organizations 22
old left 34
old political agenda 12, 34–6, 77–8, 80–1, 95–6, 165–7
  see also agenda, political; new political agenda; postmaterialism; postmodernism
older cohorts 167
open society 16
opinion clusters 79–80, 95–6, 98–9, 108–9, 123
opinion formation 107, 121
opinion leaders 12, 112, 165
opposition parties 10
order, political 17, 21, 26, 67, 151
organization 20, 32
outputs 8, 9, 136
overload 11, 17, 26, 32, 37, 71, 72, 73, 74, 77, 89, 143
oversized coalitions 168–9

panel data 44
parliament 7, 61, 102, 170
parochial attitudes 25, 98
participation, political:
  changes in 37–9, 63, 150
  and democracy 128–9, 137, 139, 146, 159, 162
  and legitimacy crisis 23, 169
  and overload 24–5
  and political values 13
  and political violence 20
  and postmaterialism 35, 42, 77, 150
  and postmodernism 29, 165
  and voting 6, 137, 143, 161
  in western Europe 50–2
  see also conventional political behaviour, political action; political repertory; protest politics; unconventional political behaviour
participatory democracy 139, 159
participatory revolution 11, 144

parties, political:
  and cleavage politics 43
  and democratic crisis 22–31, 35, 75
  evaluation of 10, 136, 168–9
  families of 113
  and government 8, 130, 132–4, 137,
    139, 143, 168
  identification with 10, 25, 41, 48, 53,
    88, 92, 96
  mass parties 17, 20, 156
  and old and new politics 48, 53, 140,
    146, 155, 171
  and opinion formation 113, 122–3
  party leaders of 113
  party manifestos 78, 113
  party systems 53, 96, 164
  and political change 48, 53, 89, 148–9,
    161
  and political linkages 53–8, 140, 154,
    156
  and postmaterialism 35, 78
  preference 6, 57, 92
  voting 11, 48, 140, 169
peace:
  and cultural pluralism 124–5
  and democracy 153
  and EU 98, 100, 114, 123
  and internationalization 134
  movement 21, 36, 57, 58
  and postmaterialism 34, 39
  and post-war Europe 17–18, 65
  and UN 103
period effects 149, 166
permissive consensus 112, 122
personal income 68, 71, 76, 82, 86, 149
  see also economic equality; taxes
petitions 23, 27, 39
  see also direct political action; protest
    politics; unconventional political
    behaviour
pluralism 5, 8, 19–20, 37, 50, 127, 132,
    154, 158–9, 162–5, 167–71
pluralist democracy 5, 20, 151, 154, 160
pluralist societies 19, 73
pocket book attitudes 85–8
  see also sociotropic voting
polarization, political 41, 53, 168

police 52, 61
policy:
  constraints 169
  distance 93, 140
  inputs 68
  integration 131
  and legitimacy crisis 22
  linkage 134
  opinion about 68–96, 135
  and opinion about international
    policies 97–125
  orientations 52, 110–11, 122, 161
  outputs 136
  overload 24–6
  priorities 162
  social 65
  and unpopular governments 19, 132
political executive 8, 130, 160
politicians 5, 6, 67, 75, 131, 134, 136,
    157, 169
politics of affluence 32
polity 50, 53, 163, 168, 170
pollution 110, 149
polyarchy 128, 151
  see also pluralism: pluralist democracy
popularity cycles 90
population replacement 6
populism 20, 27
Portugal 91, 102, 105, 115, 117
position politics 169
possessive individualism 33, 34
postmaterialism 11–13, 18, 29, 31, 34–6,
    38, 41, 43–4, 48, 60, 63, 77–8, 80,
    92, 108, 140, 144, 155, 166, 167
  see also silent revolution
postmodernism 13, 16, 28–30, 33–4, 36,
    51, 61, 73, 78–9, 89, 155, 165, 166
Poujadism 19
poverty 151, 158
power, political:
  balance of 130
  and binary codes 133
  competition for 60, 137, 150
  concentration of 153–4
  and cycles of opinion 90
  élite desire for 162
  and executive and legislative 160

of intermediary organizations 53
of international governments 14, 97
and postmaterialists 35
redistribution of 16, 31
powerlessness 20
preferences, political 92
prejudice 15, 98, 121, 158
press 111, 112
see also mass media
pressure groups 27, 37, 155
see also interest groups
privatization 67, 90
professional organizations 19
protest parties 66, 169
see also parties, political
protest politics 23, 27, 57, 74, 94, 152,
169
see also direct political action;
unconventional political behaviour
Protestant 88, 118
provision for the old 95
proximity model 77
public agenda, *see* agenda, political
public expenditure 12–13, 23–6, 65–78,
94–6
public goods 12
public interest 77, 88
public opinion, *see* attitudes, political;
demands, political; opinion clusters
public sector 66, 67, 68, 71, 73, 165

quality of life 77, 80, 147, 152

race 22
racial 27, 39
racists 81, 92
radicalism 21
ranking 81, 144
ratepayer revolts 66
rational choice 76
rational choice theory 76
rationality 79, 121, 122, 143
realism 75
redistribution 16, 88
reference group 152
referendum 14, 113, 159, 171
reform 31, 38

regime, political 9–10, 14, 60–1, 94, 126,
132–4, 143, 148, 160, 168, 171
see also authorities, political;
community, political
regime evaluation 10
region 22, 27, 118, 124, 170
religion 13, 16, 23, 27, 43, 48, 63, 153–4,
158, 163
see also Christian Democracy;
Protestant; secularization
repertory, political 50, 63, 146, 161, 169
representation, political 128, 143, 156
representative democracy 26
repression potential 41
Republicans 19
revolution of declining expectations 26
revolutionaries 81, 92
rights, political and social 5, 22, 92, 95,
126–8, 137–8, 143, 150–1, 154, 157–
8, 161–2, 171
rolling back the state 67
romantic revolt 29
rootlessness 33, 34
Roper Center 3
Rosseau 139, 153
Russia 105

Scandinavia 53, 88
scarcity of resources 75, 135, 149
Schumpeter 139
science, political 3, 36, 42, 53, 92, 128,
131, 151
scope of government 2, 12, 65–96, 104,
123, 134, 161
Second World War 42, 118, 127, 150
secondary associations, *see* voluntary
associations
secondary data 3, 4
secularization 7, 13, 43–4, 144, 154, 158,
163
security:
economic 80, 84
international 72, 82, 98–110
personal and physical 19, 144, 152–3,
163, 165, 167
social 66, 72, 77–8, 84, 86, 88, 90, 92
selective rewards 57

services, public 12, 22, 24, 65–7, 69–74,
    76, 79, 81–2, 86, 88–9, 92, 95, 135
silent revolution 18, 35, 42, 144
    see also postmaterialism
social capital 21
Social Democrats 66, 88
social differentiation 142
social expenditure 21, 134
social mobility 68, 79
social security transfers 66
social state 11, 134, 160
socialism 149, 151
sociotropic voting 85–8, 123
solidarity 30, 65, 158
Soviet bloc 15, 102, 107, 115
Soviet Union 106
Spain 61, 91, 102, 105, 115, 117
spiral of falling expectations 73
spiral of rising expectations 11, 73, 149
sport 19
stability:
    of attitudes 40, 44, 60, 63, 79–81, 96,
        98, 109–11
    of behaviour 51, 57, 140
    economics 34
    of party identification 53
    political 5, 10, 17–30, 72, 125, 133,
        141, 150, 164, 170
    of political attitudes 6, 31
    of voting patterns 48
Stalin 21
standard of living 135
    see also affluence; income; wealth
state:
    and citizens 11, 52, 118, 128, 146–9,
        151, 153–62
    crisis of 21–30, 74
    democratic 8, 126, 128–38, 151
    growth and decline of 11, 31, 65–9,
        71–2, 76, 90
    nation 97, 108, 115, 123, 129–30, 170
    and public policy 75, 85–6, 89, 107
state intervention 156
state socialism 151, 171
stereotypes 98
strata, political 142
strikes 23, 27, 39

subsidiary 14, 110, 111
superpowers 78, 80
support, political 93
supranational government, *see*
    international government
survey evidence 5, 15, 71, 72, 77, 79, 82,
    107, 136
Sweden 3, 14, 66, 90, 113
Switzerland 132, 170

tax:
    levels 65–9
    protest 22, 68–71, 76–7, 89, 94
    regimes 67, 94–5
    strain 12
television 42, 44, 140, 141, 172
    see also mass media
terrorism 30
tertiarization of the economy 42
Thatcher 90, 111, 149
The Civic Culture 3, 4, 9, 10, 63
The Impact of Values 2, 7, 13
The Scope of Government 2, 12, 68, 69,
    71, 72, 73, 74, 75, 76, 78, 79, 80, 81,
    82, 85, 86, 89, 90, 91, 92, 94, 95
theories of political change 6, 17–40, 96
Third World 111
totalitarianism 21, 150, 158
    see also authoritarian regimes;
        dictatorship
trade unions 19, 29, 57, 58, 135, 146, 171
tradition 15, 24, 36, 41, 53, 150, 163
trust:
    personal 98, 106, 112, 114, 119–21,
        124
    political 22, 25, 29–30, 38, 60, 72, 93–4
turnout, *see* voting

UN 14, 97, 103, 105, 106, 108, 122
unconventional political behaviour 35–7,
    49–50, 144
    see also civil disobedience; direct
        political action
unemployment 21, 62, 66, 70, 75, 78, 80–
    2, 84–5, 95, 109, 147, 149
unfreezing of parties 11
ungovernability 17, 22, 24–6, 32, 37, 71–3

unionization rates 56
unitary and federal government 7
United Kingdom, *see* Great Britain
United Nations 103, 105, 108, 109, 122
United States 4, 19, 25, 44, 53, 66, 85,
    99, 105, 106, 131, 133, 154
United States Information Agency 4, 99
unofficial strikes 39
unrest, political 21

valence politics 169
value change 6, 13, 42–3, 63, 140, 144,
    155
    see also materialism; postmaterialism
value voting 23–6, 43, 48
values 2, 23–6, 31, 33, 60, 68, 78, 114,
    133, 158, 159, 160, 167–8, 171
VAT/TVA 94
velvet revolution 15
Vietnam 42
violence, political 23, 31, 33, 52, 145,
    157
volatility, political 27, 29, 37, 112, 140
voluntary associations 19–20, 38, 50, 57,
    156
    see also citizen associations; interest
        groups; intermediary associations
voting 12, 35, 41, 43, 48, 50, 88, 96, 128,
    130–40, 143, 145, 161, 169–70
    see also elections; electoral volatility

Wagner's law 66
wants 75, 82
war:
    anti-war movements 58

cold war 81, 96
    political impact of 19, 42, 65–6, 118
    and support for international
        government 78, 103
war efforts 65
war years 122
wealth 16, 78, 80, 86, 135, 151, 152
    see also income
welfare capitalism 22
welfare state:
    backlash 66, 68–71, 77, 89
    crisis of 12, 21–3, 95
    and end of ideology 31
    growth and decline of 65–8, 151, 160
    and postmaterialism 77–8
    public opinion about 77–89, 95–6, 111,
        123, 167
    and rational choice 76–7
    and social state 11, 137
West Germany, *see* Germany
western Europe 1, 3, 5, 7–8, 11, 13–15,
    18, 25, 42–3, 48, 51, 56, 65–6, 71,
    75, 78–9, 82, 88, 90, 92, 94, 97,
    99–100, 103, 106, 120, 122, 135,
    143, 149, 156, 162, 166–7
women's movements 57
    see also new social movements
work ethic 23
work satisfaction 77
working class 22, 31, 68–9, 74, 131
    see also class
World Values Survey 3

young 11, 35, 67, 146, 149, 157
    see also age